JUDICIAL RESTRAINT IN AMERICA

JUDICIAL RESTRAINT IN AMERICA

HOW THE AGELESS WISDOM OF THE FEDERAL COURTS WAS INVENTED

EVAN TSEN LEE

OXFORD
UNIVERSITY PRESS

OXFORD
UNIVERSITY PRESS

Oxford University Press, Inc., publishes works that further Oxford University's objective of excellence in research, scholarship, and education.

Oxford New York
Auckland Cape Town Dar es Salaam Hong Kong Karachi Kuala Lumpur Madrid Melbourne
Mexico City Nairobi New Delhi Shanghai Taipei Toronto

With offices in
Argentina Austria Brazil Chile Czech Republic France Greece Guatemala Hungary Italy
Japan Poland Portugal Singapore South Korea Switzerland Thailand
Turkey Ukraine Vietnam

Published by Oxford University Press, Inc.
198 Madison Avenue, New York, New York 10016

Library of Congress Cataloging-in-Publication Data

Lee, Evan Tsen.
Judicial restraint in America : how the ageless wisdom of the federal courts was invented / Evan Tsen Lee.
p. cm.
Includes bibliographical references and index.
ISBN 978-0-19-534034-1 (hardback : alk. paper)
1. United States. Supreme Court–History. 2. Judicial process–United States. I. Title.
KF8742.L44 2010
347.73'–dc22

2010024771

---

1 2 3 4 5 6 7 8 9
Printed in the United States of America on acid-free paper

Note to Readers
This publication is designed to provide accurate and authoritative information in regard to the subject matter covered. It is based upon sources believed to be accurate and reliable and is intended to be current as of the time it was written. It is sold with the understanding that the publisher is not engaged in rendering legal, accounting, or other professional services. If legal advice or other expert assistance is required, the services of a competent professional person should be sought. Also, to confirm that the information has not been affected or changed by recent developments, traditional legal research techniques should be used, including checking primary sources where appropriate.

(Based on the Declaration of Principles jointly adopted by a Committee of the American Bar Association and a Committee of Publishers and Associations.)

For Susie, M. G., and Mikey

CONTENTS

PREFACE

For two decades now I have taught a law school course called "Federal Courts" (in some schools, "Federal Jurisdiction"). The value to law students is chiefly technical: I teach them the secret handshake you have to know in order to get your case into federal court. But it's more than a handshake. There's a liturgical chant that goes with it, and that chant contains eternal verities about the evils of federal court adjudication. *Federal litigation about anything other than disputes between private parties is inherently undemocratic.* This especially includes challenges to the constitutionality of legislative enactments and judicial review of administrative agency decisions. Legislatures are elected, and agencies are directly accountable to the President and Congress. Life-tenured federal judges are accountable to no one.

If a generation is 20 years, then four generations of the nation's lawyers and judges have learned the secret handshake and chant. In America, that counts as time out of mind. The credo of judicial restraint—that is, the notion that federal courts must avoid deciding challenges to majoritarian action whenever possible—is now assumed to have originated at the Founding, an ineluctable product of axioms about constitutional democracy. I have written this book to show that the story is more complicated than that. The opposition of "judicial activism" to "judicial restraint" did not generally occur to the Founders or jurists of the time. They believed that the separation of law from politics was a complete answer to any such concern. Provided that courts confined themselves to vindicating vested rights, they would stay on the law side, and what moderns would call "judicial restraint" would automatically be achieved. The first broad challenge to these assumptions did not come until the early 20th Century, when Progressives and New Dealers became outraged that courts could stop so much essential legislation and regulation on the pretense of "vested property rights" that, in their view, amounted to little more than the wishful thinking of conservatives and big business. Having championed "judicial restraint" to clear the way for progressive measures, the next generation of lawyers, judges and scholars froze up when confronted with claims of racial equality. All enlightened men recognized the moral validity of such claims, but how could one explain the *juridical* difference between these claims and those of property owners at the turn of the century? And, when the Court moved on to the rights of criminal defendants, sex equality, reproductive rights, and the environment, the mantra of judicial restraint began to resonate with a broad swath of America, not just conservatives.

The "thesis" of this book, if it has one, is banal. In the last 100 or so years, the nation has oscillated between its commitment to judicial vindication of vested rights and its commitment to government by the people. The inputs have been many—the centrality of property and land to American history; the need for regulation to deal with the problems of industrialization, mechanization, and urbanization; the dominant Protestant ethic giving way to secular and scientific pragmatism; the legacy of slavery and segregation unique to America; the professionalization of public interest litigation; and more. Each of these historical developments exerted not only a political, economic, or social force, but an influence on *moral* thinking as well. The centrality of property helped influence people to think that property rights had a moral or divine standing. The seeming senselessness of one war made people wary of moral absolutes; the justness of another made them wary of relativism. The righteousness of the civil rights movement filled many with confidence that clear moral judgments could be made; the troubled adolescence of *Roe v. Wade* and affirmative action made it appear that one person's moral judgments could not be treated as any better than another's. Some see environmental protection and measures to stop global warming as moral imperatives, while others see such issues as requiring a lengthy and fluid series of political compromises. This book is an attempt to glimpse the context in which the rules of judicial restraint have been developed.

There were many phases in the research and writing of this book, some of which are now quite hazy in my mind, and so I am sure I have forgotten many who contributed to it. I apologize for any such omissions. Beth Hillman, Susan Duncan Lee, Jim Pfander, and Reuel Schiller were kind enough to read the manuscript and give invaluable comments. Reuel Schiller spent countless hours talking me through the historiography of various periods, and I hope his association with this product does not get him drummed out of the professional historian society. Multiple conversations with my colleagues Ash Bhagwat, Bill Dodge, Geoff Hazard, Ethan Leib, David Levine, Rick Marcus, and Keith Wingate were very helpful. David Faigman gave me great advice about publication and consistent moral support when the spirit was flagging. Thanks also to workshop participants at UC Davis and to Suzanne Park, who helped me shape the Postscript. Dean Mary Kay Kane was supportive of projects that led up to the book, and Dean Nell Newton supported it by giving me the Harry and Lillian Hastings Research Chair. Academic Dean Shauna Marshall exhibited unusual patience with the slow pace of this project and has generally helped by being the best boss one could hope for, while my administrative assistant Roz Foy has enabled me to spend time on something other than event planning. Major research assistance was provided by Elisa Pandolfi, Anya Stein, Diana Hughes, Sarah Giammichele, Laureli Mallek, Ben Whiting, Michael Davis Wilson, Katie Grinold Sample, Kayla Birns, and Sarah Logue.

Finally, I wish to thank my wife Susan, my children Maria Grace and Michael, and my late father, who all believed in this book and in me when there was little reason to do so.

PROLOGUE

On September 4, 1905, a woman identified in the *United States Reports* only as "one Mrs. E. Gotcher" worked more than 10 hours at the Grand Laundry in Portland, Oregon. What made this literally a federal case was that two years earlier the Oregon Legislature had made it a misdemeanor to employ a woman in a laundry for more than 10 hours in the same day. The owner of the Grand Laundry, Curt Muller, was convicted and fined $10. The Oregon Supreme Court affirmed his conviction. Muller, who claimed that the statute violated his constitutional right to liberty of contract, appealed to the United States Supreme Court.

He had to have liked his chances. Three years earlier the Court had struck down New York's maximum hours restriction in bakeries, and the Court had only just declared unconstitutional a federal law prohibiting railroads from requiring workers to sign "yellow dog" contracts in which the workers would promise not to join a union. In both cases the Court had essentially decided in favor of liberty of contract; in the New York case, it was the liberty of parties to set the terms of employment by agreement, and, in the railroad case, the liberty of an employer to fire workers for any reason at all.[1] But in *Muller v. Oregon*, a successful corporate lawyer turned reformer named Louis D. Brandeis filed a new kind of brief—one packed not with timeless and universal principles of jurisprudence but instead with statistics depicting the real-world impact of long working hours on women and their families. Brandeis had by then become one of the nation's leading Progressives. He staunchly defended legislative attempts to ameliorate the harsh effects of industrialism on the health and welfare of working people. The wisdom and rationality of such legislation could only be assessed through empirical evidence, the "experiments of competent scientists," the knowledge-gathering of government investigations and congressional hearings.[2] Brandeis now presented the Court with a compilation of working-hours statutes and statistics that made the scientific and pragmatic case for sustaining the Oregon law.

The result was stunning. The Court unanimously upheld the law. Justice David Brewer's opinion for the Court went to the unusual length of citing the advocate Brandeis by name and reciting many of the statistics that Brandeis's brief had introduced. Brewer was obviously delighted that an advocate had

1. *See* Owen M. Fiss, Troubled Beginnings of the Modern State, 1888–1910 at 167 (Cambridge Univ. Press, 1993).

2. Edward A. Purcell, Jr., Brandeis and the Progressive Constitution 120 (Yale Univ. Press, 2000).

thought to present extrajudicial evidence of the social and economic reality underlying the legal question before the Court. Brewer had long believed that judges had both the ability and duty to canvass such information, however specialized and scientific it may be.[3] In this case, Brandeis's statistics confirmed the soundness of a proposition that Brewer knew to be true by other means, namely, his devout Christianity. Women really were different. They really did have lesser physical capacity for work. They did have a different and unique role in the family, the essential and sacred duty of childbearing and child-rearing. If we were to continue "as a race," as Brewer put it, women had to be protected from overwork in factories and other places of business. Here the scientific evidence dovetailed perfectly with the Christian values that Brewer believed underlay the Constitution. In this, his last major opinion before retiring from the Court, Brewer must have felt that he had helped in some small way to cement the place of Christian certainties in a volatile future of science and technology.

Whatever synchronicity there may have been between Brewer's and Brandeis's use for scientific evidence in *Muller v. Oregon*, however, was largely fortuitous. Brandeis was not laying out the scientific evidence before the justices because he wanted them to pass on the justifiability of the maximum-hours law. Brandeis thought judges generally incompetent, or at least untrustworthy, for such work. As a young corporate lawyer, Brandeis had been accepted into the professional and social circles of the most elite of the New England Protestant gentry, the Boston Brahmins. In the late 19th Century, upper-crust Protestant idealists dominated the federal bench, including the Supreme Court. These liberal Protestant idealists, David Josiah Brewer prominent among them, believed that the Constitution represented the enshrinement of Christian values, in particular individual liberty and individual autonomy. One had to have the freedom to choose the path to one's own salvation out of one's own volition. As a result, any reform legislation that smacked of undue paternalism had to be stricken down as unconstitutional. Although the Court had upheld much reform legislation—after all, not all paternalism was undue, as in *Muller* itself—it had also invalidated many measures that were key to the reform movement. Brandeis firmly believed that federal judges needed to be taken out of the business of evaluating legislation. Through a combination of mandatory judicial deference and restrictions on jurisdiction, the legislatures would be left with the final say on the justifiability of any particular piece of reform legislation. The legislatures—increasingly middle-class, pluralistic, and, in some parts of the country, immigrant—did not share the unyielding Protestant elitist view of the sanctity of contract. They were open-minded to the truths of lived-out experience, as chronicled in social scientific studies. Unlike courts, legislatures could conduct their own investigations and hold open-ended hearings. In *Muller*, Brandeis had put the scientific evidence

3. *See* Michael J. Brodhead, David J. Brewer: The Life of a Supreme Court Justice, 1837–1910 at 154 (Southern Ill. Univ. Press, 1994).

before the judges, but only because it was better than the judges deciding purely on the basis of their religious, cultural, and class values.

For one moment in time, Brewer's and Brandeis's jurisprudential approaches appeared to have come to rest in the same place. In fact, however, these two men and their ideas were moving past one another. Brewer was near the end of his long tenure on the Court; Brandeis was on his way to his own appointment. Brewer's devout Christianity had led him to the view that judicial review and federal equity jurisprudence—to be deployed in the protection of naturally-endowed liberty and property rights—were prior to any positive law. If liberty and property rights were given by God, then the means to protect them must have been as well. In Brewer's world, judges would always bear the ultimate responsibility for determining which liberty and property interests were inviolable. Brandeis's bedrock commitment to reform legislation, his strong aversion to concentrations of wealth, and his deep mistrust of the ruling Protestant elite that dominated the judiciary led him to the view that judges could not be permitted such a role. Legislatures, with their accountability to the working- and middle-classes, and with their ability and inclination to investigate the underlying facts of social and economic problems, had to have the final word in all but the most egregious cases. His commitment to secular pragmatism in constitutional jurisprudence led Brandeis to believe that procedural and jurisdictional doctrines should be used to pry reform legislation loose from the chokehold of Protestant idealist judges. The "standing to sue" doctrine would become foremost among those rules. In this sense, the move from Brewer to Brandeis, from Protestant idealism to secular and scientific pragmatism, is the beginning of the story of standing, and of judicial restraint in America.

1. JOHN MARSHALL AND THE INSEPARABILITY OF ACTION AND RESTRAINT

Marbury v. Madison is widely regarded as the case that established judicial review in the United States. But it is also the case that established judicial restraint in the United States, and its author, Chief Justice John Marshall, accomplished both with a single stroke. His singular genius was to reject the separation of restraint from action.

In the waning hours of its congressional majority in early 1801, the Federalists confirmed a raft of new justices of the peace for the District of Columbia. President John Adams signed the commissions on his last day in office and transmitted them to Secretary of State John Marshall for delivery to the now confirmed appointees. But Marshall, already confirmed as the next chief justice, did not have time to effect delivery. He could not find a clerk at that hour. No reason to panic, he thought; not even the wretched Thomas Jefferson (a distant cousin) could have the temerity to scuttle these signed and sealed appointments. And so he left the commissions behind for the incoming administration to deliver and moved on to his new post at the Supreme Court.

President Jefferson and new Secretary of State James Madison evidently did not share Marshall's view that delivery of the commissions was a matter of mere legal formality. They viewed it as a matter of political prerogative. Jefferson and Madison were Republicans, archenemies of Adams and Marshall. They were outraged that the defeated Federalists would take advantage of an orderly transfer of power by rushing through a large number of appointments at the last minute. Jefferson and Madison decided to withhold the commissions, one of which was reportedly bound for William Marbury. Marbury moved the U.S. Supreme Court for an order that would compel Madison to deliver the commissions, thereby handing John Marshall a trump card over his old political adversaries.

The card would never be played. With Marshall leading the way, the Court ruled that it lacked jurisdiction to issue the relief that Marbury had requested. Conventional wisdom sees *Marbury* as a brilliant gambit, with Marshall going out of his way to find a constitutional defect in Congress's jurisdictional grant to the Court.[1] The immediate result was nothing more than a scolding of the new administration for its wanton violation of vested rights, while the enduring result was the entrenchment of judicial review. It is impossible to know precisely what

---

1. For a fuller narrative, see William Michael Treanor, *The Story of* Marbury v. Madison*: Judicial Authority and Political Struggle*, *in* FEDERAL COURTS STORIES (Vicki C. Jackson & Judith Resnik eds., Foundation Press 2010).

was in Marshall's mind, but the conventional view ignores his consistent pattern of playing it straight when it came to jurisdictional inquiries. Throughout his career as chief justice, Marshall refused to rule on the merits of cases when he sincerely believed the court lacked jurisdiction, even when he believed that injustice would thereby go unredressed. By the same token, he consistently advocated reaching the merits of cases in which he sincerely believed jurisdiction existed, even if exercising jurisdiction would place the court in a politically volatile situation. It would have been uncharacteristic of Marshall to duck a case on the pretext of a jurisdictional defect. As he would write twenty years later:

> It is most true that this Court will not take jurisdiction if it should not: but it is equally true, that it must take jurisdiction if it should.... We have no more right to decline the exercise of jurisdiction which is given, than to usurp that which is not given. The one or the other would be treason to the constitution. Questions may occur that we would gladly avoid; but we cannot avoid them. All we can do is, to exercise our best judgment, and conscientiously to perform our duty.[2]

* * *

John Marshall was born September 24, 1755, the first of fifteen children, in what was then known as Germantown, Virginia, just south of what would become the Civil War battlefield of Manassas. His father was Thomas Marshall, who two years earlier had been named the agent of Lord Fairfax in the management of Fairfax's estates. John received most of his early education from his father, who gave him a solid grounding in English history, literature, and the classics. At age 18, John found a copy of Blackstone in his father's house and studied it. The book had just been exported to America. But war was about to break out, and his intellectual pursuits would have to wait.

He was a natural leader of men. After serving as a lieutenant in a regiment of minutemen who fought at Norfolk, he served in New Jersey, Pennsylvania, and New York. As a frequent judge advocate, he personally worked with George Washington and Alexander Hamilton. During that infamous winter at Valley Forge, wrote a fellow officer and messmate, Marshall was "neither discouraged nor disturbed by anything, content with whatever turned up, and cheering everybody by his exuberance of spirits" and his "inexhaustible fund of anecdote." He was "idolized by the soldiers and his brother officers."[3]

To his contemporaries, Marshall seemed to be made of stronger stuff. Here is an eyewitness account of Lieutenant Marshall drilling a company of soldiers in Fauquier County:

> He was about six feet high, straight, and rather slender, of dark complexion, showing little if any rosy red, yet good health, the outline of the face nearly a

2. Cohens v. Virginia, 6 Wheat. (19 U.S.) 264, 291 (1821).
3. James Bradley Thayer, John Marshall 11–12 (Houghton, Mifflin 1901).

> circle, and within that, eyes dark to blackness, strong and penetrating, beaming with intelligence and good nature; an upright forehead, rather low, was terminated in a horizontal line by a mass of raven-black hair, of unusual thickness and strength. The features of the face were in harmony with this outline, and the temples fully developed. The result of this combination was interesting and very agreeable. The body and limbs indicated agility rather than strength, in which, however, he was by no means deficient . . . . He went through the manual exercise by word and motion, deliberately pronounced and performed in the presence of the company, before he required the men to imitate him; and then proceeded to exercise them with the most perfect temper . . . .[4]

His athletic exploits were legendary. "It was said . . . that he surpassed any man in the army; that when the soldiers were idle at their quarters, it was usual for the officers to engage in matches of quoits, or in jumping and racing; that he would throw a quoit farther, and beat at a race any other; that he was the only man who, with a running jump, could clear a stick laid on the heads of two men as tall as himself," wrote Marshall's early biographer James Bradley Thayer.

In early 1780, his troops disbanded, Marshall resumed his education, however briefly. At the behest of Governor Thomas Jefferson, the College of William and Mary had just terminated its chair in divinity and replaced it with chairs in law ("law and police") and medicine. The faculty voted that, "for the encouragement of science, a student, on paying annually 1000 pounds of tobacco, shall be entitled to attend any school of the following professors, viz.: of Law and Police; of Natural Philosophy and Mathematics . . . ." Marshall attended a course in natural philosophy and one in law, taught by George Wythe. He was there for only one term and by the end of the summer he was licensed to practice law in Virginia.[5]

After Marshall settled in Richmond in 1784 his practice flourished. Thayer examined the case reports of the time and found that no man's name appeared more often than Marshall's; his name appeared with particular frequency in the important cases. Washington consistently tendered him federal appointments—federal prosecutor, attorney general, minister to France—and each time Marshall declined. He needed to practice law full time to support his large family, and to continue acquiring large amounts of land in the Northern Neck of Virginia. Eventually John Adams managed what Washington had been unable to do, enticing Marshall into joining Charles Pinckney and Elbridge Gerry in a mission to settle differences with the revolutionary government of France. "I will confess that the *éclat* which would attend a successful termination of the differences between the two countries had no small influence over a mind in which

4. THAYER at 7–8.
5. THAYER at 13–15.

ambition, though subjected to controul, was not absolutely extinguished," Marshall explained later.[6] From a diplomatic standpoint, the mission was a failure, thwarted by the insistence that the United States make a huge loan to France, and by the demand for a sizable sum to secure an audience with the calculating foreign minister Talleyrand. Personally, however, Marshall came out shining, having sent home dispatches attributing the diplomatic standoff to the American envoys' firm refusal to compromise American independence and sovereignty. Upon his return in 1798, it was said that Marshall was one of the four most beloved men in the United States, alongside Washington, Adams, and Pinckney. Shortly thereafter Marshall only enhanced his standing with the Federalist administration when he defended Adams's decision to surrender seaman Jonathan Robbins to the British. The British had insisted that Robbins was in reality a Royal Navy petty officer guilty of mutiny and murder on the frigate *Hermoine* in 1797. Robbins claimed that he had been wrongly impressed into British service. Upon extradition, the British promptly executed Robbins, prompting anti-Federalists in the Sixth Congress to assail Adams for shipping off a persecuted American to his certain death. In a brilliant oration on the floor of the House, Marshall argued that Adams's decision was within the sphere of the president's authority to execute treaties.[7] Adams promptly appointed Marshall secretary of state, a post he would hold until his elevation to the Supreme Court.

* * *

Marshall began the *Marbury* opinion in his customarily syllogistic fashion, laying out the three questions to be answered:

> 1st. Has the applicant a right to the commission he demands?
> 2dly. If he has a right, and that right has been violated, do the laws of his country afford him a remedy?
> 3dly. If they do afford him a remedy, is it a mandamus issuing from this court?

The first question was whether successful delivery of the commission to the appointee was essential to the legal validity of the appointment. Marshall held that it was not; otherwise, the effectiveness of an appointment could be made vulnerable to such chance events as postal mishaps. The final act of presidential appointment was the signing of the commission after Senate confirmation. The secretary of state was then legally required to affix the seal of the United States to

6. Charles F. Hobson, The Great Chief Justice: John Marshall and the Rule of Law 6 (Univ. Press of Kansas 1996).

7. On the Robbins affair, see Ruth Wedgwood, *The Revolutionary Martyrdom of Jonathan Robbins*, 100 Yale L.J. 229 (1990). On the importance and interpretation of Marshall's speech, see H. Jefferson Powell, *The Founders and the President's Authority over Foreign Affairs*, 40 Wm. & Mary L. Rev. 1471 (1999).

the commission, at which point the appointment was fully effective. Marbury, then, had a right to the document, which constituted conclusive evidence of the already effective appointment.

That brought Marshall to the second question, whether Marbury had a remedy for the violation of his right to the commission. For Marshall, the application of two great principles resolved this issue. The first was the maxim *ubi jus, ibi remedium*—that is, where there is a legal right, there must be a remedy. As authority for this proposition, Marshall quoted the third volume of Blackstone's *Commentaries*: "[I]t is a settled and invariable principle in the laws of England, that every right, when withheld, must have a remedy, and every injury its proper redress."[8] This principle went to the heart of Marshall's jurisprudence. The highest function of law (as opposed to political will) was the protection of vested property rights. Political will could and would play personal favor, rewarding the popular and the powerful. Only law was impersonal. "The government of the United States has been emphatically termed a government of laws, and not of men," Marshall wrote. "It will certainly cease to deserve this high appellation, if the laws furnish no remedy for the violation of a vested right."[9]

The second great principle likewise involved the separation of law from politics. Marbury had moved the court for a writ of mandamus against Secretary of State Madison. But how could a court issue an order to a cabinet member, an agent of the president, who sat at the apex of a coordinate and equal branch of government? The answer, wrote Marshall, was to recognize the duality of every executive official's job. Some of an official's acts were discretionary, others ministerial. If the secretary of state were to take a certain negotiating position in talks with a foreign nation, contrary to congressional declaration, there would be no remedy, because the official has discretion to carry out that portion of his duties as he sees fit. He would be answerable only to the president, and the president answerable only to the electorate.

But, said Marshall, not all of an official's duties fell into the discretionary category. Here he tapped his personal knowledge as a former secretary of state. A 1796 statute authorized "the sale of lands above the mouth of Kentucky river." The purchaser would tender payment to the treasurer, who would give him a certificate. The purchaser would then present the certificate to the secretary of state, who would countersign and record it, and, finally, issue a land patent. Following this sequence of events, the secretary's duty to issue the patent would be merely ministerial, not discretionary, Marshall stated. "If the secretary of state should choose to withhold this patent; or the patent being lost, should refuse a copy of it; can it be imagined that the law furnishes to the injured person no remedy?" Marshall asked. The delivery of Marbury's commission was likewise a

8. 1 Cranch (5 U.S.) at 163.
9. *Id.*

purely ministerial function. Having established his right to the commission, Marshall concluded that Marbury was entitled to a remedy.

This distinction between discretionary and ministerial functions corresponded perfectly with the dichotomy Marshall thought central to public adjudication—the separation of politics from law. The legal historian William E. Nelson has written:

> Chief Justice John Marshall drew a line, which nearly all citizens of his time believed ought to be drawn, between the legal and the political—between those matters on which all Americans agreed and which therefore were fixed and immutable and those matters which were subject to fluctuation and change through democratic politics.[10]

It was a theory of separate spheres. Within its domain, the legislature was supreme. It, after all, was popularly elected and operated by majority. There was no legitimate basis on which courts might second-guess the legislature's policy decisions. Legislatures might choose among policy options in an unprincipled manner; indeed, such choices might be completely resistant to principle, in which case they must be made on the basis of sheer political will. But that was the legislature's bailiwick. Somebody had to make such decisions, and in a society devoted to popular sovereignty, it had to be the popularly elected branches.

Outside its domain, however, the legislature was not supreme. Not only was it owed something less than full deference when operating beyond its proper sphere, it was owed no deference at all. It was the courts' job to see that the legislature did not cross the line. But where was that line? How to determine precisely where legislative competence ran out? Marshall and his contemporaries did not view these questions as difficult. A legislature could do whatever it thought best, provided that it disturbed no one's vested rights. The legislature could grant new lands to individuals on whatsoever basis it so chose. It could not, however, extinguish vested rights in land, or in any other private property. This principle extended to the executive as well. Though the elected branches could criminalize whatever conduct they deemed properly punishable (including seditious libel), the executive could not detain an individual without due process.

For Marshall, the reconciliation of judicial review with popular sovereignty was hardly an issue. It was true that legislation represented popular will, but it was the will of a transient majority. The Constitution was the enduring and ultimate repository of popular sovereignty. The Constitution was not, as his ideological nemesis Spencer Roane of Virginia would have it, simply a compact among the states. The force that severed America from Great Britain could have been nothing less than We the People acting in their most politically elevated capacity. The Constitution was the instrument the People chose to endow with

---

10. William E. Nelson, *Marbury v. Madison*: The Origins and Legacy of Judicial Review 8 (Univ. Press of Kansas 2000).

their sovereignty. When a court refused to enforce an unconstitutional enactment, it was upholding true popular sovereignty as against an imposter.

The challenge of judicial restraint was for courts to stay in the legal sphere, abjuring the world of politics. Roughly, if a claimant presented a court with the alleged violation of a vested legal right, the matter was legal; if he did not, the matter was political. If the matter was political, the courts must not exercise jurisdiction, for it would be to trespass into the legislature's sphere. If the matter was legal, then the courts *must* exercise jurisdiction. If a court was to refuse jurisdiction in such a case, it would be to turn its back on popular sovereignty as embodied by constitutional protections of vested rights—"treason to the Constitution."

The protection of individual vested rights had thus become "the basic doctrine of American constitutional law," declared the historian Edward S. Corwin. Yet the path to that doctrine had been strange and tortuous. The colonists of course originally received their concept of rights from the English, whose rights against the Crown had been finally secured by the Glorious Revolution of 1689. The king had always had his rights and prerogatives against his subjects, but now the people had their own set of enforceable rights against royal tyranny, and against the elite House of Lords. These rights did not extend as against the House of Commons. Why would they? Commons represented the people themselves; it was inconceivable that the people would act against their own interests.

If the very concept of rights was rooted in checks against monarchical power, what happened when there was no monarch? According to Gordon S. Wood, "In 1776 it had not been at all clear that people had rights against their own representatives." "[A] democratical despotism is a contradiction in terms," said John Adams in 1775. Within a decade, all that changed. Americans became acutely aware that the people's representatives were capable of tyranny. Wood has chronicled the divergence of views in response to this puzzle. Some hoped that the new federal government might assume a judicial-like character and become a disinterested and dispassionate umpire in disputes between and among the several states.[11] But John Marshall and others were coming to a distinctly different conclusion, and their view would prevail.

The key intellectual move was from the English notion of individual rights against the Crown to a uniquely American notion of individual rights against representative government. "The secret was to identify the popular legislatures with the former monarchical power . . . and invoke the traditional language of

11. In private correspondence, Ed Purcell has stated that Madison's views on this subject were changing and in some ways unsettled during the period from before the Convention until the publication of the Federalist Papers. See, e.g., LANCE BANNING, THE SACRED FIRE OF LIBERTY: JAMES MADISON AND THE FOUNDING OF THE FEDERAL REPUBLIC 200–01, 374, 394 (Cornell Univ. Press 1998).

the rights of Englishmen in these new republican circumstances," Wood explained.

This was an extraordinary achievement, made possible because large numbers of influential people, including John Marshall, were becoming increasingly disillusioned with democratic legislative politics in these years. Indeed, it is hard for us today to appreciate the degree to which men like Marshall became "disgusted with . . . the political world" they saw developing in America. Democracy and individual rights, public and private liberty, seemed at odds with one another. Since, unlike England, the representative legislatures were the source of the problem, not the solution, some other bulwark for individual rights would have to be found. This meant that the crucial issues of individual rights had to be taken out of the hands of the popular legislatures and placed in the hands of some other institution, which turned out to be the courts.[12]

Essential to the development of this idea was the emergence of a distinction between public and private matters. Legislation concerned matters properly in the public domain; adjudication covered those in the private sphere. According to Wood, a robust distinction between public and private matters followed ineluctably from the new doctrine of disestablishmentarianism. "Once Americans were able to limit state authority in religious matters . . . they had committed themselves to the creation of a private arena into which executives and legislatures had no business intruding."[13] Wood explained:

> The idea that there was a sphere of private rights that lay absolutely beyond the authority of government, especially a republican government, was extraordinary, to say the least. There were virtually no precedents for such an idea in the American's colonial experience. But with the Revolution Americans had prepared the way for such a radical idea by their commitment to the right of religious freedom.[14]

Until the late eighteenth century, virtually everything in colonial America was treated as a governmental concern, including personal comportment and sexuality. This was a function of the pervasive authority of the church, which regulated every aspect of life. In William E. Nelson's study of Massachusetts society, he found that more than half of the prosecutions in the Superior and General Sessions Courts between 1760 and 1774 involved sexual and religious offenses, and a good chunk of the other prosecutions involved drunkenness, slander, and violations of decency and good manners.[15] Colonial governments' involvement in what would today be seen as "private matters" was not limited to

12. Wood, *Vested Rights*, at 1435.

13. Wood, *Vested Rights*, at 1439.

14. Wood, *Vested Rights*, at 1439–40.

15. William E. Nelson, Americanization of the Common Law: The Impact of Legal Change on Massachusetts Society 37 (1975).

the courts. "Indeed, colonial assemblies still saw themselves more as courts making judgments rather than as legislatures making law," according to Wood.[16] The vast majority of this governmental activity was carried out by ordinary citizens, albeit ones who had achieved a high degree of economic and social success. Such were the public obligations of private persons. There was no real separation between the two, practically or conceptually. It was only when government ceased to derive its authority from religion and began to derive it from civil sources that the public-private distinction began to develop. As it did, courts become more and more exclusively concerned with the protection of private vested rights, both as against other individuals and as against government, even republican government, until it became their main function.

* * *

Having established that William Marbury had a vested right in his commission signed by President Adams, and that he was entitled to a writ of mandamus to vindicate that right, Chief Justice Marshall proceeded to the last question: Did the Supreme Court have jurisdiction to issue the writ of mandamus that Marbury had requested? A provision of the First Judiciary Act, passed in 1791, purported to empower the Supreme Court to "issue writs of mandamus, in cases warranted by the principles and usages of law, to any courts appointed, or persons holding office, under the authority of the United States." Certainly Secretary of State Madison qualified as a "person[] holding office, under the authority of the United States." The statute, then, clearly attempted to authorize mandamus in cases like Marbury's.

But did Article III of the Constitution give Congress the power to grant such authority to the Supreme Court? Article III states that "the supreme court shall have original jurisdiction in all cases affecting ambassadors, other public ministers and consuls, and those in which a state shall be a party. In all other cases, the supreme court shall have appellate jurisdiction." If the secretary of state were considered a "public minister," and if a mandamus to him in his purely ministerial capacity were to be considered as "affecting" him, then presumably the Court would have had original jurisdiction in the case, and mandamus would doubtless have been a proper remedy. But counsel for Marbury made no such argument, and Marshall did not consider it. Instead, Marbury's lawyer argued that Congress had the power to enlarge the original jurisdiction of the Supreme Court beyond its enumeration in Article III, to encompass a case like Marbury's.

Marbury's lawyer was Charles Lee, older brother of General Henry "Light Horse Harry" Lee. There was good reason to think that he would have credibility with Marshall. Lee was another ardent Federalist who was appointed attorney general by George Washington and continued in that position by John Adams.

16. Wood, *Vested Rights* at 1430.

(After the decision in *Marbury*, he would decline Jefferson's appointment to the Supreme Court.) "Congress is not restrained from conferring original jurisdiction in other cases than those mentioned in the constitution," Lee argued, citing three cases in support of the proposition. But in none of those three cases did the Supreme Court actually issue a writ of mandamus against a federal officer. Lee pointed out that the Court had not questioned its own jurisdiction to issue mandamus in any of these cases, from which he inferred that the Court must have believed that it did possess jurisdiction.

Lee's tenuous precedential appeal, however, was no match for Marshall's logical exegesis of Article III. "If it had been intended to leave it to the discretion of the legislature to apportion the judicial power between the superior and inferior courts according to the will of that body, it certainly would have been useless to have proceeded further than to have defined the judicial powers, and the tribunals in which it should be vested," Marshall wrote. In other words, why precisely enumerate the original jurisdiction of the Supreme Court, saving all else to its appellate jurisdiction, if Congress was free to alter that balance at any time? "The plain import of the words seems to be, that in one class of cases its jurisdiction is original, and not appellate; in the other it is appellate, and not original," he concluded. And, despite Lee's valiant attempt to argue that "appellate" should be interpreted capaciously rather than technically, Marshall made it clear that the mandamus he was requesting on Marbury's behalf appertained to original, not appellate, jurisdiction. The provision purporting to give the Supreme Court jurisdiction to issue mandamus was unconstitutional.

In demonstrating that the statute had to give way to the constitution, Marshall articulated what would prove a most durable rationale for judicial review. "It is emphatically the province and the duty of the judicial department to say what the law is," Marshall wrote, not because courts had the exclusive role of declaring the law, but because it was inextricable from adjudication of concrete cases. If courts were to decide cases according to the law, and if the constitution was paramount law, then courts *had* to have the power to ascertain that law, and they had to have the power to disregard any inferior enactment in conflict with the paramount law. This explains why every court in the United States has the "power" of judicial review, as contrasted with the practice in many countries, where only a specialized court has such power. By Marshall's thinking, to deny a court the ability to declare constitutional law was to deny it the ability to do its duty, which was to refuse enforcement of any enactment that conflicted with the paramount norm. If judicial review was a power, it was an entirely defensive power, not an aggressive one. It was not a power to "strike down" statutes so much as it was a duty to ignore them when they violated the constitution.

Therein lay the "restraint" in Marshall's conception of judicial restraint. Courts were to abstain from judicial review except when asked to enforce a norm violating the Constitution. There was to be no "reaching out" to test the constitutionality of laws not truly implicated by litigants' claims to remedies for violations of their rights. By the same token, however, if a litigant claimed the violation of a right, and if the resolution of that claim required the testing of legislative or executive action against the Constitution, then there was no option for the court to "restrain" itself from reaching the constitutional question. If a claim of right depended on the validity of a law, how *could* the court legitimately avoid the adjudication of the law's validity? To escape judicial review under such circumstances would require turning one's back on the principle that rights deserve remedies.

Cherokee Nation v. Georgia casts a similar light on Marshall's conception of judicial review. *Cherokee Nation* involved a motion in the Supreme Court's original jurisdiction to restrain the state of Georgia from enforcing a passel of laws that would have effectively destroyed the sovereignty of the Cherokee Nation. The scope of the requested relief was breathtaking:

> [The bill in equity requested that] the said state of Georgia, her governor, attorney-general, judges, magistrates, sheriffs, deputy sheriffs, constables, and all other her officers, agents, and servants, civil and military, may be enjoined and prohibited from executing the laws of that state within the boundary of the Cherokee territory . . . or interfering in any manner with the rights of self government possessed by the Cherokee nation . . . and that the state of Georgia, and all her officers, agents, and servants may be forever enjoined from interfering with the lands, mines, and other property, real and personal, of the Cherokee nation or with the persons of the Cherokee people . . . .[17]

Marshall's majority opinion did not reach the merits of the motion. It instead held that the Court lacked original jurisdiction because the Cherokee Nation was not a "foreign state" within the meaning of Article III.[18] After so holding, Marshall continued:

> A serious additional objection exists to the jurisdiction of the court. Is the matter of the bill the proper subject for judicial inquiry and decision? . . .
>
> That part of the bill which respects the land occupied by the Indians, and prays the aid of the court to protect their possession, may be more doubtful. The mere question of right might perhaps be decided by this court in a proper case with proper parties. But the court is asked to do more than decide on the title. The bill requires us to control the legislature of Georgia, and to restrain the exertion of its physical force. The propriety of such an interposition by the court may well be questioned. It savours too much of the exercise of political power to be within the proper province of the judicial department.[19]

To Marshall, *Cherokee Nation* presented the flip side of the principle applied in *Marbury*. Marbury had a vested legal right to his commission. If the Court had

---

17. 30 U.S. at 11–12.
18. 30 U.S. at 16–20.
19. 30 U.S. at 20 (emphasis added).

jurisdiction, he was entitled to his remedy. It was only the unconstitutionality of the jurisdictional statute that stood in the way. By contrast, no individual claimed the violation of any vested legal right in *Cherokee Nation*. The polity claimed the violation of its right to sovereignty, its right to political self-determination. Individuals made up the polity, and each of them suffered a loss—a diminution in their political power. But none of them made out an individual legal right, say, to citizenship in a sovereign Cherokee nation. This, for Marshall, made it a political case rather than a justiciable one. It was a political case not because it revolved around "politics," but because it did *not* revolve around an individual claim of vested legal rights.

By the late twentieth century, the orthodox view of federal judicial restraint celebrated a strategy of "ducking" controversial questions to preserve the political capital of the judiciary.[20] Whatever the legitimacy of that view, Marshall did not contribute to its pedigree. Marshall's years as chief justice presented him with multiple opportunities to decline jurisdiction in politically controversial matters, several of which he declined. A combination of jurisprudential principle and personal interests led Marshall to involve the Court in these political entanglements. The jurisprudential principle was the vindication of vested property rights, which stemmed from his study of Blackstone. This principle cohered perfectly with Marshall's personal experiences as the purchaser of vast lands in the Northern Neck of Virginia.

Alongside *Marbury*, a prime example of Marshall's willingness to place the Court in the middle of a political dispute was *Fletcher v. Peck*.[21] In the 1780s and early 1790s, the state of Georgia laid claim to a tract of land running west from the Chattahoochee River to the Mississippi and south from what is now Tennessee to western Spanish Florida. This tract, containing 35 million acres—most of what are now Alabama and Mississippi—were known as the Yazoo lands.[22] In the mid-1790s, four investor groups launched a campaign to get the state to sell them the Yazoo lands. The groups were largely made up of speculators from Georgia and Pennsylvania and included the very most respectable, and influential, of gentlemen: U.S. Senators James Gunn and Robert Morris; U.S. Representatives Thomas Carnes and Robert Goodloe Harper; and Associate Justice James Wilson of the U.S. Supreme Court, among others. Gunn, the chief promoter, knew that Spain was about to cede its claims to the Yazoo lands through the Treaty of San Lorenzo, making the territory much more attractive to speculators. He and his fellow investors embarked on a letter writing campaign, seeking to persuade the Georgia Legislature to sell its western lands to them instead of ceding them to the United States, as many other states had done.

20. *See infra* note 223.

21. 6 Cranch 115 (1810).

22. *See* C. Peter Magrath, Yazoo: Law & Politics in the New Republic 3 (1966). This is the authoritative work on the Yazoo land scandal.

Apparently these federal officeholders perceived insufficient conflict of interest to dissuade them from their entrepreneurial objective.

The investors had determined to leave nothing to chance. All but one of the legislators voting in favor of the sale had been bribed in some manner. Some of them got land, others cash. "When one representative, Thomas Raburn, was jokingly criticized for selling his vote for a mere $600 while his colleagues were getting $1,000, he blandly replied that 'it showed he was easily satisfied and was not greedy.'"[23] After an initial bout of conscience, Governor George Matthews, himself a land speculator, signed the legislation granting the investors the 35 million Yazoo acres for $500,000 in specie.

The voters of Georgia, "realizing that they had been swindled by an unholy alliance of greedy speculators and traitorous legislators," chased the corrupt legislators from office. The new legislature promptly repealed the law granting the lands to the Yazoo speculators. It was an emotional act; all documents regarding the sale were excised from state records and, along with the original copy of the act, were burned in the public square of Louisville, the site of the offending legislative session. Legend has it that the impending act of immolation was perfected when a white-haired old man made his way to the center of the square:

> Lifting up his voice, he declared that, feeble as he was, he had come there to see an act of justice performed, but he thought the fire in which the records of corruption were to be destroyed should come from heaven . . . . He drew from his bosom with trembling hands a sun glass, and in this way burned the papers. [He then] mounted his horse and rode away, and was never seen again.[24]

Thus the original Yazoo grants were repudiated on the ground of corruption. But most of the lands had been resold in the interim. It is not clear that all these were bona fide purchases—in fact, the most important resale took place on February 13, 1796, the very day the repeal was enacted. For $1,138,000, the New England Mississippi Land Company purchased 11 million acres from the Georgia Mississippi Company, one of the original investor groups. These second-generation speculators, which included some of the most prominent public officials in Connecticut and Massachusetts, insisted that they had bought the property in ignorance of the circumstances surrounding the original sale, themselves having been deceived by the dissimulations of the original purchasers. It was this transaction by the New England Mississippi Land Company that now became the focus of the Yazoo affair, and, eventually, of *Fletcher v. Peck*.[25]

---

23. MAGRATH at 6.

24. MAGRATH at 13, quoting from JOEL CHANDLER HARRIS, STORIES OF GEORGIA (New York: American Book Co. 1896).

25. MAGRATH at 15–16.

The federal courts, however, were not the first resort of the Yazoo speculators. First came pamphleteering. Robert Goodloe Harper, the South Carolina congressman who was a shareholder and lawyer for the speculators, published *The Case of the Georgia Sales on the Mississippi Considered.* It consisted of a survey purporting to prove that Georgia had good title to the land when it conveyed the property to the original buyers. It further argued that a legislature did not have the power to repeal a conveyance. That, he insisted, could only be done by a court of law. "The judicial power is to declare what the *law is*; the legislative what it *shall be*," he wrote.[26] In his appendix, Harper included a brief opinion by Alexander Hamilton, who made the same point as Harper. For the legislature to revoke a grant of property for good consideration, Hamilton wrote, constituted a "contravention of the first principles of natural justice and social policy, without any judicial decision." But the repeal violated not only natural law, in Hamilton's reckoning—it violated the Constitution, specifically, its provision prohibiting states from impairing contracts. Other pro-Yazooist literature invoked similar themes, if more crudely. The Georgia Mississippi Company, one of the original investor groups, argued that the validity of the original purchase was supported by "the eternal principles of justice founded on the laws of nature and the institutions of society."[27]

The pamphleteering accompanied an effort to obtain redress from Congress. But 1796 marked the end of the Federalist party as a dominant force in Congress, and the results of this campaign were meager. Republicans in Congress, their numbers growing, were generally not as sympathetic to the speculators' claims as were Federalists. In 1798 Congress passed a bill authorizing negotiations with Georgia for its western lands. The Yazooists viewed this with favor. They could see getting nothing so long as Georgia claimed the property; perhaps they would fare better if the United States obtained it. The road to compensation for the speculators, however, stretched on. In 1801, new President Thomas Jefferson appointed three federal commissioners (including Secretary of State James Madison) to negotiate with three Georgia commissioners over the future of the lands. In April 1802, the two governments signed an agreement whereby Georgia would convey its western lands to the United States for $1,250,000, provided that one-tenth of the lands would be set aside for satisfying the claims of others. In March 1803, Congress increased the set-aside to 5 million acres. Still, a set-aside did not in itself create any right to indemnification or other form of compensation for the speculators. That would have to await separate legislation.

C. Peter Magrath, the preeminent expert on the Yazoo scandal, remarked that the speculators who comprised the New England Mississippi Land Company "formed an almost classic illustration of a political interest group" whose dominant characteristics "were its sectionalism, its bipartisan composition,

---

26. MAGRATH at 20.
27. MAGRATH at 21–22.

and the prominence, in business and politics, of its directors and largest shareholders."[28] Mimicking the change of political forces in Washington, prominent Republicans replaced Federalists as the front men for the lobbying effort. Still, the campaign for compensation struggled. In 1804, the anti-Yazooist congressman John Randolph of Roanoke, young and shrill but unmatched in oratorical eloquence, stymied the push for a bill that would have indemnified the speculators. In each of the next two years, the Senate passed pro-Yazooist bills, but the House defeated the legislation both times. Federalists supported compensation almost to a man, but by 1806 Republicans massively outnumbered them, and they still opposed compensation by a ratio of 2–1. While continuing to condemn the speculators in principle, the Jefferson administration now supported some form of compensation in the interests of closure. The Yazooists had made some progress in four years of legislative campaigning, but they had ultimately lost every time. It was time to try something different.

Four years earlier, on June 1, 1803, Robert Fletcher, a citizen of New Hampshire, had sued John Peck, a citizen of Massachusetts, in the U.S. Circuit Court for Massachusetts, alleging that Peck had violated covenants effectively guaranteeing good title to the 15,000 acres of Yazoo land that Peck had sold to Fletcher. Magrath wrote:

> Beyond any doubt the case of Fletcher against Peck was a collusive suit, an arranged case between friendly "adversaries" acting on behalf of the New England Mississippi Land Company. Those who arrange collusive suits—less politely called faked cases—do not normally leave records but in this instance explicit documentation would provide little more than a useful footnote to the impressive circumstantial and internal evidence showing that *Fletcher v. Peck* was a rigged case.[29]

There was an almost total convergence of the parties' interests. If Peck won, everybody won: title would be upheld, meaning that Peck and his fellow speculators would have powerful ammunition to obtain compensation from Congress, and Fletcher would have 15,000 increasingly valuable acres of land, purchased for a paltry sum.

In October 1806, the case was tried to a jury that rendered an indecisive verdict, "pray[ing] the advisement of the court" on the critical issue of whether Georgia had good title to pass to the original purchasers. In October 1807, Supreme Court Justice William Cushing (riding circuit) and District Court Judge John Davis rendered judgment for Peck, ruling for him on every disputed point. The Yazooists had their judgment. But a circuit court judgment was not much to wave in the halls of the Capitol. What they needed was an affirmance on the merits from the Supreme Court. A litigation that had previously crept forward in

28. Magrath at 37–38.
29. Magrath at 54.

obscurity now emerged from the shadows. Fletcher, outwardly claiming that the circuit court had got it wrong, petitioned the Supreme Court for a writ of error.

Unlike the later-introduced writ of certiorari, the writ of error triggered mandatory jurisdiction. That is, the Supreme Court had no discretion to refuse the petitioner a plenary hearing on the merits. But this presumed the existence of an otherwise proper case; of course the Supreme Court was not obligated to entertain a case over which Article III of the Constitution did not provide for jurisdiction. *Marbury* had made that much clear. Thus it was no cinch that the Supreme Court would reach the merits of *Fletcher v. Peck*, a collusive case without truly adversary parties.

Without question the Court knew it was a feigned case. At Madison's inaugural ball, Justice Henry Brockholst Livingston commented to John Quincy Adams (who was counsel of record to Peck at the time) on "the reluctance of the Court to decide the case at all, as it appeared manifestly made up for the purpose of getting the Court's judgment upon all the points." Marshall made a similar comment to William Cranch, the Supreme Court reporter. And Justice William Johnson's concurrence stated that he had been "very unwilling" to decide the case because "it appears to me to bear strong evidence, upon the face of it, of being a mere feigned case." But the Court, Marshall in particular, very much wished to reach the merits.

Arguing for Peck was Robert Goodloe Harper, who "stood in the front rank of the lawyers of his day," and Joseph Story, a Yazooist lobbyist, John Marshall intimate, and future Supreme Court justice himself. (Story replaced John Quincy Adams, who had been appointed ambassador to Russia.) Harper and Story delivered a powerful argument that covered every critical point—that the Georgia Legislature was empowered to sell the lands and had good title; that no legislature had the power to revoke an executed grant; and that the repeal act violated the Contracts Clause of the federal constitution. Arguing for Fletcher was Luther Martin, who had successfully defended Samuel Chase in his impeachment trial and who had been a vocal member of the Aaron Burr treason defense team. But the argument in *Fletcher v. Peck* was not his finest moment. He completely passed over two of the most critical issues in the litigation—whether the corruption surrounding the original conveyance rendered it a legal nullity, and whether the repeal act violated the Contracts Clause. It seems Martin, a notorious inebriate, was so drunk during the argument that Chief Justice Marshall adjourned the proceedings until counsel could regain sobriety.[30]

It is extremely doubtful that Martin's erratic performance had any significant effect on the outcome. The Court, four Federalists and three Republicans, unanimously ruled for Peck. Unsurprisingly, Marshall delivered the opinion of the Court. He almost certainly exerted considerable intellectual influence on several of the justices, especially Bushrod Washington (widely viewed as Marshall's

30. MAGRATH at 67–69.

intellectual twin), Samuel Chase (by then politically impotent) and William Cushing (by then half senile). Henry Livingston and Thomas Todd were Republicans, but were not considered heavyweights and almost never dissented. Only William Johnson of South Carolina, a vociferous champion of natural law, could stand up to Marshall's intellect, and Johnson in fact did write a separate opinion.

Marshall's opinion ratified Peck's arguments down the line. Alluding to the bribery by which the grants were procured, he expressed doubt that a court could ever properly invalidate legislation on the ground that it had been the product of corruption. "Must it be direct corruption, or would interest or undue influence of any kind be sufficient?" Marshall asked. "Must the vitiating cause operate on a majority, or on what number of the members? Would the act be null, whatever might be the wish of the nation, or would its obligation or nullity depend upon the public sentiment?"[31] These were political questions beyond the competence of a court, Marshall implied. The Court could not, and would not, examine the motives of the legislators. This line of thinking perfectly paralleled the arguments Harper had made in his early pamphlet.

Accusing the repealing legislature of setting itself up as the "judge in its own case," Marshall insisted upon the application of the same rules that would govern in court. "The question was, in its nature, a question of title," Marshall noted. This was a legal, not political, question, and the law had a clear answer for it. Of course a conveyance could be set aside for fraud, but only as between the parties. The reliance interests of bona fide purchasers without notice of the fraud had to be protected, lest all titles become insecure and the market be destabilized. This point was central to Marshall's intellect and experience. He had absorbed it from his early study of Blackstone, and it was painfully reinforced by his own speculation in the Fairfax lands of the Northern Neck of Virginia, title to which was in flux long after his purchases.

Marshall conceded the general power of a legislature to repeal the work product of its predecessors but denied that it extended to the extinguishment of title conveyed by previous legislation. Property rights were fundamental. "It may well be doubted whether the nature of society and of government does not prescribe some limits to the legislative power; and, if any be prescribed, where are they to be found, if the property of an individual, fairly and honestly acquired, may be seized without compensation," he wrote.[32] This was the great danger of democracy, that the masses would use their numbers to expropriate and redistribute wealth simply by confiscating property without compensation. Marshall was clearly alluding to a concept of natural law.

But he did not stop there. He boldly insisted that the repeal act violated the Contracts Clause. Marshall had found a constitutional, positive-law repository for this natural and philosophical commitment to vested property rights.

31. 10 U.S. (6 Cranch) at 130.
32. *Id.* at 135.

The Contracts Clause was hardly a perfect fit; it was a stretch to see a conveyance of land as a "contract," and it was a stretch to see the Contracts Clause as covering anything more than contracts between private individuals. Justice Johnson's concurrence abjured any reliance on the Contracts Clause, preferring instead to rest entirely on natural law. The Contracts Clause rationalization stuck, though, and remained the principal constitutional means of protecting property rights until "substantive due process" rose to the task in the late nineteenth century.

The significance of *Fletcher v. Peck* should not be lost. A political interest group, frustrated in its attempts to lobby the legislature, turned to the federal courts. The litigation featured anything but the "sharp adversary presentation" and "honest, antagonistic" assertion of opposed interests that the modern orthodox wisdom insists are, and always have been, the irreducible minima of Article III adjudication. The Supreme Court provided a remedy for the violation of vested rights, and further used the litigation as an opportunity to alter constitutional law in a manner that would further protect vested rights. When C. Peter Magrath published his study of the Yazoo scandal in 1966, he could not help but note that "the Court of Earl Warren still functions in ways that are essentially the same as those of the Court of John Marshall."[33] It may be true, as one modern commentator has argued, that the collusive case was in fact a common way of bringing litigation in the early nineteenth century, and therefore that the feigned quality of *Fletcher v. Peck* should not be blown out of proportion.[34] But if collusive cases were in fact common during that period, that only cuts further into the modern orthodoxy about Article III adjudication.

Marbury and *Fletcher* evidence the linkage between John Marshall and two fundamental ideals. One is that separation of powers principles require that courts exercise jurisdiction given them, just as they forbid courts to exercise jurisdiction where it has not been given to them. The separation of law and politics was achieved when courts confined themselves to claims of vested legal rights—no further "restraint" was required, or indeed permissible. In that sense, the "action" of exercising jurisdiction over claims of vested rights was inseparable from the "restraint" against wading into politics. Marshall's second fundamental ideal, *ubi jus, ibi remedium,* was closely related to the first. It too implicated the line between law and politics. If one demonstrated a violation of his rights, it was the court's obligation to supply a remedy; the court could not withhold a remedy on grounds that society would be better off if the wrong went unredressed. To withhold a remedy under such circumstances would be to act on policy, which was politics by another name.

---

33. MAGRATH at viii.

34. *See* Lindsay Robertson, *"A Mere Feigned Case": Rethinking the Fletcher* v. *Peck Conspiracy and Early Republican Legal Culture,* 2000 UTAH L. REV. 249.

2. DAVID BREWER, NATURAL RIGHTS, AND THE TRIUMPH OF EQUITY

David Josiah Brewer was born on June 20, 1837, to an "old stock" New England family.[1] His father, Josiah Brewer of Berkshire County, Massachusetts, was a Congregationalist minister whose missionary work took him to Gibraltar, Syria, Constantinople, Malta, the Greek islands, and Smyrna (in Asia Minor), where David was born. David's mother was Emilia A. Field, whose four brothers included two legal giants—David Dudley Field and Stephen J. Field. Young David Brewer had been told he was destined for a career in the law, and he did not disappoint. After graduating Yale, he moved to Albany, New York, where he spent a year reading law in the office of his uncle David. Albany Law School was next. Brewer then headed west, to private practice in Kansas City, Missouri, and Leavenworth, Kansas.

Struggling along with most others during a severe depression, Brewer caught his first big break in 1861 when he was appointed a commissioner of the federal circuit court. Brewer was actually more interested in a legislative career than a judicial one, and the next year he thought he had won commitments from enough delegates to give him the Republican nomination for a seat. The convention turned to someone else, however, and instead nominated Brewer for the judgeship of the county probate court, which included a considerable criminal practice. He reluctantly accepted, barely won the general election, and embarked on a judicial career.[2]

In 1884, having served thirteen years on the Kansas Supreme Court, Brewer was appointed to the U.S. Circuit Court. In those days, the federal circuit courts mostly served as trial courts whose jurisdiction included a hodge-podge of cases arising under federal law—patents, trademarks, copyrights, mineral rights, Indian and railroad lands, extradition, foreign corporations, state boundary disputes, and pensions. Of course, the circuit courts also decided a broad range of diversity cases. But the case that best foretold Brewer's career on the U.S. Supreme Court involved none of the above subjects.

On September 24, 1887, Circuit Judge Brewer was presented with a bill in equity by Albert F. Parsons, the police judge of Lincoln, Nebraska. The Lincoln city council, recently elected on a reform platform, strongly suspected Parsons of misappropriating city monies. When the council launched an investigation, Parsons went to federal circuit court seeking a preliminary injunction to stop

1. BRODHEAD, *supra* at 1.
2. BRODHEAD, *supra*, Ch. 1.

the council. Parsons argued that the investigation amounted to a trial, thus depriving him of liberty without due process of law. Brewer thought the bill's allegations contained sufficient merit to justify at least a temporary injunction to preserve the status quo pending further proceedings, so he enjoined the council from continuing its investigation. The council members could scarcely believe that Brewer would issue an injunction, which they believed was beyond his jurisdiction. They decided to roll the dice and disobey.

They lost. As Brewer's biographer put it:

> Confidently expecting to be released, they were shocked when Brewer, before a packed courtroom, imposed heavy fines. "If the court should say that men occupying so high a position can disregard the process of the courts," said Brewer, "what may we expect from men having no such backing or position, respectability, and influence?" He compared their defiance of the law to the recent Haymarket Riot in Chicago.[3]

The council members immediately petitioned the U.S. Supreme Court for a writ of habeas corpus, which was granted by a vote of 6–2. Writing for the majority, Justice Horace Gray agreed with the council members that Brewer had exceeded his jurisdiction in issuing the injunction. There were many reasons why Brewer lacked jurisdiction, according to the Court. The federal equity power did not extend to injunctions against criminal proceedings, Gray stated. Nor did it extend to cases involving the issue of entitlement to state or local offices. Next, the Due Process Clause of the Fifth Amendment did not apply as against state action, only as against the United States. Even if it were to apply against state action, it would be triggered only by a deprivation of liberty or property, neither of which was involved here, in the majority's view. Returning to the matter of federal equity power, Gray emphasized that such power could only be invoked to protect property interests. Finally, because Brewer was without jurisdiction to issue the injunction, the council members' disobedience could not legally constitute contempt, and therefore the contempt punishment could not stand. Even Brewer's uncle, Justice Stephen Field, voted to grant the writ.

Thus did the Court repudiate Brewer's strident assertion of the equity power. That notwithstanding, the Lincoln city council case had revealed a great deal about Brewer's jurisprudential assumptions. He had showed little concern about the use of equity in a situation where it might impinge, albeit indirectly, upon the state's ability to vindicate its own criminal laws.[4] Strictly speaking, the council proceeding might not have been "criminal," as Chief Justice Morrison Waite and Justice John Marshall Harlan pointed out in dissent, but surely a

---

3. BRODHEAD, *supra* at 68 & nn. 75–76.

4. Almost one hundred years later, it was precisely that concern that led the Court to strike down the assertion of equity power in *Huffman v. Pursue, Ltd.*, 420 U.S. 592 (1975).

federal adjudication of the matter might have implications for a subsequent prosecution of Parsons. Quite simply, Brewer was unconcerned with notions of federalism or technical limits on jurisdiction because he believed that federal equity courts had inherent power to do whatever was necessary to vindicate constitutional rights. This power stemmed not from any congressional act, indeed not even from the Constitution itself, but from the basic principles that preexisted the Constitution and which the Framers enshrined therein. For Brewer, these basic principles came from natural law—from the principles of justice exemplified in liberal Protestant doctrine and culture. They included not only the protection of liberty of contract and private property, but all other rights that citizens could not fairly be said to have relinquished in the social contract. Surely citizens had not relinquished their right to due process before being removed from governmental office, merely to obtain the benefits of the social contract. Thus, individuals retained such a right to procedural due process, and federal equity courts possessed whatever powers were necessary to vindicate such rights.

The legal historian Edward A. Purcell, Jr., has emphasized Brewer's natural law beliefs in both the Constitution and equity jurisprudence:

> The Constitution's true authority, Brewer believed, came from the fact that it incorporated the principles of the Declaration of Independence and the divine truths of Christianity. It affirmed the "sacredness of life, of liberty, and of property," and it proclaimed that government was based on and limited by "inalienable rights" that were "given not by man to man, but granted by the Almighty."[5]

Noting that, for Brewer, "[t]he nature of the Constitution determined the role of the courts," Purcell continued:

> The federal judiciary's paramount power lay in its equity jurisdiction, and Brewer sought to defend and expand that jurisdiction wherever possible. Repeatedly, he appealed to the doctrine that federal equity was a system of "independent" remedies authorized by the Constitution itself. "It is a mistake to suppose that for the determination of equities and equitable rights we must look only to the statutes of Congress," he declared for the Court in 1906. "The principles of equity exist independently of and anterior to all Congressional legislation." Similarly, he insisted that federal equity was also insulated from state action, maintaining that the creation of new state remedies at law should not deprive a federal equity court of jurisdiction. The independence of federal equity conferred broad discretion on the national courts, and it offered Brewer a wide field where he could apply his "convictions of right and wrong." Equally important, he considered equity's classic remedy, the injunction, to be the

5. PURCELL, *supra* note 2 at 47–48.

> ideal instrument for protecting private property and enforcing public order. Declaring that he was "as much opposed to government by judges as any man," Brewer maintained that equitable relief had nothing to do with discretion or policy. "[T]he writ of injunction is not an act of legislation," he explained. "It creates no new law." Rather, it was simply the law's most useful remedy. "It only enforces rights which the Constitution and the law have theretofore declared sacred."[6]

Nowhere was Brewer's reverence for and devotion to the equity jurisprudence more clear than in the case of the Pullman strike of 1894.[7] The Pullman railroad car company had responded to the severe depression of 1893 by sharply reducing its wages. This wage reduction was not accompanied by any reduction of the rent in company-owned housing. In May 1894 the Pullman employees struck, and thus began the largest labor dispute in the history of the nation. Soon thereafter the American Railway Union, led by Eugene V. Debs from his base in Chicago, voted to require all 150,000 of its union members to stop handling trains including any Pullman car. Chicago being the hub of the nation's railroad system, the strike quickly paralyzed shipment of food, fuel, and livestock. But Pullman management would not relent.

On July 2, 1894, the federal government filed a verified bill in equity in the U.S. Circuit Court for the Northern District of Illinois against Debs and other union officials, alleging that they had conspired illegally to obstruct the transport of the U.S. mails and to prevent the railroads from fulfilling their obligations as common carriers. The court quickly issued an injunction forbidding anyone with notice of the injunction to interfere with the operation of the rail system. Few obeyed. The federal marshal called for troops, who were met with massive resistance; 20 people were killed and 2,000 railroad cars were destroyed. Eventually thousands of U.S. Army troops and federal marshals quelled the violence.

On July 17, an information (complaint) was filed in the federal circuit court alleging that Debs and other union officers had disobeyed the injunction. After a hearing, the court found Debs and others guilty of criminal contempt and sentenced them to imprisonment in the county jail for terms varying from three to six months. On January 14, 1895, Debs and his colleagues petitioned the U.S. Supreme Court for writs of habeas corpus. Lyman Trumbull and Clarence Darrow argued for Debs and his fellow union officials. Justice Brewer wrote for a unanimous Court denying the petitions.

The technical question before the Court was not whether the injunction should have been issued in the first place but whether the circuit court had

---

6. PURCELL, *supra* note 2, Ch. 1, at 48–49.
7. In Re Debs, 158 U.S. 564 (1895).

jurisdiction to issue it.[8] Despite that, the Court made a point of resting its decision on the broadest possible grounds.[9]

First, the Court established that Congress was not powerless when it came to preventing the violence associated with the strike. In fact Congress did exercise two of these powers, growing out of the Commerce Clause and the post office clause. Brewer then implied that the federal equity jurisdiction is coextensive with the government's enumerated powers under the Constitution. If the government had the power to protect interstate commerce and the post by its own enforcement, then surely it could appeal to the federal courts to enforce those powers. Citing the established federal equity jurisdiction to redress public nuisances, Brewer made it clear that the government was authorized to seek an injunction against the Pullman strike:

> [T]here is no such impotency in the national government. The entire strength of the nation may be used to enforce in any part of the land the full and free exercise of all national powers and the security of all rights entrusted by the Constitution to its care. The strong arm of the national government may be put forth to brush away all obstructions to the freedom of interstate commerce or the transportation of the mails. If the emergency arises, the army of the Nation, and all its militia, are at the service of the Nation to compel obedience to its laws.
>
> But passing to the second question, is there no other alternative than the use of force on the part of the executive authorities whenever obstructions arise to the freedom of interstate commerce or the transportation of the mails? Is the army the only instrument by which rights of the public can be enforced and the peace of the nation preserved? Grant that any public nuisance may be forcibly abated either at the instance of the authorities, or by any individual suffering private damage therefrom, the existence of this right of forcible abatement is not inconsistent with nor does it destroy the right of appeal in an orderly way to the courts for a judicial determination, and an exercise of their powers by writ of injunction and otherwise to accomplish the same result.[10]

---

8. "According to the standard rule, the Court was not to determine whether the injunction that Debs had disobeyed was appropriately issued . . . the only issue open for review was whether the circuit court had jurisdiction . . . . But this was only a formal gesture, and the Court did not confine itself to this technical question. Rather, it tried to explain why the injunction itself was a proper exercise of judicial power." Fiss, *supra* note 1, Ch. 1, at 61, citing In Re Sawyer, 124 U.S. 200 (1888). For an argument that questions of jurisdiction are not always separable from the merits, see Evan Tsen Lee, *The Dubious Concept of Jurisdiction*, 54 Hastings L. J. 1613 (2003).

9. Professor Fiss saw in *Debs* "a conscious desire to reach beyond the technical requirements of the case in order to define the powers of the state in the constitutional design." Fiss, *supra* note 1, Ch. 1, at 61.

10. 158 U.S. at 582.

Brewer had now established that equity was appropriate to restrain this breach of the peace. But was the United States really eligible to seek such a remedy? Trumbull argued that the equity jurisdiction did not cover the case because the United States had no "property" right at stake. "This is not a bill by the owner of property to prevent an irreparable injury," Trumbull pointed out. "The government does not own the railroads."[11] Indeed, a case from seven years earlier, *United States v. San Jacinto Tin Co.*,[12] seemed to have established the proposition that the United States could not sue for equitable relief unless it had a "pecuniary interest" in the outcome. Brewer, however, was undeterred. Certainly federal equity jurisdiction existed to vindicate property rights, but that was not all. Plainly the public interest was implicated here. The citizenry held certain "common rights"—he did not specify which rights these were—and the equity power was equal to their protection, whether or not the government could show a "pecuniary interest" in the matter. Brewer stated:

> [W]hile it is not the province of the government to interfere in any mere matter of private controversy between individuals, or to use its great powers to enforce the rights of one against another, yet, whenever the wrongs complained of are such as affect the public at large, and are in respect of matters which by the Constitution are entrusted to the care of the Nation, and concerning which the Nation owes the duty to all the citizens of securing to them their common rights, then the mere fact that the government has no pecuniary interest in the controversy is not sufficient to exclude it from the courts, or prevent it from taking measures therein to fully discharge those constitutional duties.[13]

For Brewer, the federal government's eligibility to invoke the federal equity jurisdiction was coterminous with its enumerated powers under the Constitution. And, even if the government could not point to any property "right" of its own, the "common rights" of the citizenry were at stake, and equity was available to vindicate them. Here was a breathtakingly broad interpretation of equity jurisprudence and the government's power to invoke it.

The notion of judicial modesty that would later characterize the era of Justices Louis Brandeis and Felix Frankfurter is conspicuously absent from Brewer's opinion in *Debs*. In answer to the argument that "a mob could not be suppressed by injunction," Brewer triumphantly quoted from a striker's testimony given to the U.S. Strike Commission:

> As soon as the employees found that we were arrested, and taken from the scene of action, they became demoralized, and that ended the strike. It was

11. 158 U.S. at 575.
12. 125 U.S. 273 (1888).
13. 158 U.S. at 586.

> not the old brotherhoods that ended the strike. It was simply the United States courts that ended the strike. [T]he strike was broken up . . . not by the army and not by any other power, but simply and solely by the action of the United States courts in restraining us from discharging our duties as officers and representatives of our employees.[14]

Brewer simply believed that courts must use the equity jurisprudence wherever necessary to protect God-given property rights. Legal remedies might be frustrated by technicalities, but not equity. He underscored this point forcefully in *United States v. Detroit Timber & Lumber Co.*, a case involving land patents.[15] Writing for the Court, Brewer stated:

> It is a mistake to suppose that for the determination of equities and equitable rights we must look only to the statutes of Congress. The principles of equity exist independently of and anterior to all Congressional legislation, and the statutes are either annunciations of those principles or limitations upon their application in particular cases. In passing upon transactions between the Government and its vendees we must bear in mind the general principles of equity and determine rights upon those principles except as they are limited by special statutory provisions. And clearly upon those principles a party purchasing an equitable right is entitled to be protected in his purchase so far as it can be done without trespassing upon the rights of other parties.[16]

In other words, the property rights that arose from general principles of jurisprudence were protected by remedies that arose of general principles of equity jurisprudence. Substantive rights rooted in natural law were to be vindicated by remedies rooted in natural law.

The reality, of course, was that these high-minded principles were being fed by outright fear—of mob rule, of mass confiscation of private property, and of the physical safety of innocent people. In his study of conservative responses to the uprisings of this period, Arnold Paul shed light on the mindset of the bar's leading men. William Ramsey of Cincinnati blamed immigration as the root of the problem—"a large infusion of ignorance and viciousness rapidly recruited from the worst elements of the population of the old world . . . and all of this in a land governed by the ideas of the majority."[17] Edward J. Phelps, former president of the American Bar Association and Kent Professor of Law at Yale, said, "The accursed warfare of classes is the danger that appears chiefly to threaten the future."[18] Seymour D. Thompson, senior editor of the prestigious American

14. 158 U.S. at 597.

15. 200 U.S. 321 (1906).

16. *Id.* at 339.

17. Arnold Paul, Conservative Crisis and the Rule of Law 66 (reprinted by Peter Smith, 1976; originally published by Cornell Univ. Press 1960).

18. *Id.* at 62–63.

Law Review and someone generally sympathetic to progressive thought, wrote: "The corporations, and especially the railway corporations, have often been in the wrong . . . . But in [the *Debs* case] they were in the right. They entered upon a struggle with an unknown and appalling force, which threatened to revolutionize the very foundations of society and to reverse all the processes by which our splendid industrial system has been built up."[19] Fear and principle coexisted in this symbiotic relationship, each intensifying the other and strengthening the resolve of Brewer and like-minded judges to put a judicial brake on the crisis.

Brewer's most frequent ally on the Court was Rufus Wheeler Peckham. Peckham was born in Albany in 1838 and named after his father, who would serve on the New York Court of Appeals. The family was full of lawyers and judges, including young Rufus's older brother Wheeler, whose nomination to the U.S. Supreme Court was defeated in committee. Rufus also became a lawyer and, following in his father's footsteps, won election to the New York Court of Appeals in 1887. Nine years later his close friend Grover Cleveland appointed him to the U.S. Supreme Court, on which he served until "dying in the full vigor of his ripe manhood in 1909."[20] Peckham was a man's man—one "of vigorous and forceful character; frank and outspoken and courageous in every relation in life."[21] He was disinclined to nuance or subtlety. His opinions often took the form of a logical *tour de force,* reasoning remorselessly from syllogisms stacked one atop the next, even when their premises were controversial. Oliver Wendell Holmes, Jr., once said the major premise of Peckham's jurisprudence was "God damn it," thereby revealing something about both men.

Holmes's most famous jab at Peckham and Brewer was that the Constitution "does not enact Mr. Herbert Spencer's Social Statics." Peckham had written the majority opinion in *Lochner v. New York,*[22] which struck down local limits on how many hours per day bakers could work, and Holmes's dissent accused the majority of having written Spencer's philosophy into the Fourteenth Amendment. Peckham's opinion, joined by Brewer, elevated the principle of liberty of contract over the government's claimed justification for hourly limits, which was to protect employee health. Holmes's witticism has forever linked the *Lochner* majority with Spencer in the public consciousness, but it is unclear how deserved the linkage is. To be sure, *Social Statics* posited a natural justification for individualism and a minimalist state. Peckham and Brewer similarly believed in individual natural rights to liberty and property. Their beliefs, however, stemmed from liberal Protestant idealism and, more remotely, from Scottish commonsense realism, not from science. It was not that Peckham and Brewer did not believe in science—they, like other elite liberal Protestants of the era, sought to

19. *Id.* at 144–45.
20. Proceedings on the Death of Mr. Justice Peckham, 215 U.S. v, xi (1909).
21. *Id.*
22. 198 U.S. 45 (1905).

adjust their religious views to accommodate the scientific discoveries of the nineteenth century, evolution in particular. They did not, however, share Spencer's harsh inferences from the observation that, among the species, there was a tendency to the "survival of the fittest" (a phrase that Darwin, in point of fact, pinched from Spencer). Spencer celebrated the eradication of the weak and complained that social intervention on their behalf would merely cause "idiots, imbeciles, drunkards, lunatics, paupers, and prostitutes" to multiply.[23] There is no evidence that Peckham and Brewer felt this animosity toward the unfortunate; indeed, their liberal Protestantism posited the inherent goodness of man and suggested Christian charity.[24] Brewer's calling cards were emblazoned with the credo, "Right is Might"—hardly the rallying cry of a Social Darwinist. Although Brewer and Peckham may have embraced the gentry's general belief that many in the lower class were consigned to lives of penury because of their poor work and saving habits, they did not believe these behaviors were strictly genetic. Anyone who adopted good work habits and the salutary practices of self-denial could live a virtuous and therefore inherently valuable life. Certainly Holmes—he of "three generations of imbeciles are enough"—was an odd candidate to be accusing others of agreement with Spencer.[25]

Peckham not only shared Brewer's deep belief in natural rights, he shared Brewer's commitment to use the equity power to enforce those rights, irrespective of technical and jurisdictional limits. It was Peckham who authored the Court's opinion in *Ex Parte Young*, a decision that was later to become the fulcrum of the Warren Court's institutional reform jurisprudence. On April 4, 1907, the Minnesota Legislature cut the maximum rates that railroads could charge passengers, lowering the ceiling from three cents per mile to two.[26] The day before the new rate was to take effect, shareholders of the Northern Pacific Railway Company brought a derivative action in federal circuit court, requesting

---

23. Steven Shapin, *Man with a Plan*, New Yorker, Aug. 13, 2007, at 77.

24. For examples of revisionist scholarship on Peckham and Brewer, see James W. Ely, Jr., *Rufus W. Peckham and Economic Liberty* (unpublished manuscript); Robert E. Gamer, *Justice Brewer and Substantive Due Process: A Conservative Court Revisited,* 18 Vanderbilt L. Rev. 615 (1965).

25. Buck v. Bell, 274 U.S. 200, 207 (1927).

26. Prior to the Civil War, state legislatures imposed safety regulations and general reporting requirements on railroads. After the war, many states created railroad commissions, which inherited the job of regulating safety and requiring reporting, but which had an all-important new mandate—regulating rates. In the antebellum period, people generally saw railroads as a positive force for progress and freedom. But as railroads gained enormous economic and political power, a demand for rate regulation developed. The federal government got involved in railroad regulation with the creation of the Interstate Commerce Commission in 1887. For a study of how railroads transformed American society, see Barbara Young Welke, Recasting American Liberty (Cambridge Univ. Press 2001).

an injunction that would prohibit the railroad from complying with the new rate and the state attorney general from enforcing it. The attorney general, Edward T. Young, moved to dismiss on the ground that the court lacked jurisdiction. The suit was nominally against him, but he had no personal interest in the matter; thus, it was in reality a suit against the state of Minnesota. The Eleventh Amendment of the U.S. Constitution, ratified in 1798, states: "The Judicial Power of the United States shall not be construed to extend to any suit in law or equity, commenced or prosecuted against one of the United States by Citizens of another State, or by Citizens or Subjects of any Foreign State." This suit was for equitable relief, brought against Minnesota, by plaintiffs at least one of whom was a citizen of another state.[27] The Eleventh Amendment deprived the circuit court of jurisdiction to proceed, Young insisted.

The circuit court disagreed and enjoined Young from attempting to enforce the new rate. Rather than appeal the entry of the injunction, Young filed an enforcement action in state court, in direct contravention of the order. When the circuit court called upon him to show cause why he should not be held in contempt of court, he repeated his original argument: the Eleventh Amendment deprived the court of jurisdiction to enter the injunction in the first place. The order was void *ab initio* (a legal nullity) and could not support a contempt judgment. The circuit court remained unmoved and held him in contempt.

With nowhere else to go, Young now turned to the U.S. Supreme Court. He filed simultaneous petitions for a writ of certiorari and a writ of habeas corpus. The Court ruled against him, 8–1, with Peckham writing for a majority that included both Brewer and Holmes. It was not Peckham's usual Spartan opinion. It exhaustively reviewed the precedents and began with unaccustomed judicial modesty:

> We recognize and appreciate to the fullest extent the very great importance of this case, not only to the parties now before the court, but also to the great mass of the citizens of this country, all of whom are interested in the practical working of the courts of justice throughout the land, both Federal and state, and in the proper exercise of the jurisdiction of the Federal courts, as limited and controlled by the Federal Constitution and the laws of Congress.
>
> That there has been room for difference of opinion with regard to such limitations the reported cases in this court bear conclusive testimony. It cannot be stated that the case before us is entirely free from any possible doubt nor that intelligent men may not differ as to the correct answer to the question we are called upon to decide.[28]

The case's importance ran along multiple lines. That Young had been held in contempt for doing no more than filing an action in state court obviously

27. Charles E. Perkins was a citizen of Iowa.
28. Ex Parte Young, 209 U.S. 123, 142 (1908).

implicated the relationship between federal and state courts. If anything, however, it even more sharply implicated the relationship between the federal courts and state legislatures. In this field, the Court had zigzagged unaccountably for the previous thirty years. In *Munn v. Illinois* and the *Granger Cases* of 1877, the Court had broadly upheld the regulation of grain elevator and railroad rates.[29] But in *Chicago, Milwaukee & St. Paul Railway v. Minnesota* (1890), the Court reversed the state supreme court's holding that railroad rates were not subject to judicial review. The decision was difficult to square with the 1877 cases; Justice Joseph P. Bradley's dissent contended that the majority had "practically overrule[d]" *Munn*. In *Budd v. New York* (1892), the Court could have embraced then-New York Court of Appeals Judge Rufus Peckham's frontal attack on *Munn* in dissent, but instead it affirmed.[30] In *Reagan v. Farmer's Loan & Trust Co.* (1894), Brewer's majority opinion swept aside an Eleventh Amendment challenge and upheld an injunction against commission-set rates. Sitting down to write the opinion in *Ex Parte Young*, Peckham knew the future of the relationship between federal courts and state legislatures was at stake.

Before the Supreme Court, Young had argued not only that the Eleventh Amendment barred federal court jurisdiction, but that the case raised no federal question to begin with. Interestingly, this brought Peckham right to the heart of the matter: Was the sufficiency of the rates a question cognizable in federal court? Peckham said yes, but he immediately spotted another ground supporting federal jurisdiction. The penalty for violating the rate regulations was ninety days in jail. There was no statutory provision for a hearing prior to enforcement. If a railroad wanted to challenge the validity of the rates, one of its employees had to disobey and defend the prosecution by attacking the rates' validity. This scheme deprived the railroads of property without due process, which constituted both a violation of the Fourteenth Amendment and a federal question sufficient to support jurisdiction. Therefore the circuit court had been right to issue the injunction—provided that the Eleventh Amendment did not bar the action.

Literally, the Eleventh Amendment did not apply. The shareholders' suit named the attorney general as defendant, not the state. Early on, the Supreme Court, speaking through no less an authority than John Marshall, had adopted such a literal approach, but the Court's practice soon became inconsistent.[31]

29. Munn v. Illinois, 94 U.S. 113 (1877); Stone v. Wisconsin, 94 U.S. 181 (1877); Winona & St. P. R. R. v. Blake, 94 U.S. 180 (1877); Chicago, M. & St. P. R. R. v. Ackley, 94 U.S. 179 (1877); Peik v. Chicago & N. W. Ry., 94 U.S. 164 (1877); Chicago, B. & Q. R. R. v. Iowa, 94 U.S. 155 (1877).

30. For a fuller narrative of these cases, see William F. Duker, *Mr. Justice Rufus W. Peckham and the Case of Ex* Parte Young: *Lochnerizing* Munn v. Illinois, 1980 B.Y.U. L. REV. 539.

31. The literal approach was endorsed in *Osborn v. Bank of the United States*, 22 U.S. (9 Wheat.) 738, 857 (1824). But only four years later the Court found the nominal

Under the literal approach, one would think the Eleventh Amendment would become a dead letter, as plaintiffs would simply learn to name state officials as defendants rather than states themselves. As the eminent constitutional scholar David Currie put it, "People are not likely to amend constitutions just to change captions on complaints."[32] And so it seemed inevitable that the courts would look past the pleadings to see whether the state was the real party in interest. In the shareholders' original suit against Young, no great insight was required to see that the state of Minnesota was the actual party in interest. Young was defending the validity of the rate regulations on behalf of the legislature. If the court were to find the regulations unconstitutional, there was no personal loss to Young; he converted it into a case of personal loss only by disobeying the injunction and thereby committing contempt.

But state legislatures could not be permitted to obscure systematic deprivations of property without due process from federal judicial view. Even the hallowed notion of Jacksonian democracy could not be permitted to overrun all vested property rights. Peckham deployed a fiction to pierce the literal shield of the Eleventh Amendment. If the law that Young was seeking to enforce was unconstitutional, then it could provide Young no shield of authority. Young insisted that his prosecution of the enforcement action was purely in his capacity as the state's representative. But if the rate regulations were a legal nullity on account of their unconstitutionality, then they could provide Young no legal cover. He was stripped of his authority, meaning that he stood before the circuit court only as a private individual – and the Eleventh Amendment says nothing about suits against private individuals. Peckham wrote:

> The answer to this is the same as made in every case where an official claims to be acting under the authority of the State. The act to be enforced is alleged to be unconstitutional, and if it be so, the use of the name of the State to enforce an unconstitutional act to the injury of complainants is a proceeding without the authority of and one which does not affect the State in its sovereign or governmental capacity. It is simply an illegal act upon the part of a state official in attempting by the use of the name of the State to enforce a legislative act which is void because unconstitutional. If the act which the state Attorney General seeks to enforce be a violation of the Federal Constitution, the officer in proceeding under such an enactment comes into conflict with the superior authority of that Constitution, and he is in that case

---

defendant not to be the real party for Eleventh Amendment purposes, see Governor of Georgia v. Madrazzo, 26 U.S. (1 Pet.) 110, 123 (1828).

32. David Currie, *Sovereign Immunity and Suits Against Government Officers*, 1984 SUP. CT. REV. 149, 151 & n. 11.

> stripped of his official or representative character and is subjected in his person to the consequences of his individual conduct.[33]

Ex Parte Young demonstrated the length to which Peckham and Brewer would go to vindicate natural rights. Despite the serious consequences for federal-state relations, they were willing to entertain the merits of the constitutional claims for the sake of protecting private property and liberty of contract. Where God-given rights were at stake, technical and jurisdictional niceties had to stand aside.

Yet there is a Peckham opinion that, like *San Jacinto Tin*, could be cited as a progenitor of the modern standing doctrine. The case is *Hooker v. Burr*.[34] In 1893, Anna and Ambrose Spencer executed a mortgage on their California property in favor of Jacob Swiggert. Swiggert subsequently assigned the debt to Charles Bishop, who commenced a foreclosure action against the Spencers. The plaintiff, John Hooker, purchased the property at the foreclosure sale for $9,500. Six months later, a judgment creditor of the Spencers tendered $10,070—Hooker's $9,500 plus interest at the statutorily prescribed rate of one percent per month—in order to redeem the property. Hooker refused the tender and sued in California for a decree requiring that a deed be executed in his favor.

Hooker's principal contention was that California unconstitutionally impaired his contract rights when it amended the statute prescribing the conditions under which property sold at foreclosure sales could be subsequently redeemed. When the Spencers executed the mortgage in 1893, the statute permitted redemption within six months of the foreclosure sale, at the interest rate of two percent per month. In 1895 and 1897, however, the California Legislature amended the statute, eventually prescribing a redemption period of twelve months at one percent interest per month. These amendments occurred prior to Hooker's purchase of the property in 1898.

The U.S. Supreme Court predictably held that Hooker's rights were to be determined as of the time he purchased the property, and not as of the time that the mortgage was originally executed. This holding was decisive, as Hooker had purchased the property after the legislature's amendment of redemption conditions. In dicta, however, the Court asserted that neither the mortgagee nor his assignee had standing to challenge the statutory amendment because Hooker had paid them fully and therefore that the subsequent redemption did not injure them "one penny." Justice Peckham, writing for the Court, stated:

> We have lately held (therein following a long line of authorities) that a party insisting upon the invalidity of a statute, as violating any constitutional provision, must show that he may be injured by the unconstitutional law before the law will listen to his complaint. *Tyler v. Judges*; *Turpin v. Lemon*. If, instead of

33. 209 U.S. at 159–60.
34. 194 U.S. 415 (1904).

> showing any injury, the plaintiff shows that he cannot possibly be injured, he cannot of course ask the interference of the court. Therefore, if the mortgagee, or his assignee, were himself the plaintiff, and complaining that the obligation of his contract had been impaired by subsequent legislation, it is plain his complaint would be dismissed when it appeared that . . . he suffered no injury, because he had proceeded with the foreclosure of his mortgage and had been paid the full amount of his contract debt, interest and costs. Under such circumstances the question becomes a moot one, and courts do not sit to decide that character of question.[35]

Why the Court found it necessary to establish that the mortgagee lacked standing to challenge the constitutionality of the legislation is unclear; neither the mortgagee nor his assignee were plaintiffs, and the purchaser could not assert the mortgagee's rights. What is clear is that, by engaging in this dictum (which was hardly, as Peckham claimed, supported by a "long line" of precedents) the Court appeared to state something very much like the modern standing doctrine.

Can *Hooker v. Burr* be squared with Peckham's approach just four years later, in *Ex Parte Young*? In *Young*, after all, he refused to allow the technical jurisdictional barrier of the Eleventh Amendment to embarrass the vindication of the railroad's natural vested property rights. In *Hooker*, Peckham averred that the mortgagee or his assignee would have been barred from challenging the constitutionality of the statute because they lacked the technical adjudicative requisite, namely, personal injury. The key to resolving this seeming paradox lies in viewing the cases from the classical legal orthodox perspective of Peckham and Brewer. Neither the mortgagee nor his assignee in *Hooker* had suffered any violation of their property rights. The question was not, as today's Court would ask, whether the rate regulations in *Young* or the statutory redemption amendments in *Hooker* "caused" the plaintiff something that could fairly be characterized as "cognizable injury." Rather, the only question was whether the plaintiff demonstrated a violation of natural liberty or property rights (which, by definition for Peckham and Brewer, were constitutional rights). There was no separate inquiry into "injury" above and beyond the question of whether substantive liberty or property rights had been transgressed. For Peckham and Brewer it was not (as today's Court would insist) some kind of threshold question that transcended the subject matter of the lawsuit. It was one and the same.

Hooker v. Burr was a case of *damnum absque injuria*, which is to say, loss without injury. In common parlance, this would be an oxymoron—how can someone suffer a loss without suffering an injury? To the eighteenth-century Anglo-American legal mind, however, the term "injuria" had a special meaning.

---

35. 194 U.S. at 419 (citations omitted).

It meant not simply harm, but *wrongful* harm. Thus, if one merchant put another out of business by way of fair and accepted competition, it was *damnum absque injuria*. The vanquished merchant had suffered "loss" but not "injury" in the sense of a wrongful harm. Fully translated into contemporary common parlance, *damnum absque injuria* meant no remedy for nonwrongful acts causing loss. Translated into modern legal concepts, it meant no remedy for injuries in the absence of an actionable wrong, or, stated even more tersely, no remedy without a valid cause of action. (To a modern Anglo-American lawyer, of course, this is a truism, for "cause of action" is essentially defined as entitlement to a remedy.)

Damnum absque injuria as a bedrock principle made perfect sense to Brewer and Peckham. Equity was available to redress injustices—violations of basic rights. If one party occasioned loss to another through nonwrongful means, there was no remedy. If the act was not wrongful, by definition it could not be said that any right was violated. The actor had breached no duty owed to the other person. By the same token, however, if the actor's conduct *had* caused wrongful harm, then a right *had* been violated, and *ubi jus, ibi remedium* then took over. The principle of God-given remedies for all violations of God-given rights cohered seamlessly with these maxims.

Marbury itself established a limit on judicial review that cohered with Brewer's and Peckham's principle. The legitimacy of judicial review was linked indissolubly to the vindication of rights. Wrote Marshall:

> [I]f a law be in opposition to the constitution; if both the law and the constitution apply to a particular case, so that the court must either decide that case conformably to the law, disregarding the constitution; or conformably to the constitution, disregarding the law; the court must determine which of these conflicting rules governs the case. This is the very essence of judicial duty.
>
> If then the courts are to regard the constitution; and the constitution is superior to any ordinary act of the legislature; the constitution, and not such ordinary act, must govern the case to which they both apply.[36]

Here Marshall not only establishes the institution of judicial review, but gives the justification for it. If a party claims that government action violates his or her constitutional right, and the question of the action's constitutionality is decisive of the case, the court has a duty to decide the constitutional question. The institution of judicial review is incident to the necessity of resolving claims of right. A court has no commission to strike down legislative enactments unless indispensable to the vindication of a right. Even then, the court has no authority to remove a statute from the books; it disregards the unconstitutional law in the course of deciding the case at bar, and *stare decisis* makes the law unenforceable in future cases.

36. 5 U.S. (1 Cranch) at 178.

The *Marbury* theory of judicial review helps to explain a much-cited Brewer opinion—*Chicago & Grand Trunk Railway v. Wellman*.[37] The facts are a bit murky, but it is clear that the railroad contrived the litigation in order to challenge the constitutionality of rate restrictions. In 1889 the Michigan Legislature enacted ceilings on railroad passenger fares. The first day the law went into effect, a litigation pigeon named Thomas Wellman "made an application" for a ticket, and a suit was immediately commenced. At trial the railroad's strategy apparently was to prove, through expert testimony, that a reduction in fares would not lead to an increase in overall revenues, but instead would lead to a decrease in such revenues, which in turn would deprive the company of the ability to cover its operating expenses and fixed charges. Apparently the railroad offered only an annual total of operating expenses, without any breakdown among items. The railroad then moved for an instruction requiring the jury to find that the statute was unconstitutional. The requested instruction was denied.

Justice Brewer's opinion for the Court questioned why the jury should be instructed that the statute was unconstitutional as a matter of law. "If the validity of such a law in its application to a particular company depends upon a question of fact as to its effect upon the earnings, may not the court properly leave that question to the jury . . . ?" asked the Court.[38] If the railroad had requested an instruction establishing unconstitutionality as a matter of law, Justice Brewer surmised, then it must in reality be contending that all regulations are unconstitutional per se. Given the precedents, that contention was a nonstarter.[39] The refusal to give the instruction was not error, and the judgment was affirmed.

This did not stop Justice Brewer from delivering a stern admonition about collusive or "friendly" litigation:

> The theory upon which, apparently, this suit was brought is that parties have an appeal from the legislature to the courts; and that the latter are given an immediate and general supervision of the constitutionality of the acts of the former. Such is not true. Whenever, in pursuance of an honest and actual antagonistic assertion of rights by one individual against another, there is presented a question involving the validity of any act of any legislature, State or Federal, and the decision necessarily rests on the competency of the legislature to so enact, the court must, in the exercise of its solemn duties, determine whether the act be constitutional or not; but such an exercise of power is the ultimate and supreme function of courts. It is legitimate only in the last resort . . . It was never the thought that, by means of a friendly suit, a

---

37. 143 U.S. 339 (1892).

38. *Id.* at 344.

39. *Id.*, citing Stone v. Farmer's Loan and Trust Co., 116 U.S. 307 (1886), and Chicago, Milwaukee &c. Railway v. Minnesota, 134 U.S. 418 (1890).

> party beaten in the legislature could transfer to the courts an inquiry into the constitutionality of the legislative act. . . .
>
> Our suggestion is only to indicate how easily courts may be misled into doing grievous wrong to the public, and how careful they should be to not declare legislative acts unconstitutional upon agreed and general statements, and without the fullest disclosure of all material facts.[40]

Brewer evidently regarded *Wellman* as a fairly straightforward application of *ubi jus, ibi remedium*. Had the railroad complied with the regulations and lost so much money that it was denied a reasonable return on its investment, presumably the Court would have held the regulations unconstitutional and affirmed an injunction against future enforcement. In that case, the railroad's property rights would have been violated, and therefore deserving of a remedy. In reality, however, the railroad had suffered no loss of property rights—not yet, at least. Instead the railroad had contrived to get the constitutional issue before the courts. Where there is a right, there must be a remedy, but here there was no "honest and actual" right involved. Because the major premise of *ubi jus, ibi remedium* was missing, no remedy was forthcoming.

There was another fatal defect with the litigation, in Brewer's estimation. The problem was one of judicial craft: because collusive suits are decided upon agreed facts, undoubtedly shaded entirely to one side, they provide a poor foundation for judicial lawmaking. Justice Brewer cited but one example, the railroad's failure to break down its operating expenses. "Of what do these operating expenses consist?" he asked. "Are they made up partially of extravagant salaries; fifty to one hundred thousand dollars to the president, and in like proportion to subordinate officers?"[41] Surely, Justice Brewer asserted, before a court decides that a rate restriction is unconstitutional on the ground that it denies shareholders a reasonable return on their investment, it should know whether exorbitant sums are being paid the officers—money that could be going back to the shareholders instead.[42] As in the 1850 decision in *Lord v. Veazie*, the Court's concern was not to permit the inadequacy of the factual record and argument in a collusive suit to skew the process of judicial lawmaking—in this case, constitutional lawmaking.

* * *

Robert Post has observed that the era of "substantive due process" was really two periods, with World War I in between.[43] The era began during the Fuller Court, led by Brewer and Peckham, which struck down numerous regulatory

---

40. *Id.* at 345.

41. *Id.* at 345.

42. *Id.*

43. Robert C. Post, *Defending the Lifeworld: Substantive Due Process in the Taft Court Era*, 78 B.U. L. Rev. 1489 (1998).

statutes in fields they deemed to be insufficiently "affected with a public interest."[44] But between *Lochner* (1905) and the end of World War I (1917), the Court upheld a considerable number of regulatory regimes. Certainly during the war the Court felt it could not exercise too exacting a brand of judicial review on emergency measures. As if to heed President Warren G. Harding's inaugural call for a return to "normalcy" after the war, however, the Court once again began to strike down regulations in fields the Court determined "private." Harding himself had a huge impact on the Court, appointing William Howard Taft as Chief Justice and George Sutherland, Pierce Butler, and Edward Sanford as Associate Justices, all within the period of less than two years. Sutherland was unquestionably one of the intellectual leaders of the conservative wing of the Taft Court.

Alexander George Sutherland, Jr., was born in Stoney Stratford, Buckinghamshire, England, on March 25, 1862. His father's ancestors were from Caithenesshire, Scotland; his mother's from England. When Sutherland was eighteen months of age, the family emigrated to Utah "because of the appeals of Mormonism."[45] Sutherland's father eventually broke with the Church of Latter Day Saints, and young Sutherland "lived as a 'Gentile' among the Mormons."[46] In 1879, he enrolled in what would become Brigham Young University, finishing his studies in only two years. Fifteen months later he enrolled in the University of Michigan Law School.

At Michigan, Sutherland studied under constitutional scholar Thomas Cooley, and under James Valentine Campbell, then the chief justice of the Michigan Supreme Court. Sutherland's first biographer confidently speculated that both Cooley's and Campbell's teachings would have been heavily laden with the laissez-faire individualism of Herbert Spencer.[47] Sutherland's second biographer, Hadley Arkes, downplayed the Spencer influence at Michigan and instead highlighted the natural rights tradition as a pedagogical theme:

> That tradition supplied the moral foundation, and the moral ground of conviction, for the teaching offered by Cooley and Campbell on the importance of a government restrained by law. . . .

---

44. Brewer was not the first to scrutinize regulations outside the public sphere. In the antebellum period, the authority of communities to police themselves through regulation of "safety, economy, property, morals, and health" was rarely overturned or even reviewed by courts. Following the Civil War, however, individual challenges to regulations became the norm. See William Novak, The People's Welfare: Law and Regulation in Nineteenth-Century America 245–46 (Univ. of No. Carolina Press 1996) ("Liberal constitutionalism thrived on (and reinforced) the separation of public from private, state power from individual right . . . . Age old regulatory issues were reexamined and redecided in a distinctly constitutional framework . . . .").

45. Hadley Arkes, The Return of George Sutherland 39 (Princeton Univ. Press 1994).

46. *Id.* at 40.

47. See Joel Francis Paschal, Mr. Justice Sutherland: A Man Against the State 9–15 (Princeton Univ. Press 1951).

> Cooley and Campbell suffered no epistemological doubts when they made the rudimentary point that the purpose of the Constitution was to protect its citizens from the "arbitrary" uses of political power. They were evidently persuaded that it was possible to make distinctions between "arbitrary" and the "plausible" uses of legislation.[48]

By Arkes's reckoning, "Sutherland's writing never depended on theories of economics even when he addressed regulations of the economy. His reasoning was always jural in nature." "Jural" meant "based on principle," and that in turn meant based on natural rights. Sutherland's opposition to unionism was based less on an economic theory than on his conviction that, just as employees were free to band together with other employees, they had no right to deny other workers the same choice, nor did they have the right to deny employers the freedom to decide that they would not associate with union employees. His willingness to join the majorities in *Meyer v. Nebraska*[49] and *Pierce v. Society of Sisters*,[50] upholding parents' rights to send their children to certain private schools, was based on natural rights informed by a theory of moral objectivity. (The right to educate one's children was hardly agnostic as to the type of education contemplated. As Arkes put it, the Court did not argue for the "right of the family, say, to enroll the children in Fagin's school of pickpocketry.")[51] When Sutherland broke with conservatives Pierce Butler and James McReynolds over the famous "Scottsboro Boys" case in 1933, it was because his version of natural rights theory led him to a conception of due process that essentially anticipated *Gideon v. Wainwright*, which was still thirty years away. Sutherland's majority opinion reversing the death sentences of the nine Black teenagers for rape certainly could not have been conjured up from existing positive law.[52]

Sutherland's natural rights jurisprudence sheds some light on his contribution to the standing doctrine. In the 1923 companion cases of *Massachusetts v. Mellon* and *Frothingham v. Mellon*, the Commonwealth of Massachusetts and an individual taxpayer, Mrs. Frothingham, sued various federal officials for an injunction to stop the continued appropriation of funds to an infant mortality program enacted by Congress. Their legal argument was that the legislation violated states' rights under the Tenth Amendment, although the true motivation for the lawsuit appears to have been a belief that funds were being mishandled during the appropriation process. A unanimous Supreme Court rejected the challenges on jurisdictional grounds. If *Frothingham* did not give birth to the modern standing doctrine, it was at least present during gestation.

---

48. Arkes, *supra* note 78 at 42–43.
49. 262 U.S. 390 (1923).
50. 268 U.S. 510 (1925).
51. Arkes, *supra* note 78 at 283.
52. *Id.* at 268–70.

The problem with Massachusetts's lawsuit had to do with the permissible uses of the *parens patriae* doctrine—that is, the rule governing when states may sue on behalf of their citizens. Although a state might sue to protect the rights of its citizens against the actions of another state, it could not sue to protect its citizens against federal action.[53] (This would become important in 2007, when Massachusetts sought to sue the federal Environmental Protection Agency over greenhouse gases and climate change.) But Mrs. Frothingham, suing entirely in her capacity as a garden-variety federal taxpayer, created a more generally applicable precedent. She filed a bill in equity before the Supreme Court of the District of Columbia praying for an injunction against the carrying out of the so-called "Maternity Act," a congressional statute providing for appropriations to states who complied with the law's provisions, for the purpose of reducing maternal and infant mortality. She argued that the effect of the statute would be to take her property, "under the guise of taxation," without due process of law.[54] The Court acknowledged that the issue of whether a federal taxpayer could sue to challenge an allegedly unconstitutional congressional appropriation presented a question of first impression. It was true that the Court had permitted municipal taxpayers to challenge municipal expenditures.[55] The suit of a federal taxpayer challenging a federal appropriation, however, was different.

Justice Sutherland wrote for the Court, concluding that Mrs. Frothingham could not maintain the suit because she "has no such interest in the subject-matter, nor is any such injury inflicted or threatened, as will enable her to sue."[56]

> It is only where the rights of persons or property are involved, and when such rights can be presented under some judicial form of proceedings, that courts of justice can interpose relief.[57]

Sutherland first examined the cases in which municipal taxpayers had been permitted to sue for injunctions against misuse of municipal funds. The reason for permitting such actions, he theorized, was that they could be directly analogized to corporate shareholders suing the corporation for the misuse of corporate funds. Indeed, municipalities were themselves specialized corporate forms. The relationship between federal taxpayers and the federal government, on the other hand, could hardly be likened to the relationship between shareholders and corporations. A shareholder might have a property right against the misuse of corporate assets, but a federal taxpayer has no analogous property right. Once a person pays his or her taxes, the property right is extinguished.

53. 262 U.S. at 485.
54. 262 U.S. at 480.
55. See Crampton v. Zabriskie, 101 U.S. 601, 609 (1880).
56. *Id.*
57. *Id.* at 484.

If there is a right to see that one's tax money is properly spent, it is some kind of political or moral right, not a legal right.

Of course, the *Frothingham* rationale swept well beyond just the "taxpayer standing" cases. It applied equally to the "citizen standing" cases, for no citizen has a legal right not to have government act illegally. In truth, Sutherland's *Frothingham* rationale consisted of little more than *ubi jus, ibi remedium*: federal taxpayers have no legal right not to have their taxes spent illegally, therefore the equity courts will provide no remedy. Still, there was something new and important about *Frothingham*: the Court explicitly tied this familiar rationale to the idea of separation of powers.

In his final paragraph, Sutherland wrote:

> The functions of government under our system are apportioned. To the legislative department has been committed the duty of making laws; to the executive the duty of executing them; and to the judiciary the duty of interpreting and applying them in cases brought before the courts. . . . We have no power per se to review and annul acts of Congress on the ground that they are unconstitutional. That question may be considered only when the justification for some direct injury suffered or threatened, presenting a justiciable issue, is made to rest upon such an act. Then the power exercised is that of ascertaining and declaring the law applicable to the controversy. It amounts to little more than the negative power to disregard an unconstitutional enactment, which otherwise would stand in the way of the enforcement of a legal right.[58]

Here, Sutherland explained that adherence to the *Marbury* principle of judicial review—constitutional questions may be entertained when and only when necessary to resolve a claim of right—is what keeps the federal judiciary within its constitutional role. (Of course, it is implied that, when reaching a constitutional question is indeed necessary to resolve a claim of right, the court has a constitutional duty to reach it.) Although in *Frothingham* the Court determined that it could not reach the constitutional question because no claim of legal right was involved, at the same time Sutherland's opinion implicitly justified reaching the constitutional questions involved in *Lochner* and *Young*, as well as in *Adkins v. Children's Hospital*,[59] handed down the same term as *Frothingham*. By refusing to exercise judicial review in *Frothingham*, and by explaining why it had to be refused in that situation, he endeavored to justify its exercise in other cases.

Frothingham could plausibly be viewed as the beginning of the modern standing doctrine. But that honor must be equally shared with a brief unanimous opinion issued the previous term. The case was *Fairchild v. Hughes*.[60] In early

58. *Id.* at 488.
59. 261 U.S. 525 (1923).
60. 258 U.S. 126 (1922).

1920, state legislatures were in the process of ratifying the Suffrage Amendment, guaranteeing women the right to vote. Thirty-five states had passed resolutions purporting to ratify the amendment, and the federal secretary of state had indicated that, upon receiving one more certification, he would declare the amendment adopted. On July 7, 1920, one Charles S. Fairchild filed a bill in equity in the Supreme Court of the District of Columbia, asking that the "so-called Suffrage Amendment be declared unconstitutional and void," and that the secretary of state be enjoined from declaring that it had been adopted. Mr. Fairchild declared himself to be a citizen and taxpayer of the United States and a member of the American Constitutional League, a voluntary association dedicated to spreading knowledge about the fundamental principles of the Constitution, "especially that which gives to each State the right to determine for itself the question as to who should exercise the elective franchise therein."[61] The trial court refused to issue the requested relief, whereupon the secretary of state announced that he had received a certificate of ratification from the thirty-sixth state and therefore that the amendment had been adopted.

Justice Louis Brandeis delivered the opinion of the Court. "Plaintiff's alleged interest in the question submitted is not such as to afford a basis for this proceeding," he wrote.[62] Brandeis's rationale broke new ground. He made it clear that the Court was not exercising some kind of discretion to disqualify Mr. Fairchild as a plaintiff; it was the *Constitution* that disqualified him. Brandeis stated:

> In form [the action] is a bill in equity; but it is not a case within the meaning of Section 2 of Article III of the Constitution, which confers judicial power on the federal courts, for no claim of plaintiff is "brought before the court[s] for determination by such regular proceedings as are established by law or custom for the protection or enforcement of rights, or the prevention, redress, or punishment of wrongs."[63]

No previous decision had attributed a plaintiff's ineligibility to go forward to Article III. Never before had the Court articulated the idea that an otherwise properly filed bill in equity might not fit the constitutional description of a "case." Brandeis now made that linkage explicit. If a matter did not fit a certain formal and historical mould of "justiciability," then the federal courts were without power to take cognizance of the matter because it was not a "case" within the meaning of Article III. With a major assist from Felix Frankfurter and the Burger Court, this would become one of the principal pillars in the pantheon of federal judicial restraint.

61. *Id.* at 127.
62. *Id.* at 129.
63. *Id.*

3. FROM PROTESTANT IDEALISM TO SCIENTIFIC PRAGMATISM

> *If we pass beyond these matters to a view of American life as expressed by its laws, its business, its customs and its society, we find everywhere a clear recognition of the same truth. . . . [T]his is a Christian nation.*[1]

This dictum has become David Brewer's most enduring legacy. The Court's actual holding in *Church of the Holy Trinity v. United States* was narrow; it held only that a federal law prohibiting the hiring of foreign laborers was limited to manual laborers and therefore did not include a pastor. But Brewer's opinion characteristically went out of its way to make a point.[2] Laws could never be construed against religion because the nation was founded on it. "[N]o purpose of action against religion can be imputed to any legislation, state or national, because this is a religious people," Brewer wrote.[3] Ever since, this language has been cited to prove that there should be no separation between church and state—that government ought to endorse Christianity without apology. Careful examination of the full opinion reveals slender support for such an interpretation. Instead, what Brewer had done was to recognize an obvious sociological fact about late nineteenth-century America. The public culture of America was Protestant.

This culture was not connected to any one denomination. According to David Hollinger, "[t]his generic, transdenominational Protestantism had come by the end of the nineteenth century to be taken for granted by nearly all of the Americans in a position to influence the character of the nation's major institutions, including those controlling public education, politics, the law, literature, the arts, scholarship, and even science."[4] By the latter half of the nineteenth century, most Protestant churches had broken from the unremitting axioms of Calvinism, which included the strict doctrine of predestination and the basic

---

1. Church of the Holy Trinity v. United States, 143 U.S. 457, 471 (1892).

2. But see Linda Przybyszewski, *Judicial Conservatism and Protestant Faith: The Case of Justice David J. Brewer*, 91 J. AMER. L. HIST. 471, 474 (2004), questioning the conventional view that Brewer's discussion of America as a religious nation constituted dictum. This stance parallels Przybyszewski's more general argument that historians have unduly deemphasized the religious character of Brewer's jurisprudence.

3. *Id.* at 465.

4. DAVID A. HOLLINGER, SCIENCE, JEWS, AND SECULAR CULTURE : STUDIES IN MID-TWENTIETH-CENTURY AMERICAN INTELLECTUAL HISTORY 20 (Princeton Univ. Press 1996).

belief in the essential depravity of man. Liberal Protestantism held that people were essentially good and that individuals could earn their way to heaven through piety and good works. This set of beliefs put a premium on individual freedom. If people were to earn their salvation on the basis of their actions, then those actions had to be freely chosen, not the products of coercion or paternalism. The principle of individual freedom was integral to Protestant idealism.

Protestant idealists dominated the nineteenth century federal bench and the elite bar that practiced before it. But the cultural norms held by these judges and lawyers was derived not only from their religious backgrounds; it was also a product of class, breeding, and education. Most of them identified with a Victorian gentry culture that celebrated civic virtue and embraced the view that the American republic was founded on universal, a priori principles grounded ultimately in Protestant Christianity. This gentry viewed itself as the guardian of that republic. In some ways Ralph Waldo Emerson, with his strident beliefs in individualism and self-reliance, and with his ardor for idealism (he was fond of Immanuel Kant), was emblematic of gentry attitudes.[5] As Daniel Ernst has noted, two classical ideals were especially important. One was public-minded citizenship. The gentry believed that they alone had the capacity to perceive the common welfare, and that this obligated them to defend it from self-interested factions. "College-educated lawyer-politicians were particularly likely to find their model republican in Cicero, the great advocate whose orations showed how 'reason and speech' could awaken listeners to peril around them," according to Ernst.[6] The second classical ideal was "the timeless nature of the public good and the corrupting nature of change."[7] Change was inherently wrong because it necessarily entailed deviation from ancient ideals.

In his fascinating book *Lawyers Against Labor*, Ernst traces the upbringing and education of Daniel Davenport, the lawyer who headed the American Anti-Boycott Association, which conducted a litigation campaign against closed union shops around the dawn of the twentieth century:

> George Davenport saw to it that his children would appreciate and participate in the genteel cultural tradition he cherished. Daniel and his two brothers followed their father into the legal profession, in Daniel's case after graduating from Yale, a stronghold of genteel education. Noah Porter, inaugurated president during Davenport's junior year, committed the college to producing men of "comprehensive thought" and refined, liberal culture, rather than

5. "The gentleman, in short, personified the great Emersonian principles of individualism and self-reliance," STOW PERSONS, THE DECLINE OF AMERICAN GENTILITY 3 (Columbia Univ. Press 1973).

6. DANIEL R. ERNST, LAWYERS AGAINST LABOR: FROM INDIVIDUAL RIGHTS TO CORPORATE LIBERALISM 27–28 (Univ. of Illinois Press 1995).

7. *Id.*

teams of "specialists." Four elements of the curriculum were especially important sources of genteel values: the civic humanism of the great works of Greek and Roman antiquity; Scottish "common-sense" moral philosophy; classical economics; and liberal political philosophy, as found in such textbooks as Francis Lieber's *Manual of Political Ethics* (1838–39) and *On Civil Liberty* (1856) and Whiggish accounts of English constitutional history.[8]

> [B]y the time Davenport left Yale he had received formal instruction in the most important components of gentry culture in Victorian America. He learned from the classical exponents of civic virtue and a clerical instructor in moral philosophy that the revolutionary generation had founded the American republic on universal, a priori principles grounded ultimately in Protestant Christianity and that he should strive wherever possible to prevent or reverse departures from these timeless precepts. He learned from classical economics and liberal political philosophy that attempts to regulate prices and output upset the providential laws of supply and demand and trampled upon the rights of employers, workers, and consumers. Sumner in particular charged him to resist such threats to the permanent welfare and "political virtue" of the country.[9]

Dorothy Ross has linked the Gilded Age gentry to the phenomenon of American exceptionalism—the notion that America and its institutions were (and should continue to be) essentially different from those of its British and European forebears. Class warfare was neither inevitable nor tolerable. Civic virtue was extolled. "Whether born into this class or entering it through education, the gentry also thought of themselves as elite guardians of the American Republic and were thus sensitive to threats to the exceptionalist ideal created by political and economic change," Ross wrote.[10] At the heart of American exceptionalism were the concepts of natural law and natural rights. Throughout the eighteenth century, European intellectuals largely embraced the belief that there were certain laws through which God governed the world, and, in some cases, established inalienable rights in man. By the nineteenth century, however, positivist natural science and historicism had largely taken sway in Europe. Evolutionary theory undermined religious orthodoxies about the origins of man, while historicism undercut the plausibility of timeless, a priori principles governing social and political conditions.

But American exceptionalism was surprisingly resistant. The gentry's commitments to natural law and natural rights remained strong, even as they sought to accommodate the discoveries of natural science. As the authority of religious

8. *Id.* at 26.

9. *Id.* at 37.

10. Dorothy Ross, The Origins of American Social Science 54 (Cambridge Univ. Press, 1991).

dogma began to ebb, the gentry sought to replace it with the authority of science. Ross explained:

> As clerical leadership became increasingly discredited, the cosmopolitan gentry were uniquely placed to offer themselves as a modern alternative. In contrast to the politicians, labor leaders, and businessmen who raised divisive claims, the gentry could call on the authority of modern science to command agreement. Science allowed them to speak with the voice of universal rationality, while bestowing special authority on its elite class of practitioners.[11]

Orthodox Christianity once proved the rightness of the gentry's timeless a priori principles governing society and economics; now it was science. "[T]heir overriding concern was to show that the social sciences could reconfirm the traditional principles of American governance and economy and replace religion as a sure guide to the exceptionalist future," according to Ross.[12] Few of the gentry intellectuals who attacked religious control actually became agnostics—"most adjusted the basis of their Christian faith to avoid cognitive conflict with natural science."[13] In some cases, there was not much adjustment necessary, as with Brewer in *Muller v. Oregon*. His Christian beliefs held that women were essentially different from men in terms of their workplace capacities, and the Brandeis brief cohered perfectly with those beliefs.

Not all the Protestant gentry reacted to science as Brewer did. John Marshall Harlan was born into a most distinguished Kentucky family, his father James a prosperous lawyer, successful Whig officeholder, and (relatively) benevolent slaveowner. John, named after the great chief justice, was a devout conservative Presbyterian who, like Brewer, generally believed that principles of Christianity underlay principles of the Constitution. According to Harlan's biographer Linda Przybyszewski, "His belief in a transcendent God who ordered the universe lay behind his belief in a transcendent law that ordered the nation."[14] At a banquet commemorating Harlan's twenty-fifth year on the Supreme Court, Brewer playfully teased that Harlan "goes to bed every night with one hand on the Constitution and the other on the Bible, and so sleeps the sweet sleep of justice and righteousness."[15] Yet Harlan refused to join Rufus Peckham and Brewer in the *Lochner* majority. Harlan instead wrote a dissent that looked as if it could have been written by Louis Brandeis, chock full of labor statistics showing the need for regulation of working hours. Nor would Harlan go along with Peckham and Brewer in *Ex Parte Young*, where Harlan stood alone in decrying what he saw as

---

11. *Id.* at 62.
12. *Id.* at 64.
13. *Id.* at 57.
14. Linda Przybyszewski, The Republic According to John Marshall Harlan 54 (Univ. of North Carolina Press, 1999).
15. *Id.*

a constitutional perversion—a single judge federal circuit court enjoining a state regulatory scheme. Scientific discoveries may not have moved Peckham and Brewer off their view that Christian principles corresponded unproblematically with constitutional ones, but they appear to have had a different effect on the equally devout Harlan.

Still, Harlan was atypical. What most characterized the so-called *Lochner* Court was its insistence on placing principle above necessity. These were not, after all, just any principles. They were universal, a priori principles, decreed by Providence and discovered by men through the use of their common sense and reasoning faculties. These principles established natural rights, which cohered with an objective moral reality. It was the received wisdom, which was not to be swept aside for every claim of exigent circumstances. Legislatures could respond to the felt necessities of the times, but they could not be permitted to violate these natural rights that had been enshrined in the Constitution.

* * *

Oliver Wendell Holmes, Jr., could have been the genteel Protestant idealist from central casting. He was related to many of New England's most aristocratic families—the Olivers, the Wendells, the Quincys, the Bradstreets, the Cabots, the Jacksons, and the Lees. His father, Dr. Oliver Wendell Holmes, was a professor who at one time served as dean of the Harvard Medical School, and was a renowned man of letters. In *The Metaphysical Club*, Louis Menand's absorbing chronicle of how secular pragmatism came to supplant Protestant idealism as the intellectual motif of early twentieth-century America, the teenage Holmes is portrayed as an idealist of sorts. In 1858, for his seventeenth birthday, his parents gave him five volumes of Ralph Waldo Emerson, which set him "on fire." He enrolled at Harvard and began to publish essays emulating Emerson's version of abolitionism, which, in Menand's words, "associate[d] the tolerance of slavery with the conformist mentality of institutionalized religion."[16] Emerson was highly individualistic—"self-reliance" his credo—and hostile toward institutions. Accordingly, the young Holmes believed that "a finer morality was possible outside organized religion than inside it."[17] By late 1860, he had closely associated himself with the abolitionist Wendell Phillips and even agreed to serve as one of Phillips's bodyguards (as fate would have it, he never actually had to hit anyone). When Fort Sumter fell in April 1861, President Abraham Lincoln called for volunteers, and Holmes quit Harvard to enlist. He returned to Harvard briefly to sit for his final exams, which allowed him to graduate, but soon he was commissioned as an officer in the Twentieth Regiment of the Massachusetts Volunteers. Moral principles had convinced him of the duty to serve. But Ball's Bluff changed Holmes forever.

---

16. Louis Menand, The Metaphysical Club: A Story of Ideas in America 25 (Farrar, Straus, & Giroux 2001).

17. *Id.* at 27.

Ball's Bluff was a "very minor engagement," but it was Holmes's first battle, and it was an experience inhospitable to idealism. Holmes was hit in the chest, suffered an agonizing trip to the hospital in a lurching, broken-down ambulance, and there was told "the chances are against you." At that moment, wrote Menand, "Holmes did an extraordinary thing: he road tested his beliefs. [W]atching his comrades dying around him and listening to rumors that the building was about to be shelled, he interrogated his philosophical convictions in order to discover whether there were any he now might wish to revise. . . ."[18] Adaptability of belief became the key. "It is curious how rapidly the mind adjusts itself under some circumstances to entirely new relations," Holmes scribbled from his hospital bed. "I thought for awhile that I was dying, and it seemed the most natural thing in the world—The moment the hope of life returned it seemed as abhorrent to nature as ever that I should die."[19] The notion of eternal verities was fast falling away. By the end of his enlistment, he would write, "I have felt for sometime that I didn't any longer believe in this being a duty & so I mean to leave at the end of the campaign as I said if I'm not killed before."[20] It was not that Holmes no longer believed in the concept of duty, but instead that hard evidence had reshaped the form of that duty. "I started in this thing a boy," he told his parents. "I am now a man and I have been coming to the conclusion for the last six months that my duty has changed."[21]

The war, and Holmes's sense perceptions of it, had undermined his confidence in the moral foundation of American social structure. He now questioned the social advantage of his own class, the gentry. And yet he was strangely unmoved by whatever injustice might be entailed. Telling his mother of the many commoners in his regiment who were dying, he wrote, "Poor devils . . . but it's odd how indifferent one gets to the sight of death—perhaps, because one gets aristocratic and don't value much a common life—Then they are apt to be so dirty it seems natural—'Dust to Dust—I would do anything that lay in my power but it doesn't much affect my feelings—and so I'll stop for the present—."[22] The loss of confidence in social structure derivatively undercut his faith in what the classical orthodoxy embraced as the abiding principles of law. "The law had broken down in America; the Constitution had gone to pieces," wrote Edmund Wilson. "It was impossible for an honest man of Holmes's probing intelligence

18. *Id.* at 36–38.

19. TOUCHED WITH FIRE: CIVIL WAR LETTERS AND DIARY OF OLIVER WENDELL HOLMES, JR., 1861–1864 at 32 (republication by De Capo Press 1969) (original published by Harvard Univ. Press 1947).

20. TOUCHED WITH FIRE, *supra* note 19, quoting a letter to Holmes's parents dated May 16, 1864.

21. EDMUND WILSON, PATRIOTIC GORE: STUDIES IN THE LITERATURE OF THE AMERICAN CIVIL WAR 753 (Farrar, Straus, & Giroux 1962).

22. TOUCHED WITH FIRE, *supra* note 19 at 78.

to pretend that the law was a sacred code, which had simply to be read correctly."[23]

In *The Metaphysical Club*, Menand went on to weave Holmes's life into the lives of three other intellectuals associated with this uniquely American strain of "pragmatism"—William James, Charles S. Peirce, and John Dewey. He attributes to them one common attitude toward ideas:

> If we strain out the differences, personal and philosophical, they had with one another, we can say that what these four thinkers had in common was not a group of ideas, but a single idea—an idea about ideas. They all believed that ideas are not "out there" waiting to be discovered, but are tools—like forks and knives and microchips—that people devise to cope with the world in which they find themselves. . . . They believed that ideas do not develop according to some inner logic of their own, but are entirely dependent, like germs, on their human carriers and the environment. And they believed that since ideas are provisional responses to particular and unreproducible circumstances, their survival depends not on their immutability but on their adaptability.[24]

Pragmatic approaches stood in direct opposition to the Protestant idealist commitment to a closed system of universal and immutable principles. If the modern workplace was causing serious social and health problems, pragmatists called out for new solutions and new criteria by which to evaluate those solutions. Idealists pleaded for a longer view, pursuant to which principles of freedom and natural rights that had proven themselves time and again would not be swept aside to extinguish the latest brush fires. In a large number of cases, there was no disagreement, as the particular government action was not deemed to violate any vested legal rights. In those cases, the idealists generally conceded that legislatures were entitled to deal with social and economic problems as they saw fit. But in other cases, the idealists did see the uprooting of natural rights, and (by their logic) equitable remedies had to be made available.[25]

The clash between Protestant idealism on the one hand and secular or scientific pragmatism on the other took place in American culture wars generally, but it had a direct counterpart in American jurisprudence. Protestant idealism corresponded closely to what has been variously labeled the "classical orthodoxy" or "Langdellian formalism." Scientific pragmatism more or less corresponded to a movement that called itself "Sociological Jurisprudence" and a later movement known as "Legal Realism." The struggle between classical legal orthodoxy on the one hand and Sociological Jurisprudence and Legal Realism on the other

23. Wilson, *supra* note 117 at 765.

24. *Id.* at xi–xii.

25. *See, e.g.*, New State Ice Co. v. Liebmann, 285 U.S. 262 (1932).

profoundly shaped the mores of judicial review and helped produce the modern standing doctrine.

According to Thomas Grey, "the heart of classical theory was its aspiration that the legal system be made complete through universal formality, and universally formal through conceptual order."[26] What he meant was a closed system consisting of a few highly abstract principles from which could be inferred a larger number of more concrete principles which, in turn, would provide demonstrably right answers to all legal questions. The system was closed in the sense that it was impervious to notions of policy or "rough justice." "Considerations of justice and convenience were relevant," Grey explained, "but only insofar as they were embodied in *principles*—abstract yet precise norms that were consistent with the other fundamental principles of the system."[27] All the answers were supposedly accessible through principles already within the system.

Incredible as this claim may seem, it was essential to the maintenance of the notion that law itself was a science. Harvard's Christopher Columbus Langdell, Joseph Beale, Samuel Williston, James Barr Ames, and others held fast to the notion that this orthodox system made law scientific.[28] Developments in natural science had created pressures on lawyers and legal academics to situate their discipline within this new world. The universities had plighted their troth to science; if law schools were to be part of the university, they would have to demonstrate their methods were scientific. As Langdell himself put it:

> If law be not a science, a university will consult its own dignity in declining to teach it. If law be not a science, it is a species of handicraft, and may best be learned by serving an apprenticeship to one who practices it. If it be a science, it will scarcely be disputed that it is one of the greatest and most difficult of sciences, and that it needs all the light that the most enlightened seat of learning can throw upon it.[29]

In what sense could it be said that law, as conceived by the classicists, was scientific? For one, Grey explained, there was an analogy to Euclidean geometry. If "Euclid's axioms are not merely human constructs, but rather obvious and indubitable physical truths about the structure of space, from which nonobvious truths (like the Pythagorean theorem) can be proved by sequences of indubitable deductive steps," then the parallel to classical legal thought is clear.[30] Although in

---

26. Thomas C. Grey, *Langdell's Orthodoxy*, 45 U. PITT. L. REV. 1, 11 (1983).

27. *Id.* at 15.

28. *Id.* at 30 n.109, citing JOSEPH BEALE, TREATISE ON THE CONFLICT OF LAWS 135 (1916) ("the one most important feature of law [is] that it is not a mere collection of arbitrary rules, but a body of scientific principle").

29. *Id.* at 38 (quoting from Langdell, Speech (Nov. 5, 1886), 3 LAW Q. REV. 123, 124 (1887)).

30. *Id.* at 17.

the twentieth century mathematicians would come to understand that Euclidean geometry did not necessarily represent objective truths in the world, that view certainly counted as scientific in the late nineteenth century. There was a second sense in which the classical legal system was thought to be scientific, namely, that it was empirical. Lawyers and judges had to research appellate decisions to discover the true principles of the common law. "For legal science," wrote Grey, "the universe of data was not the totality of sense experience of the physical world, but rather the restricted set of reported common law decisions—hence Langdell's often-reviled remark that all the materials of legal science were to be found in printed books."[31] However comical a view of empiricism this might now seem, it was not an implausible characterization even by the late nineteenth century.

There is some disagreement about whether the "substantive due process" jurisprudence of the Fuller and Taft Courts truly fit the "classical orthodoxy" mold. Duncan Kennedy argued that it did; Grey argued that it didn't.[32] Grey's point was that the true believers of classical orthodoxy within the academy were cool to the Court's "liberty of contract" jurisprudence.[33] The academic classicists did not regard "public law," including constitutional law, as "law" at all. "Constitutional law was unscientific, because hopelessly vague, as typified by the police power doctrine; the question whether a statute was 'reasonably related to safety, health or morals' could not be treated formally," Grey explained. But judges like Brewer, Peckham, and George Sutherland were not principally academics. Whether or not the scholarly mandarins of classicism regarded their judicial work product as sufficiently scientific to qualify as "formalism," these judges almost certainly viewed their reasoning as being in line with classical methodology. The essence of their reasoning, after all, was *principle.* They may have derived their abstract principles from general Protestant teachings (which they believed the Framers had enshrined into the Constitution) rather than from appellate decisions, but the methodology was otherwise classical. And there was another sense in which the "substantive due process" jurisprudence cohered with classical orthodoxy. They both held the individual as the primary moral unit. "In nineteenth-century law, as in other areas of Victorian culture, the individual was the exclusive focus of concern in legal, moral, and political reasoning," wrote William Wiecek. "Applauding Henry Maine's celebrated observation that 'the movement of the progressive societies has hitherto been a movement from Status to Contract,' they regarded the centrality of individual will as the

---

31. *Id.* at 20.

32. *Id.* at 35 & n.134, citing Duncan Kennedy, *Toward an Historical Understanding of Legal Consciousness: The Case of Classical Legal Thought in America, 1850–1940* (1975) (unpublished).

33. For example, he cites Samuel Williston, *Freedom of Contract*, 6 Cornell L. Rev. 365, 375–80 (1921) (disapproving of the "liberty of contract" decisions).

supreme achievement of modern legal systems."[34] This credo fit *Lochner* and its cohort as well as it did late nineteenth-century common law.

The first American political movement to adopt a generally scientific and pragmatic approach was Progressivism. In opposition to the timeless and universal truths of Protestant idealism, Progressives believed that society was in a constant state of flux. The simple combination of enlightened self-interest in the marketplace and judicial protection of natural liberty and property rights was not, they believed, sufficient to ensure social progress. "It was no longer enough to justify governmental indifference to economic and social inequalities by appeal to Darwinist religiosity which informed the exploited that 'God helps those who help themselves,'" wrote the noted legal historian G. Edward White. "Progressives criticized judges for being unresponsive to social and economic conditions and asked them to take greater notice of the casualties which unregulated industrialism created."[35] In the scientific and pragmatist spirit, Progressives were generally open to interventionist experimentation in the fields of rate regulation, working hours and conditions legislation, and workmen's compensation requirements. They believed in expert management of ever-changing social and economic conditions. Progressives assumed universal agreement on the common social ends and shared moral values of society—for them, it was simply a question of how best to achieve those ends and realize those values. The problem with Protestant idealism lay in its pious obstinacy toward instrumental thinking.

From within the academy, the leader of the assault on classical orthodoxy was none other than Langdell's successor as dean of the Harvard Law School, Roscoe Pound. Pound derided classical legal thought as "mechanical jurisprudence" and proposed that it be replaced by "sociological jurisprudence," which he defined as "the movement for the adjustment of principles and doctrines to the human conditions they are to govern rather than to assumed first principles."[36] This new way of thinking would insist on studying the actual effects of rules on social conditions and would consciously attempt to achieve "reasonable and just solutions of individual causes."[37] G. Edward White noted that Pound's approach was "congenial to Progressives."[38] As an illustration, White pointed to Pound's critique of the New York Court of Appeals decision in *Ives v. South Buffalo Ry. Co.*,[39]

34. William M. Wiecek, The Lost World of Classical Legal Thought: Law and Ideology in America, 1886–1937 at 8–9 (Oxford Univ. Press 1998).

35. G. Edward White, *From Sociological Jurisprudence to Realism: Jurisprudence and Social Change in Early Twentieth-Century America*, 58 Va. L. Rev. 999, 1003 (1972).

36. Roscoe Pound, *Liberty of Contract*, 18 Yale L. J. 454, 464 (1909).

37. Roscoe Pound, *The Scope and Purpose of Sociological Jurisprudence*, 25 Harv. L. Rev. 489, 515 (1912).

38. White, *supra* note 35 of this chapter, at 1005.

39. 201 N.Y. 271, 94 N.E. 431 (1911).

which had struck down a workmen's compensation statute. The statute had been arrived at after a bipartisan commission had presented the legislature with a detailed report citing mounds of statistics and the industrial practices of other nations, and recommending the adoption of a workmen's compensation law. To Pound, the Court of Appeals decision invalidating the new law was the worst sort of meddling; the legislature had taken an empirical and scientific approach to a serious social problem, and the court had ruled it out on the basis of a few hide-bound platitudes that turned a proudly blind eye to actual conditions.

Sociological Jurisprudence, then, was the application of Progressivism to law and adjudication, and it held its greatest sway in the 1920s, toward the tail end of Progressivism's heyday. In the 1930s, Progressivism was eclipsed by the New Deal, which inspired its own jurisprudential movement—Legal Realism. "Just as Sociological Jurisprudence was the jurisprudential analog to Progressivism, so Realism was the analog to the New Deal," wrote White.[40] He detected several differences between the two jurisprudential movements. One of Pound's principal visions was of "a society motivated by a search for common goals, these resting on shared moral principles."[41] He rejected classicism's dogmatic insistence upon vindicating vested rights come what may; he did not reject the notion that there were universal moral absolutes toward which social engineers should be aiming. Legal Realists, on the other hand, doubted the existence of either a monolithic society or moral absolutes. The First World War and the Great Depression had made traditional morality seem quaint, at best. "The war, with its images of holocaust and meaningless death and its mood of social instability" accelerated skepticism about the traditional Christian morality, according to White. "Earnestness, a favorite state of the prewar years, was replaced by cynicism; social responsibility gave way to alienation, virtuousness appeared as hypocrisy."[42]

A second difference between Sociological Jurisprudence and Legal Realism was the types of science they idolized. The universities of the early twentieth century became preoccupied with social sciences, such as statistics, ethnology, economics, and sociology. For Progressives, a scientific approach usually meant an approach informed by one or more of the social sciences. The Legal Realists focused less on the social sciences than on the then-emerging behavioral sciences, including psychology and cultural anthropology. The Realists Karl Llewellyn and Jerome Frank were famously fascinated with the psychological processes of judging, which, to their evident delight, they found to have very little in common with the classicist account of induction and syllogistic reasoning.[43]

---

40. White, *supra* note 35 of this chapter, at 999.

41. *Id.* at 1011.

42. *Id.* at 1013–14.

43. *See* JEROME FRANK, LAW AND THE MODERN MIND (1930); Karl Llewellyn, *A Realistic Jurisprudence—The Next Step*, 30 COLUM. L. REV. 431 (1930).

Exacerbating these substantive differences were personal animosities that developed between Pound, the founding father, and Llewellyn, the *enfant terrible.* But too much can be made of the friction between the movements. They viewed classicism and judicial review in essentially the same way. Classical legal thought was not up to the challenge of a new economic and social day in America. In a largely agrarian society, one might maintain the faith that a correct disposition of all cases could be logically deduced from a closed system of a priori universal principles, but the rapid industrialization and urbanization of America introduced problems that could not be credibly assimilated into the system. Legislatures had to experiment with regulations of railroads and employers, and courts had to be open to this process of experimentation. Indeed, they almost had to become partners in an enterprise of social engineering, with science the guiding force. It simply could no longer be maintained that vested rights were inviolable. They had to be weighed against social exigency.

In these beliefs about classical legal thought and judicial review, Sociological Jurisprudence and Legal Realism could both trace their intellectual roots back to Holmes. In his 1897 lecture, *The Path of the Law,* Holmes produced a collection of observations and aphorisms that would fuel critics of legal orthodoxy for the next century. He disdained the method of constitutional interpretation that inquired directly into the content of natural rights, as understood by Christian teachings. There was sure to be some overlap of the Constitution and Christian morality, but they were not coterminous:

> For instance, when we speak of the rights of man in a moral sense, we mean to mark the limits of interference with individual freedom which we think are prescribed by conscience, or by our ideal, however reached. Yet it is certain that many laws have been enforced in the past, and it is likely that some are enforced now, which are condemned by the most enlightened opinion of the time, or which at all events pass the limit of interference as many consciences would draw it. Manifestly, therefore, nothing but confusion of thought can result from assuming that the rights of man in a moral sense are equally rights in the sense of the Constitution and the law.[44]

(Three decades later, Karl Llewellyn would push precisely the same point by calling for the "temporary divorce of ought and is" for the purpose of studying the law, which promptly earned him and the Realists an undeserved indictment for moral relativism.)

Holmes's most-quoted aphorism, of course, is that the "life of the law has not been logic, but experience,"[45] and in *The Path of the Law* he amplified on the point.

---

44. Oliver Wendell Holmes, Jr., *The Path of the Law,* 10 Harv. L. Rev. 457, 460 (1897).
45. Oliver Wendell Holmes, Jr., The Common Law (1881).

> The danger of which I speak is . . . the notion that a given system, ours, for instance, can be worked out like mathematics from some general axioms of conduct. This is the natural error of the schools, but it is not confined to them. I once heard a very eminent judge say that he never let a decision go until he was absolutely sure that it was right. So judicial dissent often is blamed, as if it meant simply that one side or the other were not doing their sums right, and, if they would take more trouble, agreement inevitably would come.[46]

Judges could not rely on the uncomplicated application of general rules to specific fact situations. Some policy decisions were inescapable. Holmes used tort law to illustrate:

> Our law of torts comes from the old days of isolated, ungeneralized wrongs, assaults, slanders, and the like where the damages might be taken to lie where they fell by legal judgment. But the torts with which our courts are kept busy to-day are mainly the incidents of certain well known businesses. They are injuries to person or property by railroads, factories, and the like. The liability for them is estimated, and sooner or later goes into the price paid by the public. The public really pays the damages, and the question of liability, if pressed far enough, is really the question how far it is desirable that the public should insure the safety of those whose work it uses.[47]

There was, of course, no canonically formulated rule that could decide this matter of degree. The judges had to make some kind of policy judgment, and pretending not to make such a judgment only made matters worse. "[T]he result of the often proclaimed judicial aversion to deal with such considerations," Holmes wrote, "is simply to leave the very ground and foundation of judgments inarticulate, and often unconscious. . . ."[48]

Holmes was the most prominent, and most pithy, early critic of Protestant legal idealism. That did not make him an adherent to Sociological Jurisprudence or Legal Realism; Holmes's only ideology was opposition to ideology. He became a jobbist, if a philosophically-minded one.[49] He had a few clear jurisprudential commitments—for example, to objective standards of liability.[50] Hence he was opposed to inquiring into legislative motives. For the most part, however, Holmes

---

46. HOLMES, *supra* note 44 of this chapter, at 465.

47. *Id.* at 467.

48. *Id.*

49. *See* G. Edward White, *The Integrity of Holmes' Jurisprudence*, 10 HOFSTRA L. REV. 633, 668 (Holmes held a "'job mentality' that emphasized deciding cases so that they could be decided").

50. *Cf.* Robert W. Gordon, *Holmes'* Common Law *As Legal and Social Science*, 10 HOFSTRA L. REV. 719, 723 (in line with his commitment to scientific positivism, Holmes believed that "liability for crimes, torts and contract-breaking has been based decreasingly on personal, moral culpability and increasingly on an objective or external standard").

assiduously avoided monistic approaches to the law. It was others who would move forward with the critique of Protestant legal idealism, pairing that critique with an affirmative vision built on Progressivism or the New Deal.

Holmes is often considered a model of judicial deference to legislative judgments. His dissents in *Adair v. United States* and *Adkins v. Children's Hospital,* and particularly his epigrammatic dissent in *Lochner,* have probably cemented that reputation for all time. But the reputation is not entirely deserved. In his careful study of Holmes's jurisprudence, G. Edward White found a decidedly mixed record.[51] There were the First Amendment cases—*Abrams v. United States, Gitlow v. New York, Whitney v. California, United States v. Schwimmer, Near v. Minnesota*—in which Holmes refused to defer to government limits on speech. But it was not only in the area of free speech that Holmes strayed from strict deference to legislative judgments. In his *Olmstead v. United States* dissent, for example, Holmes argued that the Fourth and Fifth Amendments prohibited the use of illegally seized evidence in a criminal prosecution. And in *Pennsylvania Coal Co. v. Mahon,* Holmes wrote for the Court, holding that a company was deprived of constitutionally protected property and contract rights by a statute forbidding coal mining under circumstances that endangered structures on the surface. The Court did not defer to the legislature's balancing of the rights and governmental interests involved. White concluded that Holmes was not, in fact, "consistently an apostle of judicial self-restraint."[52]

If Holmes was not a consistent practitioner of judicial self-restraint, however, he advocated the idea memorably and became the first Supreme Court justice to be identified with it. His most effective advocacy was the *Lochner* dissent, as powerful for its brevity as for its rhetoric. The entire opinion reads:

MR. JUSTICE HOLMES dissenting.

> I regret sincerely that I am unable to agree with the judgment in this case, and that I think it my duty to express my dissent.
>
> This case is decided upon an economic theory which a large part of the country does not entertain. If it were a question whether I agreed with that theory I should desire to study it further and long before making up my mind. But I do not conceive that to be my duty, because I strongly believe that my agreement or disagreement has nothing to do with the right of a majority to embody their opinions in law. It is settled by various decisions of this court that state constitutions and state laws may regulate life in many ways which we as legislators might think as injudicious or if you like as tyrannical as this, and which equally with this interfere with the liberty to contract. Sunday laws and usury laws are ancient examples. A more modern one is the prohibition

---

51. G. Edward White, *The Integrity of Holmes' Jurisprudence,* 10 HOFSTRA L. REV. 633 (1982).

52. *Id.* at 665.

> of lotteries. The liberty of the citizen to do as he likes so long as he does not interfere with the liberty of others to do the same, which has been a shibboleth for some well-known writers, is interfered with by school laws, by the Post Office, by every state or municipal institution which takes his money for purposes thought desirable, whether he likes it or not. The Fourteenth Amendment does not enact Mr. Herbert Spencer's Social Statics. The other day we sustained the Massachusetts vaccination law. *Jacobson v. Massachusetts,* 197 U.S. 11. United States and state statutes and decisions cutting down the liberty to contract by way of combination are familiar to this court. *Northern Securities Co. v. United States,* 193 U.S. 197. Two years ago we upheld the prohibition of sales of stock on margins or for future delivery in the constitution of California. *Otis v. Parker,* 187 U.S. 606. The decision sustaining an eight hour law for miners is still recent. *Holden v. Hardy,* 169 U.S. 366. Some of these laws embody convictions or prejudices which judges are likely to share. Some may not. But a constitution is not intended to embody a particular economic theory, whether of paternalism and the organic relation of the citizen to the State or of *laissez faire.* It is made for the purpose of fundamentally differing views, and the accident of our finding certain opinions natural and familiar or novel and even shocking ought not to conclude our judgment upon the question whether statutes embodying them conflict with the Constitution of the United States.
>
> General propositions do not decide concrete cases. The decision will depend on a judgment or intuition more subtle than any articulate major premise. But I think that the proposition just stated, if it is accepted, will carry us far toward the end. Every opinion tends to become a law. I think that the word liberty in the Fourteenth Amendment is perverted when it is held to prevent the natural outcome of a dominant opinion, unless it can be said that a rational and fair man necessarily would admit that the statute proposed would infringe fundamental principles as they have been understood by the traditions of our people and our law. It does not need research to show that no such sweeping condemnation can be passed upon the statute before us. A reasonable man might think it a proper measure on the score of health. Men whom I certainly could not pronounce unreasonable would uphold it as a first installment of a general regulation of the hours of work. Whether in the latter aspect it would be open to the charge of inequality I think it unnecessary to discuss.

In this paean to judicial restraint, Holmes perfectly echoed the sentiments of Harvard law professor James Bradley Thayer, whose 1893 article, "The Origin and Scope of the American Doctrine of Constitutional Law," would become the holy scripture of judicial restraint advocates throughout much of the twentieth century. Thayer's ultimate thesis was that courts may only treat a legislative enactment as unconstitutional "when those who have the right to make laws have not merely made a mistake, but have made a very clear one,—so clear that it is not open to rational question."[53] In other words, legislation had to be given the strongest possible presumption of constitutionality. Thayer supported his thesis with a set of historical claims and a set of policy claims. Modern critics have exposed much of Thayer's history as tendentious, most notably his claim that American judicial review rested not on a written constitution or the judicial oath to uphold that constitution, but instead on the disreputable fact that the Crown had engaged in review of colonial legislation. Ted White found this claim unsupported by "one shred of evidence linking the early American decisions establishing judicial review of legislation under the Constitution to these Crown charters."[54] "Thayer's perspective in the historical sections of his *American Doctrine* essay was consistently that of the legal scientist doing 'historico-politics': employing history to prove the truth of his normative propositions," White wrote. But, in the hands of New Deal advocates, and later in the hands of social conservatives, Thayer's policy arguments proved powerful and timely.[55]

Courts were not to substitute their judgment for that of legislatures, which were uniquely equipped to deal with far-ranging matters of policy and the "great, complex, ever-unfolding exigencies of government."[56] Moreover, impudent use of judicial review led the citizenry and its elected representatives to become lazy thinkers. Rather than think hard about whether proposed legislation was just or desirable, they would be preoccupied with legality. Worse yet, it made legislatures cynical—they had a free hand to enact unconstitutional laws for demagogic reasons, knowing full well that the courts would strike the laws down. At its core, judicial review was necessary, because Congress may not force a coordinate branch of government, the judiciary, to enforce a law that violates the basic charter.[57] In that respect, at least, the first biographer of John Marshall agreed with his subject. But Thayer put a gloss on the principle that Marshall hadn't always lived by: judicial review had to be limited to the most egregious cases.

James Bradley Thayer was born in Haverhill, Massachusetts, in 1831, to a pro-Whig newspaper editor. He graduated from Harvard College in 1852, having immersed himself in the writings of Emerson, and from Harvard Law School in 1856. He married Emerson's niece and eventually became president of the American Unitarian Association. He was raised in the same Brahmin society

53. JAMES BRADLEY THAYER, JOHN MARSHALL 21 (Houghton, Mifflin 1901).

54. G. Edward White, *Revisiting James Bradley Thayer*, 88 NW. L. REV. 48, 74 (1993).

55. Not all the policy arguments were powerful. Thayer argued that a constitution entrusts the legislature with the determination of whether legislation is constitutional because a legislature cannot enact a law without first impliedly deciding that it would be constitutional. This, of course, is a non sequitur; see Mark Tushnet, *Thayer's Target: Judicial Review or Democracy?*, 88 NW. L. REV. 9 (1993). It is certainly possible for a legislature to pass a bill without inquiring into its constitutionality, whatever the morality or advisability of the practice.

56. THAYER, *supra* note 53.

57. *See also* THAYER, *supra* note 53 at ch. 3.

as Holmes. Indeed, wrote Ted White, "when Thayer joined the Harvard law faculty in 1874, he was in some respects the very personification of an antebellum New England Whig whose perspective had evolved into that of Brahmin political culture."[58]

That Brahmin culture underwent a "crisis of authority" after the war. So many of the old verities were gone—orthodox Protestantism, the dominance of agrarianism, a homogenous Anglo-Saxon white population, the antebellum conception of federalism. One way Brahmins responded to this crisis was to develop an epistemology based on science, which,

> for members of gentry communities, including Brahmins, emerged as a central and multifaceted ideal, reflected in enthusiasm for new fields of study, such as the Darwinist natural sciences and "professional" social science, and in the conversion of gentry intellectuals to scientific methodologies, such as historicism or historico-politics, through which academics were expected to make contributions as (in the words of Charles Eliot) "expounders, systematizers, and historians."[59]

The "clear error" rule was Thayer's "scientific" attempt to come to grips with judicial review in the postbellum era. He focused on legislative sovereignty. He may not have believed that legislatures had the capacity to deal with science, as Brandeis did, but for him the clear error rule was a scientific, systematic approach to judicial review.

Holmes knew Thayer well. Thayer had been a partner at the Boston firm with which Holmes was briefly associated, and Thayer later helped arrange Holmes's appointment to the Harvard Law School faculty. (Holmes left the faculty after less than a year to take a seat on the Massachusetts Supreme Judicial Court, prompting Thayer to write in his diary, "He [Holmes] is, with all his attractive qualities and his solid merits, wanting sadly in the noblest region of human character—selfish, vain, thoughtless of others.") In the early 1870s, Holmes and Thayer had both been members of the Metaphysical Club, whose roster seems to have included Henry and William James, Charles Peirce, William Dean Howells, Arthur Sedgwick, John Fiske, and Henry Adams ("the very cream of Boston manhood," proclaimed William James). Most importantly, Holmes and Thayer both knew Chauncey Wright.

Wright was the central figure in the Metaphysical Club, though he was an odd candidate to become an intellectual inspiration for the Olympian Holmes and the courtly Thayer. "Wright was a large, phlegmatic man . . . gentle, serene to the point of indolence, and, in a bland and unassuming way, a kind of genius," wrote Louis Menand. Philosophically, Wright was a positivist, by which he meant that one ought to maintain "an absolute distinction between facts and values."

58. White, *supra* note 54 of this chapter, at 65.
59. *Id.* at 68.

Facts were scientifically provable; values were not. Values were a matter for metaphysical speculation, in which men would naturally engage, but it was hopelessly groundless. According to Menand, Wright's positivism boiled down to a simple motto: "Where we cannot be certain, we must affirm nothing." One had to resist overarching social or political theories. Wright particularly abjured the idea of "trying to obey the dictates of a system of abstractions." He was a nihilist.

For Holmes, who had lost all idealism at Ball's Bluff, Wright was a breath of fresh air. "He identified with Wright's positivism," Menand wrote. "It suited perfectly his own disillusionment. He took satisfaction in the notion that values are epiphenomenal—that beneath all the talk of principles and ideals, what people do is just a fancy version of what amoebas do." After Holmes lost his taste for the views of William James, whom he eventually found too optimistic, he maintained admiration for Wright. "Chauncey Wright . . . taught me when young that I must not say *necessary* about the universe, that we don't know whether anything is necessary or not," Holmes reflected toward the end of his life.[60] Thayer's views about what legislatures do paralleled Wright's views about values as metaphysical speculation. He spoke of "that wide margin of considerations which address themselves only to the practical judgment of a legislative body."[61] Thayer thought the courts should stay out of the metaphysical world. His standard for judicial review—not merely a mistake, "but a very clear one"—speaks in epistemic terms. Rather than pronounce on the ultimate metaphysical question of constitutionality or unconstitutionality, Thayer would have courts think about the degree of certainty that the legislature had made a mistake. True, everything was uncertain, but not to the same degree. Wright's positivism resonated with Thayer, as it did with Holmes.

It was not, then, any form of idealism that animated this first push for judicial restraint. Quite the contrary, it was Chauncey Wright's type of nihilism—a pronounced distaste for idealism—that led Thayer and Holmes to call for limits to the practice of judicial review. But the baton of judicial restraint was about to be handed off to idealists, and the doctrine of standing to sue would become one of their principal tools.

60. Menand, *supra* note 112 at 217, quoting Holmes, Letter to Frederick Pollock (1929).

61. Thayer, *supra* note 53 at 9.

4. BRANDEIS AND LIMITS ON FEDERAL JUDICIAL POWER

Louis Brandeis's most famous opinion is *Erie R.R. v. Tompkins*, where the Court finally put an end to the regime under which federal courts sitting in diversity fashioned their own liability rules. In *Erie*, Brandeis (quoting Oliver Wendell Holmes, Jr.) mocked the notion of a general federal common law as a "brooding omnipresence in the sky" and held that, going forward, federal courts were to apply state liability rules in cases where there was no federal basis for suit. Brandeis and Holmes had long detested the general federal common law doctrine, but for quite different reasons. The positivist in Holmes rebelled against the august office of the federal judiciary pretending to discover enduring principles immanent in some kind of system of right reason—hence the epithet about a "brooding omnipresence in the sky." Legislatures could make up such principles as they wished; they at least, had some claim to social consensus. It wasn't that legislatures would be less arbitrary, and certainly not that they were more enlightened. Rather, for Holmes, the fabrication of norms was intellectually dirty business, and federal judges should not be sullying their hands with it.

Brandeis's opposition to a general federal common law shared one rationale with Holmes—the normative weight of social consensus. America was the quintessential modern democracy, and Brandeis had highly American sensibilities. Elected legislatures (or at least state judges, who were more politically accountable than life-tenured federal judges) should be the normgivers. But a commitment to democracy was not the only, or even principal, source of Brandeis's opposition to the regime overturned in *Erie*. The main problem with federal judicial lawmaking was that federal judges were insufficiently forward looking. They were insufficiently receptive to Progressive measures.

There is perhaps an enduring myth of Louis Brandeis as a radical among turn-of-the-century American lawyers and judges. In fact, a better case could be made for Brandeis as a conservative, or even as a reactionary of sorts. He was an indefatigable reformer, bringing savings bank life insurance to low-income workers and rooting out corruption in the New York, New Haven, and Hartford Railroad. But these reforms were never motivated by socialism, Marxism, or any kind of radical egalitarianism. Brandeis was the product, after an early immigration, of an idyllic small-town childhood in Kentucky. He believed passionately in the small-town values of American Protestantism—self-reliance, thrift, hard work, fair dealing, and, above all, the individual as the primary moral unit of society. He abhorred the domination of the American economy by huge trusts, corporations, and chain stores. The only way of staving off these evils was legislation that broke up, or at least regulated the reach of, these massive aggregations of capital. Brandeis believed in a reasonable return on capital, but he also thought that laissez-faire capitalism inexorably led to the destruction of the small-town America that Brandeis so cherished.

Adolph Brandeis had come to the United States from Prague in the aftermath of the 1848 revolution in search of freedom and, at least initially, the agrarian utopia of which he had heard. After some disillusionment with farm life in Ohio, Adolph decided to go into business. American starch, he had discovered, was based on wheat, and was not very satisfactory. In Bohemia they made starch from corn, and the product was far better. Adolph settled on Madison, Indiana, for his cornstarch factory and in 1849 married Frederika Dembitz, a distant cousin to whom he had become engaged in Prague. The starch factory was not a great success, but in 1851 Adolph moved to Louisville, Kentucky, and established a wholesale grain and produce business that caught on.

Louis David Brandeis was born in 1856, the youngest of four children. As the family business grew, Adolph and Frederika moved their brood to a large limestone-fronted house in an exclusive neighborhood. The Brandeises were unpopular in late '50s and early '60s Louisville owing to their decidedly abolitionist stance, but the family was little bothered by this cool reception. Biographer Phillipa Strum described an all-American childhood:

> Louis grew up in a house of books, music, sociability, and warmth. . . . A flourishing business, a large home filled with happy children and a retinue of servants, an extended family that remained close as it prospered: Adolph and Frederika had no reason to question the reality of the American dream. Neither did their children, then or later.[1]

Louisville, a bustling center of commerce on the Ohio River, may not literally have been a small town, but in many ways Louis Brandeis could not have had a more quintessentially small-town childhood experience.

The Brandeis household was an intellectually elevated place. Adolph loved to talk politics, and public affairs was a regular subject of family conversation. Frederika pushed literature on her children and "banned all discussion of money and other vulgar matters" from the dinner table. Strum found one letter from fourteen-year-old Louis to his mother particularly characteristic:

> September 7, 1870
>
> My dear darling Ma:
>
> As I can't write to you tomorrow morning, I use my time tonight to write a few lines and congratulate my dear Ma on her wedding day, the first one I have not been with you . . .
>
> Today the regular lessons began and there was yawning down in our room which would have done justice to Pa. I study only French, Latin, Chemistry,

1. Phillipa Strum, Louis D. Brandeis: Justice for the People 7 (Schocken Books 1984).

German, Algebra, Composition, Trigonometry: Mathematics and Languages being the principal studies.

We went out riding with Aunt Rosa on the river road yesterday . . . Pa is at the Opera House meeting tonight. [Older sister] Fanny is going to the Prussian meeting tomorrow afternoon. Mr. Hirschbull is going to raffle off the picture HEIDELBERG he used to have hanging in his store, for the wounded. Has Pa written you of his proposed punishment for Napoleon? It is this: He should be put in prison with no book but Kinglake's Crimea . . . Hoping you will soon be back to your

Loving son

Louis[2]

This letter describes Louis's course of study at Louisville Male High School. He consistently made top marks and, two years hence, he was awarded the gold medal "for pre-eminence in all his studies."

The most powerful adult male influence on Louis was not his father but Frederika's brother, Lewis Naphtali Dembitz. A diminutive physical presence at five feet and one hundred pounds, Dembitz was a powerful intellect and regular visitor to the Brandeis household. According to Strum, he was a

> lawyer, legal writer, civil servant, political activist, astronomer, linguist [and] mathematician. He was a follower of Henry Clay, after whom he named his oldest son, as well as of Lincoln, after whom he named his second son. He read a dozen languages; he forecast the 1869 eclipse of the sun to the minute, using his own calculations; he contributed to encyclopedias and wrote authoritative works on Kentucky law and jurisprudence. He was absent-minded, good-humored, a natural teacher, and particularly fond of children.[3]

Louis admired his namesake so much that he took Dembitz as his middle name and followed his uncle into the law. Apparently, however, Lewis Dembitz's impression on his nephew was not strictly confined to scholarly matters. Unlike Brandeis, who was being raised in a secular household that "practiced what might be called the secular Christianity of the United States, sending each other Christmas greetings and gifts," Dembitz was an observant Orthodox Jew. Phillipa Strum quotes Brandeis's remembrances of his uncle observing the Sabbath:

> [T]he joy and awe with which [he] welcomed the arrival of the day and the piety with which he observed it. I remember the extra delicacies, lighting of the candles, prayers over a cup of wine, quaint chants, and Uncle Lewis poring over books most of the day. I remember more particularly an elusive something about him which was spoken of as the "Sabbath peace" and which years later brought to my mind a passage from Addison in which he speaks of

2. *Id.* at 8–9 n.19.
3. *Id.* at 10.

stealing a day out of life to live . . . Uncle Lewis used to say that he was enjoying a foretaste of heaven.[4]

While these experiences undoubtedly gave some impetus to Brandeis's well-documented Zionist activities later in life, they did not convert him to Judaism or make him devout in any religious belief. He remained secular his entire life. There is something poignant, however, about young Brandeis marveling over his uncle's earnest observances, as if connecting him in some way with a Jewish identity. One thing is certain: the Brandeises were one of many Jewish families that emigrated to the United States during the mid to late nineteenth century. Like the Brandeis family, which came over in 1849, many of the mid-century Jewish immigrants were of German extraction—relatively well-educated, cultured, and tending toward a belief in the stability of social and political institutions. This was to be contrasted with the heavy immigration of Jews from the villages and small cities of Russia and Eastern Europe between 1880 and 1924. This group of newcomers was generally less educated and rougher around the edges, with a not inconsiderable penchant for radicalism. Alongside the massive immigration of Irish at mid-century and Italians after 1880, the demographics of America were undergoing a sea change. The most urban areas for the first time accumulated large non–Anglo-Saxon populations, which in turn led to a degree of racial and religious diversity in some city councils and a few statehouses. The lawmaking bodies of urban America ceased to be exclusive preserves for Protestant aristocrat statesmen. The political process took on an increasingly polyglot quality. But the bench, and the federal bench in particular, remained a predominantly WASP (White Anglo-Saxon Protestant) affair.

Judicial invalidation of progressive legislative measures, therefore, often had a none-too-subtle racial dimension. Such legislation often benefited immigrant workers, renters, and ratepayers. It is not that all Progressives were racial egalitarians; many, such as Theodore Roosevelt, held certain racial groups in low esteem. Even Roscoe Pound, the leading Progressive among legal academicians, was not motivated by a quest for racial justice. The Progressives were mostly genteel Anglo-Saxons out to protect small-town and agrarian American values in the face of urbanization and industrialization. Whether Italian or Eastern European immigrants benefited was therefore frequently a matter of indifference to advocates of Progressive legislation. But when proudly genteel Anglo-Saxon judges struck down such measures, the beneficiaries of judicial review were usually proudly genteel Anglo-Saxon factory owners, landlords, or railroad shareholders. Judicial restraint, in this era, was generally the friend of the have-nots, including racial minorities.

If Brandeis was one of the principal forces in the movement away from robust judicial review, he was also a central figure in what David Hollinger has called

4. *Id. at* 11 n. 23.

the "De-Christianization of American public culture." Hollinger has traced the disproportionately large influence that free-thinking Jews had on the secularization of thinking in American public institutions. Six men played a particularly large role in this transition: Horace M. Kallen, Randolph Bourne, Walter Lippmann, Morris R. Cohen, Louis Brandeis, and Felix Frankfurter. Kallen and Bourne argued against equating America with Anglo-Saxonism. In *Transnational America*, which grew out of his personal experiences at Columbia University and Greenwich Village, Bourne advocated a "cosmopolitan America" that would accommodate immigrant cultures rather than force them to assimilate into Anglo-Saxon culture. Kallen's *Democracy Versus the Melting Pot* was widely credited with having coined the phrase "cultural pluralism" to describe this idea, and it strongly influenced Bourne. Cohen "wrote with special eloquence then and later about the passion with which Jewish youth on the Lower East Side were determined to absorb all of the benefits of 'the Age of Reason.'"[5]

Instrumental in this move from Protestant idealism to secular pragmatism was the apotheosis of Holmes. Hollinger explains:

> Holmes's greatness was hailed by American intellectuals of a variety of backgrounds, but Jews did the most to establish Holmes in the public mind as more than just a great judge and scholar. Responsibility for effectively promoting Holmes as a cultural hero is often assigned above all to Frankfurter and Harold J. Laski. Grant Gilmore has argued that these two "concocted the picture of the tolerant aristocrat, the great liberal, the eloquent defender of our liberties, the Yankee from Olympus." From his strategic position at the Harvard Law School, Frankfurter affirmed his reverence for Holmes repeatedly. . . . The representation of Holmes as the Complete American Liberal was carried on by Cohen, and later by Jerome Frank and Max Lerner. In Lerner's 1943 rendition, Holmes was "perhaps the most complete personality in the history of American thought."
>
> Holmes was a good choice. His influence promised to help release American culture from a Christian bias that most Jewish intellectuals found provincial at best, and at worst a basis for continued discrimination against Jews and other non-Christians. The old Brahmin was about as "American" as it was possible to get, but he had put great distance between himself and exactly those parts of Protestant culture most oppressive to Jews. Holmes was aloof from Anglo-Saxon nativism and from the genteel tradition in literature for which his father remained an enduring symbol. Moreover, the Olympian Holmes had actually befriended Frankfurter, Laski, and Cohen at a time when Jews felt deeply the sting of social and professional rejection by most men and women of Holmes's milieu. Holmes was not noticeably Christian, and what echoes of heroic Calvinism he carried were easily detached from quotas for

5. Hollinger, *supra* note 4, Ch. 3, at 25.

Jews at Harvard and Columbia. Jewish intellectuals had a real enemy to fight, and they knew Holmes was no part of it. Hence it is not surprising that of the various specific projects moving the public culture of the United States more decisively in a secular, cosmopolitan direction, the particular project of managing the reputation of Holmes should become one in which Jewish intellectuals took the lead. The making of the agnostic Holmes into an emblem for American life was one step in the construction of a secular vision of American culture—a vision de-emphasizing that culture's historically Protestant components.[6]

Over the next two or three decades, scientific pragmatism became the public culture of America. Americans did not cease to be a religious people; church attendance continued to be strong well into the 1960s. But secular pragmatism better fit the nation America had become. The gentility of Daniel Davenport and the Gilded Age, of the Olivers and the Wendells, and even the exceptionalist individualism of Frederick Jackson Turner's frontier, no longer resonated with large groups of Americans. The population was becoming too diverse for that. Catholics and Jews now comprised large segments of the population, especially in urban areas. South Boston and the Lower East Side were not Beacon Hill or Fifth Avenue, nor was either of them the frontier. Protestant idealism was insufficiently cosmopolitan, culturally and methodologically, to address the everyday problems facing densely settled immigrants from Ireland, Italy, and Eastern Europe. Enlightenment rationalism, not Christian pieties, seemed the more promising path to addressing what Holmes called the "felt necessities of the time."

The displacement of Protestant idealism by scientific pragmatism was not, however, evenly paced throughout the elites. It occurred much earlier in city halls and statehouses than in the courthouses. And among the life-tenured ranks of federal judges it occurred most slowly of all, not only because of slower turnover in seats, but because of the ranks from which candidates were drawn. The vast majority of federal judges were business litigators from the silk-stocking law firms. They were not subject to appointment by governors or election by the general electorate; they were chosen primarily by members of that most exclusive gentlemen's club, the U.S. Senate. The social and cultural homogeneity of the federal bench in the late nineteenth century and very early twentieth century was greater than, or as great as, that of any other institution in America. Gilded Age gentry values and Victorian legal culture continued to hold sway in federal courthouses long after they had faded from many municipal governments and state legislatures.

Brandeis had access to the social and professional circles that clung to these genteel values. He graduated from the Harvard Law School in 1878 with the

6. *Id.* at 26–27.

highest scholastic record in the school's history, having obtained special dispensation to graduate at an age younger than permitted by school rules. After a false start in St. Louis (he felt he should get away from Cambridge but did not want to return to Louisville), Brandeis returned to join the Boston law firm of Samuel Dennis Warren. Warren had finished runner-up to Brandeis in their graduating class and hailed from a wealthy and socially prominent New England family. Brandeis's exceptional academic achievements, coupled with Warren's social reputation, gained Brandeis admission to the exclusive social clubs of Boston. Brahminism in the late 1870s and early 1880s frowned upon discrimination against Jews. Puritanism, from which Brahminism descended, viewed Jews as among the "chosen people." Well-educated Puritans read Hebrew. It was only at the turn of the century, with large-scale immigration from Eastern Europe, Italy, and Ireland, that Boston became highly xenophobic. The Brahmins of the late 1870s were accepting so long as one shared their brand of intellectualism and their values, and Brandeis did. According to Phillipa Strum, "The Boston Brahmins retained the Puritans' emphasis on the individual, on self-reliance, and on making the most of one's abilities—all elements of Frederika Brandeis's code, and all enshrined in the works of Brandeis's favorite Boston author, Ralph Waldo Emerson, the great advocate of Self-Reliance."[7] In the ensuing four decades tension developed between Brandeis and genteel society. Some of it was simply the xenophobia that developed in reaction to mass immigration. But to a far greater degree it was the fact that, after making a small fortune representing small manufacturers and retailers, he gradually became a Progressive crusader, the "People's Attorney."

In 1916, President Woodrow Wilson nominated Brandeis to the U.S. Supreme Court. The nomination generated considerable opposition. The most elite stratum of the bar was almost completely dominated by East Coast Establishment WASPs, many of whom harbored strong anti-Semitic sentiments. Worse still, Brandeis was a Progressive who strongly favored legislative attempts to ameliorate social and economic problems brought on by technology and urbanization.[8] Brandeis was "anti-big." He opposed corporate oligopoly, chain stores, and concentrations of wealth in general. His political philosophy was a clear threat to corporate America and other entrenched interests. In his Progressivism, Brandeis was out of step with the majority of federal judges, who harbored deep skepticism or outright antipathy toward railroad rate regulations, maximum working hours laws, workplace health and safety regulations, and workmen's compensation laws. Most federal judges were strongly committed to freedom of contract and believed that such reform laws abridged it. The reasons for their commitment to freedom of contract varied. Some were reacting to a history of

7. Strum, *supra* note 158 at 16.

8. *See generally* Alfred Lief, The Social and Economic Views of Mr. Justice Brandeis (1930).

restrictions on alienation that were thought to keep poor people from upward economic mobility. Others sought to preserve the rule of law in a society that could otherwise be overrun by mobs seeking massive redistribution of wealth through legislation. Still others simply believed in a form of social Darwinism and thought that laissez-faire economics were vital to weeding out the weak. But whatever their reasons, federal judges used judicial review aggressively in the late nineteenth and early twentieth centuries to strike down Progressive legislation. Despite strong opposition from much of the silk-stocking legal establishment, Brandeis was confirmed.

As legislatures came forth with Progressive solutions to the ills of industrialization and urbanization, it became clear that federal judges formed a large obstacle. Brandeis's principal broadside against this hegemony of hidebound federal judges was *Erie*. Corporations and other business interests had long used the diversity jurisdiction as a way around whatever Progressive legislation or state case law might benefit the little guy. But the federal constitution, especially the Due Process Clause, had harbored its share of business interests. *Lochner* and *Ex Parte Young* were the most visible, but hardly the only, examples. Brandeis favored the repeal of the Due Process Clause and directed his protégé, Felix Frankfurter, to advocate repeal in his public writings. More realistically, Brandeis adopted Holmes's and James Bradley Thayer's remonstrations against broad judicial review. Federal judges should be leaving legislation untouched except in the most egregious cases. Yet from a tactical standpoint Brandeis went far beyond Holmes. Whereas Holmes largely confined his advocacy of judicial restraint in constitutional litigation to the standard of review—that is, Thayer's "clear error" test—Brandeis pushed forward a cornucopia of procedural devices, some of which would prevent federal courts from reaching constitutional questions altogether.

In his book *Brandeis and the Progressive Constitution*, Ed Purcell illuminated the causal link between Brandeis's Progressive beliefs and his beliefs in judicial restraint:

> Brandeis's Progressivism helped insure the second major theme of his judicial career, the desirability of judicial restraint. . . .
>
> Judicial restraint for Brandeis took three forms. First on the level of judicial review, he believed with Holmes that legislatures possessed broad power and that the courts should sustain statutes unless unquestionably contrary to the Constitution. . . . Second, quite different from Holmes, he emphasized the importance of keeping the courts strictly within the confines of their jurisdiction, not merely the clear limits imposed by statutes but also the vaguer limits implied by the "case" or "controversy" clause of Article III. Courts should not hear suits unless they constituted "actual" disputes between concretely adverse parties, where the claim was "ripe" for adjudication and the court could render an effective judgment. Finally, Brandeis urged the

necessity of restraint in the application and elaboration of constitutional doctrine. Opinions should be written narrowly to deal with the specific case presented, and the Court should avoid ruling on constitutional issues if any valid alternative ground was available.[9]

Brandeis's commitment to judicial restraint was not fueled exclusively by his Progressivism. His professional indoctrination had made him especially receptive to the idea that courts should exercise judicial review most reluctantly. At the Harvard Law School, Brandeis had been strongly influenced by the teachings of Thayer, whom Brandeis regarded as his best friend on the faculty.[10] In addition to historical arguments, Thayer had made frankly utilitarian arguments for heavily restrained judicial review:

> No doubt our doctrine of constitutional law has had a tendency to drive out questions of justice and right, and to fill the mind of legislators with thoughts of mere legality. . . . Meantime they and the people whom they represent, not being thrown back on themselves, on the responsible exercise of their own prudence, moral sense, and honor, lose much of what is best in the political experience of any nation . . . . [T]he safe and permanent road towards reform is that of impressing upon our people a far stronger sense than they have of the great range of possible mischief that our system leaves open, and must leave open, to the legislatures, and of the clear limits of judicial power; so that responsibility may be brought sharply home where it belongs. The checking and cutting down of legislative power, by numerous detailed prohibitions in the constitution, cannot be accomplished without making the government petty and incompetent. . . . Under no system can the power of courts go far to save a people from ruin; our chief protection lies elsewhere.[11]

From all this, Thayer inferred the following rule of "clear error"—that the courts may only set aside legislation "when those who have the right to make laws have not merely made a mistake, but have made a very clear one,—so clear that it is not open to rational question."[12] The notion that Alex Bickel would later

---

9. Edward A. Purcell, Jr., Brandeis and the Progressive Constitution 120–21 (2000) (footnotes omitted). For another of Purcell's accounts of how Brandeis and Frankfurter shaped federal court jurisprudence to serve Progressive purposes, see Edward Purcell, *Reconsidering the Frankfurterian Principle,* 24 Law & Social Inquiry 679, 698–706 (1999).

10. *See* Alexander M. Bickel, The Least Dangerous Branch: The Supreme Court at the Bar of Politics 35 (2d ed. 1986).

11. *Id.* at 39.

12. *Id.* at 21.

refer to as "the countermajoritarian difficulty" had been born,[13] and Brandeis would be the first Supreme Court justice to expound fully on the thesis.

Principal among Brandeis's judicial restraint devices was the doctrine of standing, linked to the "case or controversy" clause in Article III and to the concept of separation of powers. Brandeis himself wrote for the Court in *Fairchild v. Hughes*, the Suffrage Amendment case, and Brandeis joined George Sutherland's opinion for the Court in *Frothingham v. Mellon*, the Maternity Act case. A thorough explication of his views about judicial restraint would, however, have to await his now-legendary concurrence in *Ashwander v. Tennessee Valley Authority*, handed down in 1936.[14] The Alabama Power Company had agreed to sell transmission lines and substations to the Tennessee Valley Authority, a federal agency created to generate, transmit, and sell electricity. A group of preferred stockholders, arguing that the contract was "injurious to the corporate interests,"[15] petitioned the Alabama Power board of directors to annul the transaction. When the board refused, the preferred stockholders sued both the company and the Tennessee Valley Authority (TVA) in federal court, again seeking to have the transaction rescinded. Not only was the contract inimical to the corporation's interests, it was invalid because the federal government lacked the constitutional authority to enter into it, according to the plaintiffs. The true motivation of the plaintiffs, of course, had nothing to do with the welfare of the Alabama Power Company. They were simply opposed to the federal government getting into the electric power business—opposed, in short, to the continuing expansion of federal activity during the New Deal. As Justice James McReynolds's dissent put it, "If under the thin mask of disposing of property the United States can enter the business of generating, transmitting and selling power as, when and wherever some board may specify, with the definite design to accomplish ends wholly beyond the sphere marked out for them by the Constitution, an easy way has been found for breaking down the limitations heretofore supposed to guarantee

13. BICKEL, *supra* note 167 at 16–23. For a fascinating series of articles attempting to put the notion of the "countermajoritarian difficulty" in its rightful historical place, see Barry Friedman, *The History of the Countermajoritarian Difficulty, Part One: The Road to Judicial Supremacy*, 73 N.Y.U. L. REV. 333 (1998); *The History of the Countermajoritarian Difficulty, Part Two: Reconstruction's Political Court*, 91 GEO. L. J. 1 (2002); *The History of the Countermajoritarian Difficulty, Part Three: The Lesson of Lochner*, 76 N.Y.U. L. REV. 1383 (2001); *The History of the Countermajoritarian Difficulty, Part Four: Law's Politics*, 148 U. PA. L. REV. 971 (2000); *The Birth of an Academic Obsession: The History of the Countermajoritarian Difficulty, Part Five*, 112 YALE L. J. 153 (2002). The series culminated in a book, THE WILL OF THE PEOPLE (Farrar Straus 2010).

14. 297 U.S. 288, 341 (Brandeis, J., concurring). For a sample of the accolades accorded the opinion over the years, see Philip P. Frickey, *Getting from Joe to Gene (McCarthy): The Avoidance Canon, Legal Process Theory, and Narrowing Statutory Interpretation in the Early Warren Court*, 93 CALIF. L. REV. 397, 399 (2005).

15. 297 U.S. at 316.

protection against aggression."[16] In other words, *Ashwander* was a public interest lawsuit brought by laissez-faire conservatives.[17]

The majority, led by Chief Justice Charles Evans Hughes, upheld the validity of the TVA's activities on the merits. Brandeis concurred in the result only; he would have found that the plaintiffs lacked standing to challenge the validity of the TVA. His opinion, however, went well beyond the matter of standing. He gave seven reasons, or sets of reasons, why the Court should not reach the merits. After adverting to Article III limits on federal court adjudication, Brandeis purported to restate a series of rules that the Court had imposed upon itself in constitutional litigation:

1. The Court will not pass upon the constitutionality of legislation in a friendly, nonadversary, proceeding.
2. The Court will not "anticipate a question of constitutional law in advance of the necessity of deciding it."
3. The Court will not "formulate a rule of constitutional law broader than is required by the precise facts to which it is to be applied."
4. The Court will not pass upon a constitutional question although properly presented by the record, if there is also present some other ground upon which the case may be disposed of.
5. The Court will not pass upon the validity of a statute upon complaint of one who fails to show that he is injured by its operation. Among the many applications of this rule, none is more striking than the denial of the right of challenge to one who lacks a personal or property right.
6. The Court will not pass upon the constitutionality of a statute at the instance of one who has availed himself of its benefits.
7. "When the validity of an act of the Congress is drawn in question, and even if a serious doubt of constitutionality is raised, it is a cardinal principle that this Court will first ascertain whether a construction of the statute is fairly possible by which the question may be avoided."[18]

In this list, Brandeis indissolubly linked standing (fifth on the list) with the policy of judicial restraint. It was now clear that the doctrine of standing was a tool to protect the ability of the executive and legislative branches to deal with modern social and economic problems. Whether it was companies challenging agency orders to protect their competitive advantages or corporate shareholders challenging legislation out of philosophical opposition to big government,

16. 297 U.S. at 372 (McReynolds, J., dissenting).

17. Though, it should be noted, not a particularly compelling one, as the other three-quarters of the "Four Horsemen"—Justices Butler, Sutherland, and Van Devanter—voted to uphold the TVA.

18. 297 U.S. at 346–48 (citations omitted).

Brandeis felt the standing doctrine should be deployed to keep these plaintiffs out of federal court.

But in fact the Supreme Court had not consistently used the standing doctrine to block the shareholder cases. Indeed, the Court had many times permitted stockholders to challenge progressive legislation on behalf of quiescent corporations. Brandeis now confronted these cases. *Pollock v. Farmers' Loan & Trust Co.* and *Brushaber v. Union Pacific R. Co.* each involved allegedly invalid taxes that the corporations had decided not to challenge.[19] *Cotting v. Kansas City Stock Yards Co.* and *Chicago v. Mills* each involved allegedly unconstitutional rate regulations with which the corporations had determined to comply.[20] *Smith v. Kansas City Title & Trust Co.* permitted a stockholder to sue to enjoin investment by the company in bonds issued under the Federal Farm Loan Act; of course, the stockholder alleged that the Act itself was beyond Congress's enumerated powers.[21] *Hill v. Wallace* was a suit by members of the Board of Trade of Chicago to restrain enforcement of the Future Trading Act, which they alleged to be beyond Congress's powers.[22] After half-heartedly attempting to distinguish these cases from *Ashwander*, Brandeis candidly argued that they should be overruled.[23] The shareholder suit in federal court had been a constant thorn in the side of Progressivism. In his view, the fact that corporate management had resolved not to challenge legislation demonstrated that the corporation and its investors had no real pecuniary interests at stake. Under these circumstances, the shareholder suit was nothing more than a thinly veiled public interest lawsuit by those who believed burgeoning government programs and regulations threatened the future of liberty in America. Brandeis was ready to ban such lawsuits altogether.

Brandeis's *Ashwander* opinion was more successful at inculcating "judicial restraint" than he could possibly have dreamed. The standing doctrine alone has kept thousands of plaintiffs or would-be plaintiffs in federal equity outside the courthouse. And, following Brandeis' last-mentioned item, many a court has twisted a federal statute into the shape of a pretzel in order to avoid a

19. 157 U.S. 429 (1895) and 240 U.S. 1 (1916).

20. 183 U.S. 79 (1901) and 204 U.S. 321 (1907). Interestingly, Brandeis did not confront the two most famous cases in which shareholders of railroads were permitted to challenge rate regulations over the heads of corporate management—*Smyth v. Ames*, 169 U.S. 166 (1898) and *Ex Parte Young*, 209 U.S. 123 (1908). Chief Justice Hughes's opinion for the majority in *Ashwander* did cite these cases as support for the existence of standing, 297 U.S. at 320.

21. 255 U.S. 180 (1921).

22. 259 U.S. 44 (1922).

23. 297 U.S. at 352 (Brandeis, J., concurring) ("If, or in so far as, any of the cases discussed may be deemed authority for sustaining this bill, they should now be disapproved").

constitutional question.[24] Not only have modern federal courts routinely cited many of the seven points in his concurrence, they have relied on the opinion as authority for other methods of decision avoidance.[25] The standing doctrine pioneered in *Fairchild* may have been among the most potent and oft-utilized of Brandeis's judicial restraint arrows, but it was hardly alone in the quiver.

* * *

The confrontation between reformers and the courts was taking place on two fronts. There were lawsuits for injunctions, often shareholder derivative actions, to block the enforcement of reform legislation. An emerging second front was litigation to challenge the decisions of administrative agencies, primarily the Interstate Commerce Commission. Brandeis and the Supreme Court significantly limited these challenges by use of the standing doctrine.

In the same term that *Fairchild v. Hughes* was handed down, the Court denied standing in *Edward Hines Yellow Pine Trustees v. United States*.[26] In 1919, the Director General of Railroads issued an order authorizing railroads to charge a penalty on the storage of lumber in train cars at reconsignment points. About a year later, the American Wholesale Lumber Association, which represented jobbers, instituted proceedings before the Interstate Commerce Commission (ICC) to have the penalty charge canceled. The charge was hurting jobbers because they had no yards in which to store lumber; they had to use transit cars for storage. The ICC ultimately found that conditions had changed during the intervening year, and it canceled the penalty charge, although maintaining the right to reinstitute it as future conditions required.

The plaintiffs in *Edward Hines* were large manufacturers and dealers who customarily shipped straight from the lumber mills to ultimate destinations. They generally had no use for storage cars, and so were not aggrieved by the penalty charge. On the contrary, they welcomed the charge, which greatly hurt their competitors, the jobbers. The manufacturers and dealers accordingly brought an action in federal district court to set aside the ICC order rescinding the penalty charge. The order was beyond the Commission's authority, the plaintiffs claimed.

Justice Brandeis, writing for a unanimous Court, held that the plaintiffs lacked standing to challenge the order:

> [P]laintiffs could not maintain this suit merely by showing (if true) that the Commission was without power to order the penalty charges canceled. They must also show that the order alleged to be void subjects them to legal injury,

24. *See, e.g.*, International Association of Machinists v. Street, 367 U.S. 740 (1961) (Black, J., dissenting) (accusing majority of distorting statute to avoid reaching constitutional question).

25. *See, e.g.*, Railroad Comm'n of Texas v. Pullman Co., 312 U.S. 496 (1941).

26. 263 U.S. 143 (1923).

actual or threatened. This they have wholly failed to do. . . . Cancellation of a charge by which plaintiffs' rivals in business have been relieved of the handicap theretofore imposed may conceivably have subjected plaintiffs to such losses as are incident to more effective competition. But plaintiffs have no absolute right to require carriers to impose penalty charges. Plaintiffs' right is limited to protection against unjust discrimination.[27]

Justice Brandeis went on to dismiss the plaintiffs' claims of future harm, such as that (without the penalty charges) there might occur a shortage of railroad cars that would harm manufacturers and dealers. If such a shortage ever occurred, plaintiffs could challenge the Commission's authority to cancel the penalty charges at that time, the Court stated.[28] This appears to have been an application of what today would be called the ripeness doctrine.

The standing requirement imposed in *Edward Hines* was not the same requirement as now exists. The plaintiffs in *Edward Hines* clearly alleged the "injury-in-fact" that would be required under today's standing doctrine—namely, that they lost the competitive advantage over jobbers they had enjoyed under the penalty charge regime. There was no question but that the rescission of the penalty charge caused the loss of this competitive advantage, or that the reinstatement of the charge would restore the advantage. Instead, the Court insisted on a different kind of showing. The plaintiffs had to allege injury to a right that they possessed either at common law or under a statute. They had no common law or statutory right to the competitive advantage created by the penalty charge, so they lacked standing to challenge the Commission's authority to rescind it. This was the "legally protected right" test for standing, and it would endure for the next four decades.[29]

If the "legally protected right" doctrine differed sharply from the "injury-in-fact" test that would eventually take its place, it was quite consistent with the Blackstonian/Marshallian regime of *ubi jus, ibi remedium* that was being applied

27. 263 U.S. at 148.

28. *Id.* at 148-49.

29. See, e.g., the Chicago Junction Case, 264 U.S. 258 (1924), decided the very next term. The plaintiff railroads suffered competitive injury when the ICC granted a competitor control over certain terminal railroads. This time, the Court permitted a suit to challenge the Commission's authority because the Commission had discriminated in favor of the competitor and against the plaintiffs. This violated the plaintiffs' rights under the Interstate Commerce Act. *Id.* at 267. Justice Brandeis wrote for the Court, with Justices Sutherland, McReynolds, and Edward Terry Sanford dissenting on the ground that the plaintiffs lacked standing. According to the dissenters, standing required violation of the plaintiffs' common law rights, which could not be shown in the instant case. 264 U.S. at 271–72. Thus, all Justices agreed on the plaintiffs' need to show a violation of a legal right, with the majority recognizing violation of a statutory right and the dissent insisting upon violation of a common law right.

outside the administrative agency context. Consider *Fairchild v. Hughes* and *Frothingham v. Mellon.* Under *ubi jus, ibi remedium,* the plaintiff in *Fairchild* should have been turned away because the ratification of the Suffrage Amendment, even if illegal, did not violate any legally protected right of his. One may have a moral or political right not to have one's government violate its own charter, but it is quite another thing to say that one is entitled to a judicial remedy for every such violation. (One might argue that the illegal votes of women would dilute the legal votes of males, but it is doubtful that this sort of dilution was remediable, quite apart from the standing doctrine.) By the same token, *ubi jus, ibi remedium* would keep Mrs. Frothingham out of court because the passage of the Maternity Act, even if illegal, did not violate any legally protected right of hers. Again, one might have a moral or political right not to have government spend one's tax dollars illegally, but that is emphatically not to say that one has a judicial remedy for every such illegal expenditure. Of course, the opinion in *Frothingham* does not speak of *ubi jus, ibi remedium*; it operates more on a theory of *de minimus non curat lex.* The point, however, is that neither *Fairchild* nor *Frothingham* violated *Marbury*'s injunction to the effect that where a legally protected right has been violated, the courts must make available a remedy. In the agency review cases, the "legally protected right" doctrine substantially captured the maxim.

During the remainder of Brandeis's tenure, the Court handed down five decisions applying the "legally protected right" test of *Edward Hines.* The first was *Interstate Busses Corp. v. Holyoke Street Railway Co.,* decided in 1927. The advent of motor vehicle buses had cut deeply into the street railway business in parts of Massachusetts. The street railways urged district attorneys to enforce a statute requiring bus companies to obtain licenses before they ran buses on lines already covered by street railways. The plaintiff bus company filed a bill in equity in federal court to enjoin the street railways and district attorneys from enforcing the law. The bus company claimed that the statute violated the Commerce Clause insofar as it affected interstate commerce. The Supreme Court, per Justice Pierce Butler, held that the statute did not violate the Commerce Clause. At the tail end of the opinion, however, the Court further noted that the plaintiff bus company had never even applied for a license, and therefore that it "lacked standing" to challenge the statute (a ground that today would probably be labeled "ripeness" rather than "standing"). The Court found no standing despite the fact that the bus company's employees had already been arrested for operating buses without a license, and—by the Court's own admission—authorities intended to pursue prosecution. (On materially indistinguishable facts, the modern Court found the existence of standing and ripeness on the part of the plaintiff in *Steffel v. Thompson.*[30]) *Interstate Busses* again demonstrated the Court's eagerness during

30. 415 U.S.452 (1974).

the Brandeis era to advance a standing/ripeness doctrine that was markedly more stringent than today's.

Brandeis himself wrote for the Court in *Alexander Sprunt & Son, Inc. v. United States.*[31] The Interstate Commerce Commission had ordered several railroads in Texas, Arkansas, and Louisiana to stop discriminating in their rates. For reasons not disclosed by the Court, the railroads' rate structures had discriminated against firms who shipped cotton from the interior to the coast, thereby according a competitive advantage to wharfside warehousers such as Alexander Sprunt. When the ICC ordered a stop to this discrimination, Sprunt and the railroads sued in federal court to enjoin enforcement of the order. Although the plaintiffs secured a preliminary injunction, the court eventually upheld the agency's order and dissolved the injunction. From that decree, only Sprunt appealed; the railroads capitulated and implemented a nondiscriminatory rate structure.

Brandeis and the majority held that Sprunt lacked standing to challenge the order because it alleged no violation of its legal rights. Without question the order "worsened the economic position" of Sprunt, which is to say, caused Sprunt what would today be referred to as "injury-in-fact." Sprunt had been deprived of a pronounced competitive advantage. But Sprunt had no legal right to that advantage. If the railroads themselves had decided to terminate the discriminatory rates, Sprunt would have had no legal recourse. Brandeis stated:

> [Sprunt's] present position resembles in all essentials one which was put forward in *Edward Hines*. . . . There, as here, the plaintiffs were deprived by the order of the Commission of a competitive advantage. But the plaintiffs there, as here, were not subjected to or threatened with any legal wrong.[32]

Later that term, in another railroad case, the Court again denied standing on the "legal right" rationale. In *Pittsburgh & West Virginia Railroad v. United States,*[33] a consortium of railroads proposed to construct a new terminal in Cleveland. The project required either an easement or outright acquisition of a property owned by the Wheeling railroad. The Wheeling agreed to an acquisition and applied to the ICC for approval. The Pittsburgh & West Virginia intervened before the Commission, opposing approval. After the ICC issued an order approving the transaction, the Pittsburgh & West Virginia filed a bill in equity in federal court to set it aside. Brandeis, writing for the Court, denied standing. "The mere fact that appellant was permitted to intervene before the Commission does not entitle it to institute an independent suit to set aside the Commission's order in the absence of resulting actual or threatened legal injury to it," Brandeis wrote, citing *Alexander Sprunt.*[34] It was acknowledged that the Pittsburgh & West

31. 281 U.S. 249 (1930).
32. 281 U.S. at 256 (citation omitted).
33. 281 U.S. 479 (1930).
34. 281 U.S. at 487.

Virginia was going to lose money as a result of the approved transaction, which is to say that it surely could demonstrate the "injury-in-fact" that would be deemed sufficient for standing from the 1970s on. Yet the Supreme Court, Brandeis again writing, denied standing:

> The mere fact that appellant was permitted to intervene before the Commission does not entitle it to institute an independent suit to set aside the Commission's order in the absence of resulting actual or threatened legal injury to it, *Alexander Sprunt*. . . . Finally, the claim that the order threatens the Wheeling's financial stability, and consequently appellant's financial interest as a minority stockholder is not sufficient to show a threat of the legal injury necessary to entitle it to bring a suit to set aside the order. This financial interest does not differ from that of every investor in Wheeling securities or from an investor's interest in any business transaction or lawsuit of his corporation. Unlike orders entered in cases of reorganization, and in some cases of acquisition of control of one carrier by another, the order under attack does not deal with the interests of investors. The injury feared is the indirect harm which may result to every stockholder from harm to the corporation. Such stockholder's interest is clearly insufficient to give the Pittsburgh a standing independently to institute suit to annul this order. The bill should have been dismissed without inquiry into the merits.[35]

In this passage it is clear that Brandeis applied the "legal right" test of *Edward Hines* and *Alexander Sprunt*. Less obvious is that he also applied the notion of a generalized grievance set forth in *Fairchild v. Hughes*. Brandeis's opinion conceded that the Pittsburgh, as a minority shareholder, would suffer financially if the Wheeling lost money. But that financial interest "d[id] not differ" from that of other, numerous Wheeling shareholders, thus depriving all of them of standing to sue.

The fourth decision in this line was *Moffat Tunnel League v. United States*,[36] decided in 1933. It too carries forward the themes of *Edward Hines* and *Fairchild v. Hughes*. The Moffat Road was a 232-mile stretch of railroad track over extremely challenging terrain in northwestern Colorado. Originally, the line was planned to extend another 250 miles into Utah, but such plans were eventually abandoned as infeasible. The Denver and Rio Grande Western Railroad Company saw an opportunity to connect one of its lines with the Moffat Road, thus reducing the distance between Denver and points west, and avoiding some of the heavy grades over the Continental Divide. The Denver and Rio Grande asked the ICC to approve its acquisition of control over the Moffat Road, and the Commission granted the request. The Moffat Tunnel League was an unincorporated voluntary association dedicated to promoting commercial development, including

35. *Id.*
36. 289 U.S. 113 (1933).

adequate transportation, in certain counties in northwest Colorado. It appears to have been something like a regional chamber of commerce. The League had opposed the Denver and Rio Grande's application before the ICC because it saw the project as dooming any chances that the Moffat Road would eventually be extended to Utah. The League sued in federal court to have the ICC's order set aside.

Justice Butler wrote for the Court denying standing, as he had in *Interstate Busses*. First, he held that the League had "no capacity to sue" because it was not a "corporation[], quasi-corporation[], or organized pursuant to or recognized by any law." Next, he stated that no federal statute "purports to give any unincorporated voluntary association standing to bring suit to set aside an order of the Commission." Finally, Butler stated:

> [T]he complaint must show that plaintiff has, or represents others having, a legal right or interest that will be injuriously affected by the order. *Edward Hines, Alexander Sprunt, Pittsburgh & W. Va. Ry.* Plaintiffs have failed to show that they are so qualified. Their interest is not a legal one. It is no more than a sentiment, such as may be entertained by members of the public in the territory west of Craig, that the improvement of transportation facilities authorized by the Commission will lessen the possibility of construction by a rival of the Rio Grande of an extension of the Moffat to Utah common points.[37]

Today, the League would probably be denied standing on the ground that its claimed injury—the lessened possibility of an extension of the Moffat Road to Utah—was too speculative. Moreover, under current standing doctrine, the setting aside the ICC's order approving the Denver and Rio Grande's acquisition of control over the Moffat Road would not necessarily "redress" the League's injury. Justice Butler's opinion, in contrast, denied standing on the ground that the League had alleged no violation of any legal right, as well as on the ground that the League had failed to differentiate itself from other "members of the public in the territory west of Craig," thus making it a generalized grievance of sorts.

In 1938, the year prior to Frankfurter's arrival, the Court handed down *Alabama Power Co. v. Ickes*.[38] The Federal Emergency Administrator of Public Works financed the construction of electricity distribution systems by four municipal corporations. Alabama Power sued to enjoin the federal government from aiding such construction, alleging that it would suffer ruinous financial losses if it had to compete with municipal power plants. The Court, per Justice Sutherland, held that Alabama Power lacked standing to sue because it had no legal right to be free of competition. But, while Sutherland's rationale almost

---

37. 289 U.S. at 119.
38. 302 U.S. 464 (1938).

perfectly recreated that of Brandeis in *Edward Hines,* Sutherland reached back even further to an 1882 case, *Railroad Company v. Ellerman*:

> The damage is attributable to the competition, and to that alone. But the competition is not illegal. . . . The only injury of which he can be heard is the invasion of some legal or equitable right. If he asserts that the competition of the railroad company damages him, the answer is, that it does not abridge or impair any such right.[39]

The tenor of Justice Sutherland's *Alabama Power* opinion, and his primary reliance on *Ellerman* rather than *Edward Hines,* suggest that he saw the "legal right" doctrine as being grounded not in Article III or a policy of judicial restraint, but instead in the principles of the common law. Alabama Power had presented a classic case of *damnum absque injuria* (damage without injury), Sutherland stated. Surely Alabama Power had alleged what would today be called "injury-in-fact," for it would suffer enormous economic losses from the competition of municipal power plants. But that "damage" would be occasioned without any "legal injury," which is to say, without the violation of any of Alabama Power's legal rights.

Reuel E. Schiller has chronicled the triumph of scientific pragmatism in New Deal–era thinking about the role of the courts in the administrative state. New Dealers rejected the vested rights and substantive due process mentality that characterized the Protestant idealist federal bench, instead embracing the notion of expertise. Judges should not revert to subconscious background assumptions about God-given rights to reasonable rates of return. They should have to defer to the empirical and secular rationality of agencies populated by social engineers. As Schiller put it:

> Courts, these thinkers believed, should stay out of the administrative process as much as possible because they did not possess the specialized knowledge necessary to second-guess expert administrators. Courts applied general rules that were inappropriate for the practical nature of the administrative state. According to Frankfurter, requiring judicial review of administrative acts took judges out of their proper element and involved them in "matters of fact and opinion not peculiarly within the special competence of judges."[40]

Long before the New Deal, Brandeis himself had touted deference to agency decisions, not only in the standing decisions of *Edward Hines* and its progeny, but in terms of the standards of review to be employed when standing was present.

39. 105 U.S. 173-74 (1882), quoted in *Alabama Power,* 302 U.S. at 481–83. It should be noted that Justice Sutherland's opinion did cite *Edward Hines* and *Alexander Sprunt,* but as secondary authorities. 302 U.S. at 483.

40. Reuel E. Schiller, *The Era of Deference: Courts, Expertise, and the Emergence of New Deal Administrative Law,* 106 Mich. L. Rev. 399, 419 (2007).

In *Ohio Valley Water Co. v. Ben Avon Borough*,[41] the U.S. Supreme Court reversed a state supreme court opinion deferring to the expertise of the Pennsylvania Public Service Commission on the question of whether certain waters were being extracted from the Ohio River or from an aquifer known to geologists as the Wisconsin Glacial Flow. The trial court had correctly exercised independent judgment on the facts of the case. "For progressive proponents of the administrative state, the Supreme Court's ruling in Ben Avon was a nightmare come to life," wrote Schiller. "Was the Court really suggesting that courts not defer to agencies even on technical" issues such as the hydrological features of the Ohio River Valley?[42] Brandeis, joined by Holmes, dissented. "Here, it is clear, there was substantial evidence to support the findings of the Commission; and no adequate reason is shown for declining to accept as conclusive the facts found by the state tribunals," he wrote.[43] In time, Brandeis's deferential "substantial evidence" standard would carry the day.[44]

Even Brandeis's "substantial evidence" doctrine, however, was not completely deferential to agencies. Under that standard, it was still possible for courts to invalidate rate regulations ultimately determined to be "confiscatory." Brandeis was a pragmatist and an instrumentalist. He was not essentially an ideologue; he did not generally push to the logical extremes. After his departure, with the advent of the New Deal and the demise of substantive due process, federal court deference to agencies became more extreme. By 1940, the Supreme Court was reversing lower federal courts and reinstating the Texas Railroad Commission's drastic limits on oil production in the face of a due process challenge. The Court handed down a "fresh reminder that courts must not substitute their notions of expediency and fairness for those which have guided the agencies," and concluded, "[i]t is not for the federal courts to supplant the Commission's judgment even in the face of convincing proof that a different result would have been better."[45] It is difficult to imagine a more doctrinaire stance toward judicial review of agency action (albeit the action of a state, rather than federal, agency). This was beyond a desire to see Progressivism or the New Deal succeed. It reflected the author's deep-seated beliefs about the proper roles of courts, legislatures, and agencies in a democratic society. The author was Felix Frankfurter.

41. 253 U.S. 287 (1920).

42. Schiller, *supra* note 40 of this chapter, at 402–03.

43. 253 U.S. at 298 (Brandeis, J., dissenting).

44. *See* Barry Cushman, *Some Varieties and Vicissitudes of Lochnerism*, 85 B.U. L. Rev. 881, 908–18 (2005) (and cases discussed therein).

45. R.R. Comm'n of Tex. v. Rowan & Nichols Oil Co., 310 U.S. 573, 581, 584 (1940).

5. FRANKFURTER AND THE INTELLECTUALIZATION OF JUDICIAL RESTRAINT

If Louis Brandeis's advocacy of the judicial restraint credo was primarily instrumental, that was not always the case with Felix Frankfurter.[1] Although there was a lengthy stretch of time before his appointment to the Court when Frankfurter acted as Brandeis's lieutenant, publishing several major scholarly works as part of Brandeis's Progressivist campaign–and although clearly his allegiance to Franklin Delano Roosevelt (FDR) and the New Deal helped fuel his zeal for judicial restraint—Frankfurter's qualms about the vigorous use of judicial review were a product of deep professional indoctrination as well as political expediency.

Frankfurter was born in Vienna in 1882, the third of six children. His father, Leopold, was a rather ineffectual man, a romantic and connoisseur of the finer things in life, but a guileless and sometimes indolent businessman who could barely keep the family financially afloat in the rough economic waters of late nineteenth-century Vienna. His mother Emma was stouter and more practical, pushing the boys toward education and directing them away from their ne'er-do-well father and toward their Uncle Solomon, a highly accomplished scholar who had been appointed director of the state library. Young Felix particularly admired that Solomon had become "a spokesman for Jewish interests in the city and a *shtadlan* (backstairs petitioner) with the gentile power structure."[2] In 1894, Emma reluctantly packed up the children and followed Leopold to New York, where he sought to start afresh.

The Frankfurters settled on the predominantly Jewish Lower East Side. In his magisterial biography of Frankfurter's pre-Court years, Michael Parrish documented how the Frankfurters "settled initially on Seventh Street, near Tompkins Square and Cooper Union, in the heavily German-speaking neighborhood where the sober residents voted Republican, admired their wealthy coreligionists—the Seligmans, Warburgs, and Strauses—and hoped to maintain a comfortable distance from the boisterous, Yiddish-speaking masses on Henry and Cherry Streets."[3] The German Jews on the Lower East Side were attracted to gentility, which carried with it a certain social conservatism and respect for pedigreed institutions and practices; the Eastern European Jews were generally

1. *But see generally* Stephen W. Baskerville, Of Laws and Limitations: An Intellectual Portrait of Louis Dembitz Brandeis (Assoc. Univ. Presses 1994).

2. Michael E. Parrish, Felix Frankfurter and His Times: The Reform Years 9 (1982).

3. *Id.* at 11.

poorer, more ideological, more political, more devout, and often more radical. Young Felix adopted the values of the German-Jewish community pretty much down the line, with one glaring exception. Like his Uncle Solomon, he loved politics.

Though he struggled to understand the devoutness of the Eastern Europeans (to his mother's everlasting consternation, Felix had inherited his father's agnosticism), he found the Eastern Europeans intellectually fascinating. At City College, Frankfurter had his first real exposure to these idealistic and bohemian thinkers, whose "conversations often turned to anarchism, revolution, Emma Goldman, dialectical materialism, and free love."[4] This was a far cry from the German-Jewish students whose company he usually kept, immersed in their quest for respectability and personal achievement. Frankfurter could see the virtues and vices on both sides, and throughout his career he sought to marry that passion for justice and social change with a profound respect for history and institutions. It eventually led him to forsake the dreamier professions of journalist or poet in favor of becoming a reform-minded lawyer.

First, however, there was the matter of legal training, and after two dull stints in night classes at local schools, Frankfurter in fall 1902 enrolled in the Harvard Law School. There, in "high-ceilinged Austin Hall . . . the waistcoated doyens of the legal profession—James Barr Ames, Samuel Williston, John Chipman Gray, Joseph Doddridge Branna, and Joseph Henry Beale—attempted to make gentlemen and lawyers out of the scions of the Anglo-Saxon establishment and a handful of immigrants."[5]

Among these faculty members, Gray was a strong influence. He hired Frankfurter as a research assistant. Frankfurter undoubtedly read Gray's *The Nature and Sources of the Law*, which rejected the jurisprudence of natural rights "in favor of a pragmatic interpretation of the origin of legal rules that located them in the shifting configurations of social life and the varying responses of judges to these changing circumstances."[6] Like his friend Oliver Wendell Holmes, Jr., Gray had breathed the deep skepticism that led both of them to scorn Christopher Columbus Langdell's orthodoxy and David Brewer's and George Sutherland's views of natural rights. Another intellectual force pushing Frankfurter toward skepticism was John Morley's *On Compromise*. Morley urged a "wise suspense in forming opinions, wise reserve in expressing them, and wise tardiness in trying to realise them." Young Frankfurter studied the volume intently and later often acknowledged its influence on him.[7]

---

4. *Id.* at 15 n.18.

5. *Id.* at 16–17.

6. *Id.* at 20.

7. Alexander M. Bickel, The Supreme Court and the Idea of Progress 31 (Harper & Row 1970).

Frankfurter would develop a habit of personal adulation for and loyalty to certain figures (Holmes, Brandeis, FDR), but his absorption of the ideas of James Bradley Thayer cannot be attributed to a personal relationship between the two. Thayer had died the year Frankfurter got to Harvard. Yet, according to Parrish, "Thayer had a profound influence upon Frankfurter, who read the latter's 'The Origin and Scope of the American Doctrine of Constitutional Law' so many times that he could recite whole passages from memory." Thayer's rule of "clear error" became a cornerstone of Frankfurter's professional and intellectual identity. He held this belief uncritically, as a first principle of American constitutionalism, in need of no justification. In this respect, his commitment to judicial restraint was different from that of Brandeis, whose advocacy of judicial restraint was more instrumental, and that of Holmes, whose endorsement of judicial restraint only grew out of his (and Chauncey Wright's) positivism. For Frankfurter, judicial restraint became an article of faith.

In 1939, Brandeis's most prominent protégé assumed his seat on the Supreme Court. Although the close personal relationship between Brandeis and Frankfurter would never quite recover from Brandeis' bitter disappointment in Frankfurter's refusal to publicly attack FDR's so-called "court-packing" plan,[8] Frankfurter's Progressive, New Deal, and judicial restraint credentials were beyond reproach. It would not take Justice Frankfurter long to disseminate his views on justiciability generally and standing in particular. *Coleman v. Miller* involved a challenge to Kansas's ratification of the Child Labor Amendment to the federal constitution. In 1924, Congress proposed the amendment, which would have given Congress the power to "limit, regulate, and prohibit" the labor of those under eighteen years of age. The next year, the Kansas Legislature rejected the amendment. In 1937, however, the Kansas Legislature enacted a bill ratifying the amendment. Several legislators on the losing side sued in federal court to enjoin certification of the vote.

Frankfurter's concurrence made four fundamental assertions about the standing doctrine. First, Frankfurter tied standing to the "case or controversy" requirement of Article III, and then in turn tied the "case or controversy" clause to English practice. Previous cases had linked standing to "case or controversy," but never to the original intent of the framers. Frankfurter stated that their intent was to limit federal court jurisdiction to the universe of matters that could properly come before the courts at Westminster:

> In endowing this Court with "judicial Power" the Constitution presupposed an historic content for that phrase and relied on assumption by the judiciary of authority only over issues which are appropriate for disposition by judges. The Constitution further explicitly indicated the limited area within which judicial action was to move—however far-reaching the consequences of action

8. Parrish, *supra* note 2 at 273–74.

> within that area—by extending "judicial Power" only to "Cases" and "Controversies." Both by what they said and by what they implied, the framers of the Judiciary Article gave merely the outlines of what were to them the familiar operations of the English judicial system and its manifestations on this side of the ocean before the Union. Judicial power could come into play only in matters that were the traditional concern of the courts at Westminster and only if they arose in ways that to the expert feel of lawyers constituted "Cases" or "Controversies."[9]

Remarkably, Frankfurter cited no evidence to support his representation of the framers' intentions.

Second, Frankfurter stated that the English practice excluded predominantly political matters and purely intellectual matters:

> It was not for courts to meddle with matters that required no subtlety to be identified as political issues. And even as to the kinds of questions which were the staple of judicial business, it was not for courts to pass upon them as abstract, intellectual problems but only if a concrete, living contest between adversaries called for the arbitrament of law.[10]

As evidence that English courts avoided political issues, Frankfurter cited a single *sui generis* case, the Duke of York's claim to the Crown.[11] To support the assertion regarding abstract and intellectual problems, he cited only Supreme Court precedents.[12]

The next important assertion in Frankfurter's *Coleman* concurrence was that the standing doctrine should never be applied mechanically, but rather should be used pragmatically to limit judicial review to cases where the federal courts could be useful in the political process:

> Since . . . considerations governing the exercise of judicial power are not mechanical criteria but derive from conceptions regarding the distribution of governmental powers in their manifold, changing guises, differences in the application of canons of jurisdiction have arisen from the beginning of the Court's history. Conscious or unconscious leanings toward the serviceability of the judicial process in the adjustment of public controversies clothed in the form of private litigation inevitably affect decisions. For they influence awareness in recognizing the relevance of conceded doctrines of judicial self-limitation and rigor in enforcing them.[13]

---

9. 307 U.S. at 460.

10. *Id.*

11. *Id.*

12. The precedents were *Muskrat v. United States*, 219 U.S. 346 (1911); *Tutun v. United States*, 270 U.S. 568 (1926); *Willing v. Chicago Auditorium Assn.*, 277 U.S. 274 (1928); and *Nashville C. & St L. Ry. Co. v. Wallace*, 288 U.S. 249 (1933).

13. 307 U.S. at 461 (footnote omitted).

This aspect of the opinion is most fascinating for the light it sheds on Frankfurter's view of courts—not just as neutral umpires or temples of justice, but as self-conscious tools of the government in making necessary social and economic adjustments.[14]

Finally, Frankfurter's *Coleman* concurrence portrayed the standing doctrine in a particular conceptual light—that of a prohibition against generalized grievances. He said nothing, for the moment, about the concept of standing as a requirement that legal rights be violated. Over the next three decades and beyond, however, the law of standing would continue on those two tracks—the generalized grievance track, involving cases outside the context of agency review, and the legal rights track, involving agency review.

* * *

Every standing decision after 1922 falls along either the track created by *Fairchild v. Hughes* or the track exemplified by *Edward Hines*. The *Fairchild* line of decisions includes what are modernly considered the Article III standing cases, most of which have involved challenges to legislative and executive action. The *Edward Hines* line of decisions exclusively involved challenges to federal administrative agency action.

The same term it decided *Coleman*, the Court handed down *Tennessee Electric Power v. Tennessee Valley Authority* and *Atlanta v. Ickes*, and then, in 1940, *Perkins v. Lukens Steel*. In each of these cases, the Court held that the plaintiff lacked standing to challenge an administrative agency order because the agency action violated no legal right belonging to the plaintiff. All three cases involved a straightforward application of *Edward Hines*. In 1940, however, the Court also handed down its decision in *FCC v. Sanders Brothers Radio Station*.[15] Today, everyone agrees that *Sanders Brothers* broke from the *Edward Hines* mold, but the real question is, in what way?

On January 20, 1936, the *Dubuque Telegraph Herald* petitioned the FCC for a permit to construct a radio station in Dubuque, Iowa. About four months later, the radio station WKBB—which had been operating for several years out of East Dubuque, Illinois, directly across the Mississippi River—petitioned the Federal Communications Commission (FCC) for permission to move its operations to Dubuque. Both parties argued that they should be given exclusive permission to operate a radio station out of Dubuque, but the broadcasting division of the FCC decided that both parties should be allowed to operate simultaneously. Sanders Brothers requested rehearing before the agency, but the petition was denied.

Under the *Edward Hines* test, Sanders Brothers clearly would not have had standing to obtain judicial review of the FCC's action. Neither WKBB nor the

---

14. *See, e.g.*, 10 East 40th Street Bldg., Inc. v. Callus, 325 U.S. 578, 583 (1945); Scripps-Howard v. FCC, 316 U.S. 4, 15: "Courts no less than administrative bodies are agencies of government. Both are instruments for realizing public purposes."

15. 309 U.S. 470 (1940).

FCC had violated any legal entitlement belonging to Sanders Brothers. Naturally, Sanders Brothers was unhappy with the agency's decision not to give them a monopoly on Dubuque airwaves, but they had no legal right to any such monopoly. The facts were materially indistinguishable from *Edward Hines* and its progeny: one party, enjoying a market advantage created by the then-existing regulatory regime, wished to obtain judicial review of a new, much less advantageous, regime. Yet there was one key difference between *Sanders Brothers* and the previous cases. In the previous cases, the plaintiffs were unable to invoke any statutory authorization for judicial review. They had to rely upon common law for their suits. In *Sanders Brothers*, Section 402(b) of the Federal Communications Act authorized an appeal to the U.S. Court of Appeals for the District of Columbia "(1) by an applicant for a license or permit, or (2) by any other person aggrieved or whose interests are adversely affected by any decision of the Commission granting or refusing any such application." Precisely what significance did the Court assign to this explicit statutory authorization to sue?

The agency argued that this provision did not alter the old "legal right" doctrine of *Edward Hines*. But in a unanimous decision, with FDR appointee Owen Roberts writing, the Court disagreed. Congress must have meant to authorize standing for more than just those whose legal rights were violated, or it would not have included the second subsection, he wrote. A disappointed applicant who could allege that the agency had violated a legal right by the denying the application had standing to challenge the denial in court under the first subsection. But what if the agency's improvident *grant* of an application harmed the public generally? Congress "may have been of opinion that one likely to be financially injured by the issue of a license would be the only person having a sufficient interest" to sue, Roberts asserted. "It is within the power of Congress to confer such standing to prosecute an appeal."[16]

The Court had now ruled that a person suffering some competitive injury could challenge agency action even if the action did not violate that person's legal rights. Elizabeth Magill has demonstrated that the Court and others clearly understood this doctrine as allowing plaintiffs "standing for the public."[17] In *Scripps-Howard Radio v. FCC*, Frankfurter's majority opinion stated that plaintiffs suing under Section 402(b)(2) "have standing only as representatives of the public interest."[18] The prominent appellate judge Jerome Frank, corresponding privately with Justice William O. Douglas, characterized *Sanders Brothers* as allowing "Congress to deputize 'private Attorney Generals' to bring cases before the federal courts that would not otherwise be cognizable."[19] If Congress could

16. *Id.* at 477.

17. Elizabeth Magill, *Standing for the Public: A Lost History*, 95 VA. L. REV. 1131 (2009).

18. 316 U.S. 4, 14 (1943).

19. Magill, 95 VA. L. REV. at 1144.

authorize the attorney general of the United States to bring cases to vindicate the interests of the public, why could it not authorize private individuals to do the same?

But the "private attorney general" device was in some tension with *Fairchild* and *Frothingham*, the early 1920s cases in which the Court had refused standing to ideological plaintiffs who believed they were suing in the public interest. The plaintiff in *Fairchild* was suing to protect the public from what he believed was illegal voting by women; the plaintiff in *Frothingham* was suing to protect the public from a violation of the Tenth Amendment and, derivatively, of states' rights. Both were found not to have standing. There was the one key distinction: Congress had not authorized private citizens to sue on the public's behalf in those two cases, whereas it had explicitly authorized such suits in *Sanders Brothers*. Still, the Court had rested its holdings in *Fairchild* and *Frothingham* on the "case or controversy" limitations of Article III. Read broadly, these precedents meant that a grievance shared by the entire public simply did not fall within the federal judicial power, at least when brought at the behest of a private litigant. Surely Congress could not enlarge the concept of "case or controversy" by simply enacting a statute authorizing "any aggrieved person" to challenge agency action.

Some respected federal judges thought that *Sanders Brothers* contravened Article III. Henry Edgerton of the District of Columbia Circuit portrayed *Sanders Brothers* as permitting an intervening competitor to appear "as a kind of King's proctor, to vindicate the public interest,"[20] prompting Jerome Frank to ask, "Where is there any constitutional power to confer on any citizen" that type of standing? Frank asserted that because the plaintiff in *Sanders Brothers* had no legal injury, they therefore "had no cause of action and there was no case or controversy before the court."[21] Justice Douglas too had qualms. "All constitutional questions aside, we should require explicit, unequivocal authorization before we permit[] an appellant who has no individual substantive right at stake in the litigation to obtain a stay to protect the public interest," he wrote in his *Scripps-Howard* dissent.[22]

Sanders Brothers was troubling from the Marshallian perspective of *ubi jus, ibi remedium*. In *Marbury*, Marshall had established that the essence of amenability to judicial resolution was an honest and antagonistic assertion of vested *rights*, not a clash of mere expectancy interests. The Court had reaffirmed that principle many times since. Sanders Brothers could not point to a vested property right, or any legal right at all, that the granting of WKBB's license would violate. At most, the license threatened a diminution in Sanders Brothers' expected revenue

20. Colorado Radio Corp. v. Federal Communications Comm'n, 118 F.2d 24, 28 (1941) (Edgerton, J., concurring).

21. Magill, 95 VA. L. REV. at 1143.

22. 316 U.S. at 20 (Douglas, J., dissenting).

and profits. If Congress had created new substantive rights and vested them in parties like Sanders Brothers, that would be one thing. But, as Frankfurter wrote in *Scripps-Howard*, "The Communications Act of 1934 did not create new private rights. The purpose of the Act was to protect the public interest in communications."[23]

In Frankfurter's estimation, the "private attorney general" scheme approved in *Sanders Brothers* passed Article III muster because such "standing for the public" was limited to those whose "interests were substantially impaired" by the challenged agency action.[24] Presumably this ruled out purely ideological plaintiffs of the sort in *Fairchild* and *Frothingham*. Sanders Brothers had a clear economic and competitive interest in the denial of WKBB's application for a license to operate out of Dubuque. Although this private economic interest was not a proper basis for the agency's decision, it provided Sanders Brothers with the pedigree necessary to act as a "private attorney general." Douglas held the same view. "[I]f we accept as constitutionally valid a system of judicial review invoked by a private person who has no individual substantive right to protect but who has standing only as a representative of the public interest, then I think we must be exceedingly scrupulous to see to it that his interest in the matter is substantial and immediate."[25] In other words, a private individual could properly act as a representative of the public, but only if he could demonstrate some personal interest in the litigation.

On the surface of things, this was an odd position: one became qualified to represent the public by having a private interest in the matter. Political theory, or perhaps simple common sense, would suggest the opposite. A prosecutor who was related to the victim in a case would generally be thought less, not more, qualified to represent the public than a prosecutor unrelated to anyone in the litigation. The head of a regulatory agency would be thought less qualified to guard the public interest—indeed, probably *dis*qualified from guarding it—if he or she had a personal fortune at stake in the market being regulated. What made the Court think that the presence of a private interest was prerequisite to representing the public interest in challenging agency action?

One likely factor was the structure of the adversary system. In litigation with potentially broad society-wide effects, it is crucial for the parties to represent their positions zealously, to bring out the most powerful arguments possible. If the case has been feigned by one or more parties, if the litigation is collusive, then the court might decide an important matter of law with only one side being represented. The presence of a private interest is a proxy for litigating initiative. A person with no private stake in the matter might not have a sufficient incentive to contest the agency action with the degree of zeal necessary to protect the public

23. 316 U.S. at 14–15.

24. FCC v. NBC (KOA), 319 U.S. 239, 260 (Frankfurter, J., dissenting).

25. 319 U.S. at 265 (Douglas, J., dissenting).

interest from a bad precedent. According to the Court, one of the main purposes of the "case or controversy" requirement was to ensure the presence of that litigating incentive.

Surely the Court was right to fear the effects of feigned or collusive litigation in matters of great public importance. But was the Court right to equate a lack of private interest with a lack of litigating initiative? Plaintiffs who pursue litigation for ideological reasons, the Court was saying, cannot be relied upon to proceed with the same zeal as plaintiffs who sue for pecuniary or other self-interested reasons. In light of the boom of public interest litigation of the late 1960s and early 1970s, this empirical supposition seems quite unfounded. One could easily conclude that the supposition was never well founded. Certainly the plaintiffs in *Fairchild* and *Frothingham* were hardly dogging it; despite their lack of pecuniary self-interest, they had sufficient motivation to take their cases all the way to the U.S. Supreme Court.

By moving from the test of "legal right" to one of "substantial impairment of a private interest," the Court was moving from a conceptually bright-line test to a conceptually vague one. The new test was conceptually vague on two counts: how much impairment was "substantial"; and what counted as an "interest"? More importantly, by insisting upon substantial impairment of a private interest in lieu of a legal right, the Court was reserving for itself the power to disallow congressional assignments of standing to "private attorneys general." In any case where the Court felt that Congress had gone too far in permitting standing for the public, it would not be difficult to say that the impairment was too insubstantial, or that the private interest at issue was not "cognizable," which is to say not of the type that would sustain litigation. Out-of-pocket pecuniary losses would always be cognizable, but economic expectancy interests could easily be denominated "too remote," and noneconomic interests could easily be characterized as insufficiently "concrete." By requiring a private interest, the Court was ensuring that it would always have the last word on standing to challenge agency action.

Sanders Brothers was thus a qualified victory for the principle of congressional control over federal court jurisdiction. Presumably the Court could have stuck to its "legal right" doctrine by simply interpreting the statutory phrase "any aggrieved party" as meaning any party showing violation of a legal right. Under the new rule, Congress was empowered to permit those with mere competitive injury to challenge agency action. On the other hand, the Court could have found that Congress was empowered to permit anyone—whether suffering private injury or not—to obtain judicial review of agency action. The "case or controversy" requirement could have been deemed satisfied by adequate demonstration of ideological zeal in pursuing the litigation. *Fairchild* and *Frothingham* may have rejected the notion of ideological plaintiffs, but the plaintiffs in those cases had no statutory authorization to sue. The Court could have found that the presence of such congressional authorization changed the calculus of when one satisfies the "case or controversy" requirement. Its decision to abjure that approach meant that *Sanders Brothers* was, at best, a modest victory for the principle of congressional control over federal court jurisdiction.

Modest as the *Sanders Brothers* development may have been, even it was not immediately and fully accepted. Frankfurter's dissent in *Stark v. Wickard*[26] illustrates the point. In August 1941, pursuant to the Agricultural Agreement Marketing Act, the Secretary of Agriculture issued an order placing minimum prices on the marketing of milk in the Boston area. The order authorized certain deductions (essentially taxes) from funds paid by milk producers. Without question, the deduction had the effect of reducing the amount actually received by producers for their milk.[27] The producers filed a class action in federal district court, seeking to enjoin the deductions. Unfortunately, the statute was silent on the question of whether producers had a private right of action. Justice Stanley Reed, speaking for the majority, asserted a presumption in favor of a private right of action under the circumstances: "When . . . definite personal rights are created by federal statute, similar in kind to those customarily treated in courts of law, the silence of Congress as to judicial review is . . . not to be construed as a denial of authority to the aggrieved person to seek appropriate relief in the federal courts in the exercise of their general jurisdiction," Reed wrote.[28]

Justice Frankfurter alone dissented. The majority had missed the nub of the matter, which was congressional intent. Unless the Constitution itself requires the availability of judicial review of certain agency action, the matter is left entirely to Congress. "There is no such thing as a common law of judicial review in the federal courts," Frankfurter chided the majority.[29] He may have been too hard on his colleagues; Justice Reed's opinion can be read as an attempt to discern the most likely intent of Congress.[30] The point, however, was that the *Edward Hines* notion of "legal right" was yoked to the question of congressional intent, not to some abstract concept of when judicial review is available.

Frankfurter's *Stark v. Wickard* dissent was apparently lost on Justice Frank Murphy. In *American Power & Light Co. v. SEC*, the plaintiff corporation owned all the common stock of Florida Power & Light Co. The Securities and Exchange

---

26. 321 U.S. 288 (1944).

27. 321 U.S. at 302.

28. *Id.* at 309.

29. 321 U.S. at 312 (Frankfurter, J., dissenting).

30. The argument between Frankfurter and Reed in *Stark v. Wickard* foreshadows the implied private right of action cases of the 1960s and 1970s. *See, e.g.*, J. I. Case v. Borak, 377 U.S. 426 (1964); Cort v. Ash, 422 U.S. 66 (1975); Cannon v. University of Chicago, 441 U.S. 677 (1979); Sierra Club v. California, 451 U.S. 287 (1981). The "legal right" doctrine of *Edward Hines* is intellectually indistinguishable from the implied private right of action doctrine. *Cf.* William A. Fletcher, *The Structure of Standing*, 98 YALE L. J. 221 (1988) (arguing that standing should be analyzed as a question of whether the underlying law creates a right on behalf of the plaintiff).

Commission issued an order requiring Florida Power to make certain accounting entries that would have the effect of reducing the amount of dividends available for distribution to the sole stockholder, plaintiff American Power. Pursuant to Section 24(a) of the Public Utility Holding Company Act, American petitioned the First Circuit to set aside the order, claiming that it was a "person or party aggrieved." The Commission moved to dismiss the petition, arguing that American lacked standing to sue. The First Circuit granted the motion to dismiss, but the Supreme Court disagreed: "We hold that a stockholder having a substantial financial or economic interest distinct from that of the corporation which is directly and adversely affected by an order of the Commission, irrespective of any effect the order may have on the corporation, is a 'person aggrieved' within the meaning of Section 24(a)."[31]

Justice Murphy dissented. His disagreement with the majority was on two levels, one peculiar to the facts of the case, one broader. The narrow disagreement was over whether American's legal interests were indistinguishable from that of Florida's. Murphy argued that they were, at least in the absence of a formal declaration of dividend. The majority argued that the interests of American and Florida diverged; Florida was not harmed in any way by the mandated accounting change, for the money was still there, albeit in a different column. But American was harmed by the diminution in funds available for dividend distribution.

In this narrow disagreement lay the seeds of a much larger and more important disagreement. Murphy clung to the original *Edward Hines* conceptualization of the standing problem: did American suffer a violation of any legal right distinguishable from rights held by Florida? The majority, however, had moved on—whether consciously or unconsciously—to a new question: did American suffer harm not suffered by Florida? Subtle as the difference may seem, the majority had started the all-important transition from the "legal right" doctrine to the "injury-in-fact" doctrine. "The Commission does not question that American, as sole stockholder of Florida, has a *substantial economic interest* which is affected by the order," wrote Justice Owen Roberts for the Court.[32] The Court did not say that American had a legal interest, but rather an economic one. The statutory language, "any person or party aggrieved," was sufficiently broad to include not only those whose legal rights were violated, but those who merely suffered economic harm. By negative implication, those who had not even suffered any economic harm could not sue. The Court was not called upon to speculate whether Congress could authorize those who had suffered no harm whatsoever, or only some kind of noneconomic harm, to sue. Section 24(a) of the Public Utility Holding Company Act applied only to those who suffered at least some economic harm. But the locus of the standing inquiry had shifted from violations of legal rights to the suffering of some kind of harm.

31. *Id.* at 388.
32. *Id.* (emphasis added).

This is such an important turn of events that it bears recapitulation. The *Edward Hines* line of cases constituted a common law of standing. Up to that point, Congress had not sought to exert any control over who was permitted to sue to challenge agency action, and the Court filled the void with the "legal right" doctrine. When Congress began to pass statutes that did attempt to exert such control—most commonly through the words "any person or party aggrieved"—the Court was called upon to discern how far Congress intended to go in permitting standing. A majority of the Court instantly conceded Congress's power to go beyond legal rights, to mere "economic" harms. But the acknowledgment of any measure of congressional control over standing made inevitable the question still being debated today: how far may Congress go?

Here was the collision of two intellectual worlds. One was the post–Legal Realist world in which legislative primacy was fully recognized, where statutes "in derogation of the common law" were not simply ignored but instead were given their full due. This legislative supremacy quite logically extended to judicial review of agency action—if Congress wanted the courts to see that statutory mandates were in fact being realized, then the courts had to stand ready to fulfill that duty. This was the intellectual world inhabited by Brandeis and Frankfurter, among others. The other world was the one never entirely vanquished by Legal Realism, that of Langdellian orthodoxy. Of course legislatures could enact statutes, but they always legislated against the backdrop of a seamless web of principles comprising the common law. A court's job was to blend these statutory newcomers into that preexisting landscape as best it could. Congress could invoke judicial review for some purposes, but the courts were not to be used as mere legislative adjuncts. The entire concept of "courtness" presupposed the exercise of independent judgment, including determinations about the occasions appropriate for the exercise of such judgment. Not even two world wars, the New Deal, and Legal Realism could completely eradicate these formalist sensibilities in most judges.

Thus, when Congress began to exercise control over the scope of judicial review of agency action, the Court's response was understandably conflicted. These new words—"any person or party aggrieved"—were so deliberate that Congress could not have meant for the same old "legal right" test to govern. And yet most of the justices could not accept a principle of limitless congressional control over federal court jurisdiction. "Injury-in-fact," although it would not be called that until the 1970s, was a reaction to more and more aggressive congressional assertions of control over the scope of judicial review of agency action. And, as we shall see, it became embedded in Article III and was transplanted to the realm of challenges against *legislative* action to prevent the possibility of unlimited standing in that arena.

* * *

Immediately following the war, the Court handed down a major decision on the *Fairchild v. Hughes* track. In *Colegrove v. Green,* three voters from urban Illinois claimed that their votes had been diluted by malapportionment in districting. The story was a familiar one around the country. Urbanization had created gross disparities in the population of congressional districts, and incumbents had little incentive to redress the problem. The plaintiffs' districts in *Colegrove* had roughly eight times as many voters as those in the least populated districts in Illinois. The plaintiffs sought a judicial declaration to the effect that this malapportionment violated the federal Reapportionment Act of 1911, which required districts to have roughly equal populations.

The three-judge district court flatly stated that the legislature's refusal to act was both disgraceful and unconstitutional. But there was a 1932 Supreme Court precedent squarely on point, *Wood v. Broom,*[33] holding that subsequent legislation had impliedly repealed the provision of the Reapportionment Act of 1911 that required districts to have equal populations. In light of this decision, the district court said, it had no choice but to dismiss. The district court was unabashed in its hope that the Supreme Court, now chock full of FDR appointees, would overrule *Wood v. Broom.*

The hope was in vain. The Supreme Court affirmed the dismissal of the plaintiff's suit, 4–3. Frankfurter's majority opinion made it clear that *Wood* was settled law and that the Court would not upset it. Then, surreally, he went on to say that the Court would not even formally reach the question he had just answered. The problem was not that the Court lacked jurisdiction to proceed ("This is one of those demands on judicial power which cannot be met by verbal fencing about 'jurisdiction,'" said Frankfurter). Instead, the Court should act in a statesmanlike manner and exercise its discretion to stay out of a controversy like this one. "This is not an action to recover for damage because of the discriminatory exclusion of a plaintiff from rights enjoyed by other citizens," he stated. "The basis for the suit is not a private wrong, but a wrong suffered by Illinois as a polity."[34] Frankfurter's opinion was designedly ambiguous about the precise basis on which the Court was foregoing a decision on the merits. He might have meant that the plaintiffs lacked standing because their grievance was generalized, in much the same way as the plaintiffs' claims in *Fairchild* and *Frothingham* were generalized. Or he may have been saying that the plaintiffs were not entitled to a remedy because they had suffered no legal wrong, much as in the agency review cases exemplified by *Edward Hines.* Or he may have been saying neither—indeed, most of the brief opinion is dedicated to a "political question" rationale. The proper redress for these plaintiffs was not in the courts, but in the political process. "The remedy for unfairness in districting is to secure State legislatures that will apportion properly," Frankfurter wrote. "Courts ought not to enter this political thicket."[35]

33. 287 U.S. 1 (1932).
34. 328 U.S. at 552.
35. 328 U.S. at 556.

The opaqueness of *Colegrove* was quite intentional. If the Court, in the best Brandeisian manner, were to preserve for itself the greatest flexibility in deciding whether to confront or avoid controversial social issues, it could not bind itself to a transparent set of rules regarding when decisions had to be rendered. It needed to create a mystique about the process of divining the proper conditions for justiciability, as if it were performing a sort of casuistry open only to the sagest of oracles. Sixteen years later, Frankfurter protégé Alexander Bickel would tout these as "the passive virtues" by which the Supreme Court should husband its political capital and make it possible to delay adjudication of controversial cases until such time as social consensus evolved and the Court could render a principled decision. Bickel was forthcoming about the paradox; he was advocating that the Court be unprincipled in its decisions about when to confront or avoid controversial issues so that it could be principled when finally reaching them. It was pure Frankfurter.

If Frankfurter's verbalizing about the wisdom of decision avoidance was gratuitous in *Colegrove*—he had, after all, already made it clear that the district court's dismissal would be affirmed on the basis of *Wood*—it seems to have been equally gratuitous in *United Public Workers v. Mitchell*,[36] decided the next term. A large number of federal civil service employees joined with a labor union to challenge the core of the Hatch Act, which consisted of the following sentence: "No officer or employee in the executive branch of the Federal Government . . . shall take any active part in political management or in political campaigns."[37] The plaintiffs brought an action in federal district court for a declaration that this provision violated their constitutional rights. Most of the plaintiffs proposed to engage in partisan political activities that presumably would have violated the Act. One affidavit that the Court characterized as typical stated that the plaintiff wished to

> engag[e] in discussion, by speeches to conventions, rallies and other assemblages, by publicizing my views in letters and articles for publication in newspapers and other periodicals, by aiding in the campaign of candidates for political office by posting banners and posters in public places, by distributing leaflets, by "ringing doorbells," by addressing campaign literature, and by doing any and all acts of like character reasonably designed to assist in the election of candidates I favor.[38]

The affiant further stated that he had obtained a poll watcher's certificate for the previous election but refrained from using it out of fear that he would be dismissed by the Civil Service Commission pursuant to the Hatch Act.[39]

---

36. 330 U.S. 75 (1947).
37. 330 U.S. at 82, quoting 28 U.S.C. Section 380(a) (ellipses in original).
38. 330 U.S. at 87 n.18.
39. *Id.* at 87–88 n.18.

On these facts, the Court held that the case was both unripe and moot. The affidavits "declare a desire to act contrary to the rule against political activity but not that the rule has been violated," wrote Justice Stanley Reed in a portion of the opinion that had Frankfurter's fingerprints all over it.[40] Previous cases found to be ripe involved "direct threat[s] of punishment against a named organization for a completed act," whereas the instant case involved only a "general threat by officials to enforce those laws which they are charged to administer."[41] The Court professed to be bothered by the contrived appearance of the lawsuit. "The affidavits, it will be noticed, follow the generality of purpose expressed by the complaint," Justice Reed wrote. "Such generality of objection is really an attack on the political expediency of the Hatch Act, not the presentation of legal issues."[42] Whereupon the Court launched into a lengthy lecture on the federal courts' incapacity to render advisory opinions in hypothetical cases—a subject on which Professor Frankfurter, not coincidentally, had once written.[43]

The Court went on, however, to find that one of the plaintiffs was in an entirely different situation. George Poole was a roller at the U.S. Mint in Philadelphia who had been a Ward Executive Committeeman. Upon learning of Poole's party activities, the Civil Service Commission served notice on Poole that, unless he could refute the allegations, he would be dismissed from federal employment. With actual charges having been proffered, the Court found that Poole's application for declaratory relief was ripe.

On the merits, the Court held that the portion of the Hatch Act in question did not violate the Constitution. "To declare that the present supposed evils of political activity are beyond the power of Congress to redress would leave the nation impotent to deal with what many sincere men believe is a material threat to the democratic system," Justice Reed stated.[44] But Poole argued that the means employed by the Hatch Act to meet that threat were overbroad. Some federal employees had considerable contact with the public, and it might have been justifiable to think that these employees had to appear politically neutral, the plaintiffs conceded. Yet other federal employees held highly technical or manual jobs the performance of which entailed little or no contact with the public. Poole was a perfect example of this second type of employee—he was a roller at the mint.

Even so, stated Justice Reed, Congress was entitled to find that such employees had to be restrained from political activity in order to prevent rank-and-file positions from becoming the currency of patronage. "There are hundreds of thousands of United States employees with positions no more influential upon

---

40. *Id.* at 88.
41. *Id.*
42. *Id.* at 89.
43. Felix Frankfurter, *Advisory Opinions*, 1 Encyclopedia of the Social Sciences 475 (1930).
44. *Id.* at 99.

policy determination than that of Mr. Poole," Reed continued. "Evidently what Congress feared was the cumulative effect on employee morale of political activity by all employees who could be induced to participate actively. It does not seem to us an unconstitutional basis for legislation."[45] What seems ironic is that, after taking great pains to explain why it could not deal with the far-ranging hypothetical cases presented by Poole's fellow plaintiffs, the Court decided Poole's claim in the most far-reaching and doctrinaire way possible. Given its treatment of Poole, it seems inconceivable that the Court could have held that the relevant provision of the Hatch Act was unconstitutional as applied to any of the other plaintiffs or their proposed conduct. The Court had left itself no wiggle room at all. The "passive virtues" that led the Court to abjure the claims of the plaintiffs other than Poole had not, at the end of the day, made for any narrower a constitutional decision. In both *Colegrove* and *Mitchell*, Frankfurter was sowing the seeds of decision avoidance for the future.[46]

---

45. *Id.* at 101.

46. That same day, the Court handed down another Hatch Act case, *Oklahoma v. United States Civil Service Commission*, 330 U.S. 127 (1947). France Paris was a member of the State Highway Commission of Oklahoma, which was financed by the federal government. At the same time, he served as Chairman of the Democratic State Central Committee. Pursuant to Section 12 of the Hatch Act, the federal Civil Service Commission determined that Paris had taken an "active part in political management or in political campaigns" and therefore that he should be removed from the highway commission. The Civil Service Commission served notice of its action on both Paris and the state of Oklahoma. The notice warned that, if Paris was not removed from the highway commission, federal highway grants to Oklahoma would be withheld.

The state of Oklahoma brought an action in federal district court challenging the Civil Service Commission's order. The state argued that the Hatch Act violated state sovereignty because it "attempt[ed] to regulate the internal affairs of a state. . . ." If the Act were valid to any degree, it would be only insofar as it applied to "active" political participation, which was not present in the instant case, the state argued. Oklahoma sued under Section 12(c) of the Hatch Act, which gave to "any party aggrieved" judicial review of commission orders.

The federal government challenged Oklahoma's standing to sue under this provision. Citing *Massachusetts v. Mellon* and *Alabama Power Co. v. Ickes*, the federal government argued that Oklahoma lacked "legal capacity to question the manner in which the United States limits the appropriation of funds. . . ." But Justice Reed, again writing for the majority, held that Oklahoma had standing to sue. Under the relevant appropriations statutes, Oklahoma had a legal right to receive its share of federal highway funds; at this point, it was not a matter of discretion or beneficence on the part of any federal official. If the Hatch Act was unconstitutional and therefore incapable of authorizing the Civil Service Commission from making deductions from Oklahoma's share of funds, then any such deduction would violate Oklahoma's legal rights. Perhaps more importantly, Congress had authorized "any aggrieved party" to sue under Section 12(c); whether or not Oklahoma had a legal right to the funds, it surely was an interested party. In sum, the case was distinguishable from *Massachusetts v. Mellon* and *Alabama Power* "by the authority for statutory review and by the existence of the legally enforceable right to receive allocated grants without unlawful deductions."

* * *

In the years immediately following World War II, very little in American constitutional adjudication can be understood outside the context of the anticommunist movement that swept the nation, and certainly *Mitchell* is no exception. The period from 1945 to 1956, popularly known as the "McCarthy era," was the last and most intense phase of anticommunist fervor in the United States, but it was hardly the first. At the turn of the century, immigrants become the main target of the American right wing, partly on the theory that immigrants brought subversive ideas with them to America. President William McKinley was assassinated in 1901 by an alien anarchist. Between 1907 and 1917, Congress passed several laws restricting the rights of aliens. Eugene Debs was convicted under the Espionage Act of 1917 for making a speech interfering with army recruitment. When the Bolsheviks seized power in 1917, the Soviet program "horrified all who cherished private property, democracy, and pluralism."[47] It galvanized the xenophobic, antisubversive sentiments latent in much of the American public and gave it a new focus—communism. By 1919, Attorney General A. Mitchell Palmer was ordering the raids of the offices of radical organizations in twelve cities, resulting in some three hundred arrests and many deportations to the Soviet Union. The evidence supporting these raids consisted of little more than the expression of radical views. When it became clear that the violent radical uprising that Palmer had predicted was not going to happen, most of the deportations and arrests were terminated, and the hysteria known as the first Red Scare subsided. For most of the next four decades, however, anticommunist fervor was never very far below the surface of American politics.

One of the high points of that fervor came in 1939 when Adolf Hitler and Joseph Stalin signed their "Pact of Steel." Now fascism and communism were the same thing. It was in this atmosphere, amid the drumbeats of world war, that Congress passed the Hatch Act, prohibiting government employees from engaging in most political activities, and the Smith Act, which made it a crime to knowingly advocate the overthrow of the government by force or violence. When Hitler turned on the Soviet Union in 1941, most American communists instantly became patriots, working hard to defeat the Nazis. For the moment, this reversal took the edge off anticommunism. But as soon as the war ended, American-Soviet relations chilled, and anticommunism once again came to the fore.

Just as anticommunism was closely related to anti-immigrant sentiments, it was inextricably bound up with fears about organized labor and about unrest among Blacks. The American Communist Party of course made diligent efforts to organize workers, controlling or substantially influencing a number of key unions. It also agitated for a radical view of racial equality, generally insisting not merely that individual Black workers be given an equal opportunity to get work,

47. Richard M. Fried, Nightmare in Red: The McCarthy Era in Perspective 39 (Oxford 1990).

but that they be given work in proportion to their representation in the general population. *Mitchell* and *Colegrove* would certainly have been controversial decisions had they come out the other way—that is, if the Court had struck down some key aspect of the Hatch Act or permitted a challenge to the Illinois Legislature's failure to reapportion. A ruling for the plaintiffs in *Mitchell* would have inflamed already rising fears about a "fifth column" within American institutions; only one year after *Mitchell,* Whittaker Chambers would accuse former State Department official (and Frankfurter protégé) Alger Hiss of having been a communist spy. (Hiss was later convicted of having perjured himself before the House Un-American Affairs Committee.) A ruling for the plaintiffs in *Colegrove* would have created the specter of judicially mandated reapportionment, leading to a loss of electoral power in WASP-dominated rural areas and an increase in power for minority-heavy urban areas, to say nothing of the possibility of reapportionment in the Deep South. Although the Court did not need the Brandeisian tools of decision avoidance in these cases, mustering a working majority against the plaintiffs on the merits, Frankfurter could see trouble down the line. There would be plaintiffs in future cases whose claims would be harder to deny on the merits. The Court had to have an escape hatch.

Anticommunism continued to intensify. In 1949 the Soviets exploded an atom bomb and the Chinese communists ran Chiang Kai-shek's Nationalists into Taiwan. In June 1950, the North Korean army crossed the 38th parallel into South Korea. The dominoes were falling. Stalin was testing America's mettle—or so it seemed. A previously obscure senator from Wisconsin named Joseph McCarthy rose to prominence on the strength of sensational accusations that communists were undermining the government from within. McCarthy played the press masterfully, stirring the public into a paranoid frenzy. In 1950, over President Harry S. Truman's veto, Congress passed the Subversive Activities Control Act (also known as the "McCarran Act," after Senator Pat McCarran, a Nevada conservative powerhouse). The Act barred certain individuals from government or defense jobs or from holding passports; tightened espionage laws; denied entrance to aliens who had ever belonged to communist or totalitarian parties or advocated violent overthrow of the government; banned obstructive picketing of federal courts; and mandated detention of likely spies and saboteurs.[48] Moreover, the Act created a Subversive Activities Control Board (SACB), which was authorized to denominate certain groups as "communist" or as "communist front-groups," which would then be required to register with the attorney general.

By 1950, Frank Murphy and Wiley Rutledge, two key liberal FDR appointees, had been replaced by more conservative Truman appointees, Tom Clark and Sherman Minton, making the Court more receptive to the claims of national

48. *Id.* at 117.

security that the government offered in defense of antisubversive legislation. In *American Communications Assn. v. Douds,*[49] the plaintiff unions challenged the provision of the Taft-Hartley Act requiring each union officer to file an affidavit swearing that he "is not a member of the Communist Party or affiliated with such party, and that he does not believe in, and is not a member of or support[] any organization that believes in or teaches, the overthrow of the United States Government by force or by any illegal or unconstitutional means."[50] In the absence of the required affidavits, the National Labor Relations Board (NLRB) was forbidden to engage its investigatory machinery on the union's behalf. The Court affirmed the lower court ruling in favor of constitutionality by an equally divided vote. Chief Justice Fred Vinson, joined by Stanley Reed and Harold Burton, upheld the constitutionality of the affidavit requirement. The Court's principal rationale was deference to Congress in matters involving national security. Congress was entitled to conclude that the Communist Party was simply different from other political parties—that it really was committed to bringing about the overthrow of the U.S. government. Congress was justified in conditioning NLRB action on proof of loyalty because of the prospect that communist-dominated unions would call primary strikes with the aim of crippling American resistance to Soviet aggression.[51] Vinson conceded that the provision concerning belief in overthrow of the government would raise a serious constitutional question if "it were read very literally to include all persons who might, under any conceivable circumstances, subscribe to that belief." But Vinson reached into the Brandeisian decision avoidance bag, insisting that the provision be interpreted narrowly to sidestep the constitutional question.

Frankfurter dissented in part, finding the affidavit provision unconstitutionally vague. He hated being eclipsed in the contest to avoid the most constitutional questions, though. "No one could believe more strongly than I do that every rational indulgence should be made in favor of the constitutionality of an enactment by Congress," Frankfurter wrote indignantly. "I deem it my duty to go to the farthest possible limits in so construing legislation as to avoid a finding that Congress has exceeded the limits of its powers. But what Congress has written does not permit such a gloss nor deletion of what it has written."[52] He did not

49. 339 U.S. 382 (1950).

50. American Communications Assn. v. Douds, 339 U.S. 382, 385 (1950).

51. As Vinson's opinion pointed out, Congress was clearly influenced by the 76-day walkout by United Auto Workers Local 248 at the Allis-Chalmers plant in Wisconsin in spring 1941. Management was virulently anticommunist and many of Local 248's leaders were in fact communists. The company claimed, and most observers believed, that the communists in the union had called the strike to sabotage the nation's defense efforts. The affidavit requirement of Taft-Hartley was only one of many government actions based on the perceived communist motivation behind the Allis-Chalmers strike.

52. 339 U.S. at 421 (Frankfurter, J., concurring in part and dissenting in part).

explain how Vinson's narrowing construction had gone beyond "the farthest possible limits."

Douds was the beginning of the Court's aid and comfort to the anticommunist movement, but the real help came the next term in *Dennis v. United States*. Even as the war drew toward its conclusion, FBI director J. Edgar Hoover was planning a criminal prosecution that would have the effect of declaring the Communist Party illegal. It soon became clear that the vehicle for that prosecution would be the Smith Act, which prohibited the knowing advocacy of the overthrow of the government by force or violence. In July 1948, the Justice Department indicted the national secretary of the American Communist Party, Eugene Dennis, and ten other top party officials for violation of the Smith Act. The Court of Appeals affirmed their convictions, and the Supreme Court granted certiorari, limited to the question of whether the Act violated the First Amendment.

By so limiting its scope of review, the Court had successfully avoided a thorny question—whether the evidence at trial was sufficient to support the convictions. From the standpoint of criminal law, the big issue was whether the government had proven that the party advocated force and violence. The FBI had been scavenging for such evidence for years, without much luck. In a memo to his second-in-command, even Hoover confided that it would "be a tough case at its best."[53] The government's case dangled from a string of tenuous inferences. First, the party's penchant for secrecy demonstrated that it had to be planning illegal activity, which meant force and violence. Second, the doctrines of Marxism-Leninism inherently called for violent overthrow. In order to connect these intellectual doctrines to the operations of the American Communist Party, the government sought to show that the American party adhered slavishly to Soviet dictates in other matters. Then there was the problem of what party officials had actually said, namely, that they did *not* endorse overthrow by force and violence. Indeed, the party's constitution explicitly foreswore revolutionary violence and called for the expulsion of members who advocated it. To combat these inconvenient facts, the government insisted that party members were merely following a statement that Lenin himself had once made in the preface to a later edition of one of his early works. There, he had said that sometimes he had had to make observations in "Aesopian language" in order to evade Tsarist censorship. So, the Justice Department argued, these renunciations of force and violence were merely red herrings strewn about to throw off the dogs. These prosecutorial tactics, aided immeasurably by the defendants' insistence upon putting up a blustery political defense rather than a technical legal one, secured convictions in a case where reasonable jurors could well have harbored reasonable doubts about guilt.

---

53. Ellen Schrecker, The Age of McCarthyism: A Brief History with Documents 192 (2d ed. Bedford/St. Martin's 2002).

When the Court limited its grant of certiorari to the First Amendment questions, it did precisely the opposite of the Brandeisian credo: it passed over a narrow question (the sufficiency of the evidence at trial) to reach a set of broad constitutional ones. As he had done in *Douds*, Chief Justice Vinson delivered the opinion of the Court, again joined by Reed and Burton, and now, Sherman Minton. Again the rationale was national security, this time expressed through Judge Learned Hand's formulation of the "clear and present danger" test. The effect of the Court's ruling was politically seismic. It gave anticommunism a badly needed judicial imprimatur. *Dennis* effectively rendered membership in the Communist Party illegal and made anticommunism legitimate in the eyes of the public.

Frankfurter refused to join Vinson's opinion, concurring in the result only. In a rambling, almost schizoid, opinion, he preached the need for judicial restraint. Without citing him by name, Frankfurter called on Thayer for the view that over-reliance on judicial review is destructive of a society's deliberative capacity: "Preoccupation by our people with the constitutionality, instead of with the wisdom, of legislation or of executive action is preoccupation with a false value." But in *Dennis* Frankfurter used the rhetoric of judicial restraint on behalf of a very different operation than the Court had performed in *Fairchild* or *Frothingham*. The "judicial restraint" going on in *Dennis* was not the same sort of judicial restraint that Frankfurter had advocated in *Colegrove*. In those previous cases, judicial restraint meant avoiding a decision on the merits of the constitutional question. When a court punts in that way, no precedent is made. In *Dennis*, by contrast, the "restraint" took the form of deference to Congress. "We may take judicial notice that the Communist doctrines which these defendants have conspired to advocate are in the ascendency in powerful nations who cannot be acquitted of unfriendliness to the institutions of this country," wrote Frankfurter. "In sum, it would amply justify a legislature in concluding that recruitment of additional members for the Party would create a substantial danger to national security."[54] This was just the opposite of punting; the Court was deliberately and powerfully ratifying legislative fact-finding that had been based on questionable inferences. When Frankfurter reassured his readers that "in sustaining the power of Congress in a case like this nothing irrevocable is done," he was exactly wrong. "Because of the importance of the case and the prestige of the high court, the case shaped the way in which people like intellectuals and educators came to view Communism," wrote Karen Schrecker. "[T]he Court's findings not only ratified the FBI's contention that the party was a criminal conspiracy, but also opened it up to additional sanctions."[55] And, of course, there was an even more obvious sense in which Frankfurter was wrong when he said that

54. Dennis v. United States, 341 U.S. 494, 547 (1951) (Frankfurter, J., concurring in result).

55. SCHRECKER, *supra* note 53 at 200.

"nothing irrevocable was done" in *Dennis*. The defendants' convictions were finally and irrevocably affirmed.

Politically, *Dennis* was the most important of the Court's anticommunist decisions. In terms of the intellectual structure of judicial restraint doctrine, however, the more important case had come down two months earlier. The case was *Joint Anti-Fascist Committee v. McGrath*, in which Frankfurter issued the most illuminating opinion on justiciability in his career, and perhaps in the entire history of the Court. Claiming to act pursuant to an executive order, Attorney General Tom Clark[56] designated three civic organizations as "Communist" in a list furnished to the Loyalty Review Board. The three organizations sued Clark and the Board in federal district court, asking for a judicial declaration that the executive order was unconstitutional, and for an injunction against its enforcement. The district court granted a motion to dismiss for failure to state a claim upon which relief could be granted, and the court of appeals affirmed. By a 5–3 vote, the Supreme Court reversed and remanded for consideration of the merits.

Justice Burton's plurality opinion (joined only by Justice Douglas) explicitly found that the plaintiffs had standing to sue. "The touchstone to justiciability is injury to a legally protected right and the right of a bona fide charitable organization to carry on its work, free from defamatory statements of the kind discussed, is such a right," Burton wrote.[57] Justice Frankfurter, concurring only in the judgment, could not accept the plurality's simple explanation regarding standing. In order to demonstrate why the plaintiffs had standing to proceed, Frankfurter found it necessary to write a small treatise on the subject.

The treatise began by explicitly tying the law of standing to two distinct phrases in Article III, and by emphasizing the conceptual similarity of all the doctrines that would eventually be grouped under the aegis of "justiciability":

> Limitation on "the judicial Power of the United States" is expressed by the requirement that a litigant must have "standing to sue" or, more comprehensively, that a federal court may entertain a controversy only if it is "justiciable." Both characterizations mean that a court will not decide a question unless the nature of the action challenged, the kind of injury inflicted, and the relationship between the parties are such that judicial determination is consonant with what was, generally speaking, the business of the Colonial courts and the courts of Westminster when the Constitution was framed. The jurisdiction of

56. During the pendency of the litigation Clark was elevated to the Supreme Court and his successor, Howard McGrath, was substituted as party defendant. Clark, of course, did not participate in the decision.

57. 341 U.S. at 140–41, citing Utah Fuel Co. v. National Bituminous Coal Commission, 306 U.S. 56 (1939); Shields v. Utah Idaho Central R. Co., 305 U.S. 177 (1938); Philadelphia Co. v. Stimson, 223 U.S. 605 (1912).

the federal courts can be invoked only under circumstances which to the expert feel of lawyers constitute a "case or controversy."[58]

Having situated the standing and justiciability doctrines in the Constitution, Frankfurter identified what it was that the Constitution required of a litigant: "[a]dverse personal interest, [which] is ordinarily sufficient to meet constitutional standards of justiciability."[59] Furthermore, Frankfurter stated, the litigant's interest "must be of a personal and not of an official nature."[60] Frankfurter conceded that this statement did not take account of the "innumerable cases recogniz[ing] the standing of an administrative or executive official to defend the constitutionality of the legislation which he is charged with administering or enforcing."[61] Next, citing *Frothingham v. Mellon*, Frankfurter stated that "[t]he interest must not be wholly negligible, as that of a taxpayer of the Federal Government is considered to be. . . . A litigant must show more than that 'he suffers in some indefinite way in common with people generally.'"[62] Here Justice Frankfurter abstracted the federal taxpayer cases beyond their context and thereby implied the existence of what would later become known as the "prohibition against generalized grievances."

Frankfurter's next point was central to his beliefs about judicial restraint. The "adverse personal interest" required by Article III did not have to be direct. Instead, such an interest, "even of such an indirect sort as arises from competition," is ordinarily sufficient. "The courts may therefore by statute be given jurisdiction over claims based on such interests," he continued, citing the *Sanders* decision from 1940.[63] If Congress wished to confer standing upon any person "aggrieved" by agency action, it was free to do so. This belief dovetailed with Frankfurter's and Brandeis's commitment to legislative supremacy, including congressional control over the scope of federal court jurisdiction. It was not that Frankfurter necessarily believed in broad standing to challenge federal administrative action, but rather that he believed it was Congress's call.

Where there was no congressional authorization, however, the same principle of judicial restraint led Frankfurter to a constricted view of standing. "To require a court to intervene in the absence of a statute, however, either on constitutional grounds or in the exercise of inherent equitable powers, something more than

---

58. 341 U.S. at 150 (Frankfurter, J., concurring). Justice Frankfurter cited no authorities in this passage.

59. 341 U.S. at 151 (Frankfurter, J., concurring).

60. 341 U.S. at 151 (Frankfurter, J., concurring), citing Braxton County Court v. West Virginia, 208 U.S. 192, 197 (1908) and Massachusetts v. Mellon, 262 U.S. 447 (1923).

61. Henry Hart & Herbert Wechsler, The Federal Courts and the Federal System 162 (1st ed. 1953).

62. 341 U.S. at 151 (Frankfurter, J., concurring).

63. 341 U.S. at 151 (Frankfurter, J., concurring), citing FCC v. Sanders Brothers Radio Station, *supra* note 15.

adverse personal interest is needed," he wrote.[64] Under these circumstances, the plaintiff does not have standing to sue unless the defendant's conduct "directly results in the violation of a legal right."[65] Yet the meaning of "legal right" had a protean quality, Frankfurter noted. In his view, it could be deciphered only by asking and answering a battery of questions. Will the action challenged at any time substantially affect the "legal" interests of any person? Does the action challenged affect the petitioner with sufficient "directness"? Is the action challenged sufficiently "final"?[66]

With respect to the first question, Justice Frankfurter asserted that one ordinarily possesses standing to "challenge governmental action of a sort that, if taken by a private person, would create a right of action cognizable by the courts."[67] After a lengthy discussion, Frankfurter concluded that this rule encompassed the case at bar—that the government was alleged to have defamed the plaintiff organizations, and to have tortiously interfered with the business advantage of their members. If, however, the plaintiffs could not point to any common law right that the government had violated, then they would lack standing to challenge the governmental action, despite the fact that they had suffered "adverse personal interest."

With respect to the second question—whether the effect of the governmental action on the plaintiff was sufficiently direct—Justice Frankfurter viewed this as an inquiry into the government's intent. "Frequently governmental action directly affects the legal interests of some person, and causes only a consequential detriment to another," he wrote. "When those consequentially affected may resort to an administrative agency charged with their protection, courts are especially reluctant to give them "standing" to claim judicial review."[68] Government action has a "sufficiently direct effect" to give rise to standing, then, when it is intended to affect the plaintiff.

As a general rule, unintended impact on a person is insufficient to support standing in federal court, particularly when that person has an administrative remedy. In theory, the effect of this second inquiry ("sufficient directness") is to further constrict nonstatutory standing, since the first inquiry (judicial cognizability) does not exclude cases in which the government is alleged to have recklessly or negligently harmed people under circumstances that would support a cause of action under tort law if the action were performed by a private person. But there were exceptions to the general rule, Justice Frankfurter observed. Here he appears to have been thinking primarily of the cases in which plaintiffs have sometimes been permitted to assert the legal rights of persons

---

64. 341 U.S. at 151 (Frankfurter, J., concurring).
65. 341 U.S. at 152 (Frankfurter, J., concurring).
66. 341 U.S. at 152 (Frankfurter, J., concurring).
67. *Id.*, citing United States v. Lee, 106 U.S. 196 (1882).
68. 341 U.S. at 153 (Frankfurter, J., concurring).

not before the court. In *Truax v. Raich*, for example, an alien employee was allowed to challenge a state law requiring his employer to discharge all but a specified proportion of alien employees.[69] In *Pierce v. Society of Sisters*, a private school was permitted to sue for an injunction against a statute requiring parents to send their children to public schools.[70] Though the employees in *Truax* and the schools in *Pierce* were only indirect subjects of the statutes involved, they were permitted to sue because the direct subjects could not be counted on to vigorously represent the interests of the plaintiffs, and because of the "nature of the relationship involved," Justice Frankfurter opined.[71]

The third question—whether the challenged action is sufficiently final—was probably the most important in Frankfurter's eyes. He began his discussion of this topic with a broad statement of policy: "Courts do not review issues, especially constitutional issues, until they have to," he stated, citing Brandeis's *Ashwander* concurrence.[72] This dictum was based on the practical wisdom of not coming prematurely or needlessly in conflict with the executive or legislature.[73] Of course, Frankfurter was describing what is now known as the "ripeness" doctrine. He considered it simply another dimension of standing, which itself was part and parcel of the larger concept of justiciability. "There is no 'standing' to challenge a preliminary administrative determination, although the determination itself causes some detriment to the litigant," he stated.[74] As was so characteristic of Frankfurter's jurisprudence, however, he went on to stress that the finality norm should be applied flexibly. "If the ultimate impact of the challenged action on the petitioner is sufficiently probable and not too distant, and if the procedure by which that ultimate action may be questioned is too onerous or hazardous, 'standing' is given to challenge the action at a preliminary stage."[75]

* * *

In 1952, the Court returned to the theme it had begun in 1923 in *Fairchild v. Hughes* and *Frothingham v. Mellon*—ideological challenges to the constitutionality of government action, albeit now in the context of state action. One case was *Doremus v. Board of Education*.[76] A New Jersey statute provided for the reading of five verses of the Old Testament at the opening of each public school day. The readings were to be done without comment, and no student was obligated to stay for the readings. A father and daughter in the Borough of Hawthorne brought an action in New Jersey trial court, seeking a declaration

---

69. 239 U.S. 33 (1915).
70. 268 U.S. 510 (1925).
71. 341 U.S. at 154 (Frankfurter, J., concurring).
72. 341 U.S. at 155 (Frankfurter, J., concurring).
73. *Id.*
74. *Id.* (quotation marks in original).
75. *Id.* (quotation marks in original).
76. 342 U.S. 429 (1952).

of the statute's unconstitutionality. No trial was held and there were no findings of fact. The trial court denied the requested relief on the merits of the constitutional question. The Supreme Court of New Jersey, while noting that the lawsuit felt more like an effort to change public policy than an effort to protect private rights, affirmed on the merits.

The U.S. Supreme Court dismissed the appeal for want of jurisdiction. Justice Robert H. Jackson's opinion for the majority rejected all possible bases for standing. The problem with the daughter's action was mootness; she had already graduated. The father had sued in two capacities—as a parent and as a taxpayer. As a parent, his position was no better than hers. If the daughter's claim was moot, then so was the parent's. But Justice Jackson went further: "There is no assertion that she was injured or even offended thereby or that she was compelled to accept, approve or confess agreement with any dogma or creed or even to listen when the Scriptures were read."[77] Thus, as it had done in *American Power & Light*, the Court had again seemed to imply that "injury" or "harm" was required for standing, whether or not violation of a "legal right" was also required. And, as with the opinion in *American Power & Light*, there was no discussion of the matter.

With respect to ideological lawsuits, Justice Jackson wrote:

> The taxpayer's action can meet [the "case or controversy"] test, but only when it is a good-faith pocketbook action. It is apparent that the grievance which it is sought to litigate here is not a direct dollars-and-cents injury but is a religious difference. If appellants established the requisite special injury necessary to a taxpayer's case or controversy, it would not matter that their dominant inducement to action was more religious than mercenary. It is not a question of motivation but of possession of the requisite financial interest that is, or is threatened to be, injured by the unconstitutional conduct.[78]

In 1952, nearing the height of McCarthyism, one could understand why the Court might not relish a challenge to mandatory Bible reading in the public schoolroom. Communists were conspicuously and despicably godless. Requiring scripture in public schools was a way of smoking them out and alienating them. The Court may not have wanted to either ratify or disapprove such a law. From that perspective, however, it is difficult to reconcile *Adler v. Board of Education*,[79] handed down the same day. *Adler* involved a preenforcement attack by municipal taxpayers on the constitutionality of a state antisubversive law. The Court not only fully reached the merits of the constitutional question, but did not make so much as a mention of standing or ripeness. In 1949, New York passed something known as the "Feinberg Law," whose purpose was to toughen up the

77. 342 U.S. at 432.
78. 342 U.S. at 434–35.
79. 342 U.S. 485 (1952).

enforcement of existing laws prohibiting the employment of Communist Party members by the public schools. A group of plaintiffs, including municipal taxpayers, parents of public schoolchildren, and public school teachers, sued in New York trial court for a declaration that the Feinberg Law and the underlying antisubversive statute were unconstitutional. The trial court granted summary judgment for the plaintiffs, but the New York appellate courts disagreed, and the plaintiffs appealed to the U.S. Supreme Court.

After reviewing the procedural posture of the case and the statutory materials, Justice Minton's opinion for the Court launched straight into the constitutional question. Though teachers had a right to freedom of speech and assembly, they had no right to work for the state. The Feinberg Law did not violate the First Amendment. The Court did not explain why the plaintiffs here had standing to sue.

Justice Frankfurter alone discerned justiciability problems.[80] As to the plaintiffs whom the trial court found to have standing as municipal taxpayers, Frankfurter pointed to the Court's language in *Doremus*: "This is not a 'pocketbook action,'" he asserted.[81] "[Plaintiffs] have neither alleged nor shown that our decision on the issues they tender would have the slightest effect on their tax bills or even on the aggregate bill of all the City's taxpayers whom they claim to represent."[82] With respect to the parents of public schoolchildren, Frankfurter asserted that they could demonstrate no violation of any legal right:

> [I]t is like catching butterflies without a net to try to find a legal interest, indispensable for our jurisdiction, in a parent's desire to have his child educated in schools free from such restrictions. The hurt to parents' sensibilities is too tenuous or the inroad upon rightful claims to public education too argumentative to serve as the earthy stuff required for a legal right judicially enforceable.[83]

Finally, as to the teachers, Frankfurter found their claims unripe. The teachers had alleged neither that they were subject to dismissal or that they wished to engage in conduct that would subject them to dismissal. "They do not suggest that they have been, or are, deterred from supporting causes or from joining organizations for fear of the Feinberg Law's interdict, except to say generally that the system complained of will have this effect on teachers as a group," Frankfurter stated.[84] The alleged harm in *Adler* was even less immediate than the one in *United Mine Workers v. Mitchell,* which the Court had found unripe, he said.

---

80. Justices Black and Douglas dissented on the merits and did not join Frankfurter's dissent.

81. 342 U.S. at 501 (Frankfurter, J., dissenting).

82. *Id.* at 502 (Frankfurter, J., dissenting).

83. *Id.* at 502–03 (Frankfurter, J., dissenting).

84. *Id.* at 504 (Frankfurter, J., dissenting).

It is hard to argue with Justice Frankfurter's dissent in *Adler*. The taxpayer plaintiffs in *Adler* could show no larger or more certain impact on their tax liability than the plaintiffs in *Doremus* or *Frothingham*. If the claims of the civil service employees in *Mitchell* were unripe, the claims of the teachers in *Adler* presented an *a fortiori* case. And, although one might disagree with Justice Frankfurter's assertion that parents had no legal right to have their children educated in public schools free of the unconstitutional ideological screening of teachers, surely the question was not free from doubt. Yet Justice Minton's majority opinion in *Adler* said nothing at all about standing or ripeness. The opinion's embarrassingly oversimple reasoning—that no one has a right to work for the state, therefore the state must be able to restrict state employment in any way it wishes[85]—leaves little doubt that the majority was champing at the bit to show that it would protect schoolchildren from the Communist threat.[86] But the opinion demonstrated something intellectual, as well: although most of his colleagues tolerated Frankfurter's professorial lectures on standing and justiciability, few of them really internalized the lessons. For all of Frankfurter's homilies about the impropriety of rendering constitutional decisions in anything but the most factually concrete and immediate situations, the *Adler* majority did not so much as nod in his direction. Jackson may have been persuaded by Frankfurter's "case or controversy" sermons, and probably John Harlan was later, but most of Frankfurter's contemporaries evidently regarded them as just another way for Frankfurter to show off his academic credentials. Certainly Hugo Black, Douglas, Murphy, and Reed showed no signs of taking Frankfurter's line seriously in any case where they wished to reach the merits. As we shall see, some future Justices, often educated by Frankfurter's protégés, internalized the Frankfurter credo to a much greater degree than most of those who served with him.

It may even have taken Frankfurter some years to believe the credo completely himself. In 1940, having served on the Court only one year, Frankfurter voted with the majority in *Thornhill v. Alabama* to uphold a facial attack on an antipicketing law.[87] The statute prohibited persons from loitering around a business establishment with the intent to dissuade others from dealing with it. The facts are not clear from Justice Murphy's majority opinion. The union had called a strike against the Brown Wood Preserving Company, and defendant Byron Thornhill, along with others, were walking a picket line on an access road to the plant. On the day that the company had scheduled resumption of operations,

85. Imagine a state statute conditioning state employment on an agreement not to vote in elections, or not to travel outside the state.

86. See FRIED, *supra* note 47 at 144. The Communists' long-running control of the New York Teachers Union led the Board of Education to a new purge, which between 1950 and 1953 led to the firing of twenty-four teachers and the resignations of thirty-four more who were under investigation. *Id.* at 153.

87. 310 U.S. 88 (1940).

Thornhill apparently confronted one Clarence Simpson, a nonunion employee, and told him "they were on strike and did not want anybody to go up there to work."[88] Simpson turned around and went back home. One witness said Thornhill was alone and never raised his voice while conversing with Simpson. Simpson's testimony apparently implied that Thornhill was accompanied by six or eight other picketers while talking to Simpson.[89]

Justice Murphy's opinion (joined by all members of the Court except the virtually sociopathic James McReynolds) showed no interest in the facts. Whether Thornhill confronted Simpson alone or in the presence of other picketers was "immaterial in our view of the case," wrote Murphy.[90] The statute was simply too broad for its stated purpose, which was to protect the public from violence that might ensue from picketing. "Proof of an abuse of power in the particular case has never been deemed a requisite for attack on the constitutionality of a statute purporting to license the dissemination of ideas," the Court stated.[91] This necessarily meant that the Court was testing the statute's constitutionality based on hypothetical facts—or, to put it differently, that it was permitting Thornhill to assert the First Amendment rights of hypothetical third persons not before the Court. *Thornhill* and its so-called "First Amendment overbreadth doctrine" would become one of the critical precedents on which the Warren Court would later rely.

It is not clear why Frankfurter joined an opinion so willing to entertain factual scenarios not presented by the record. Perhaps it was his belief in the need to protect union picketing—he had, after all, been instrumental in drafting the Norris-LaGuardia Act.[92] Whatever the reason, it proved less than durable. By 1957, Frankfurter and the Court had completely reversed course with respect to permitting facial attacks in situations like *Thornhill*. In *International Brotherhood of Teamsters v. Vogt*, Justice Frankfurter's opinion for the Court upheld a state court injunction against picketing aimed at unlawfully coercing an employer to put pressure on his employees to join the union.[93] In doing so, Frankfurter chronicled the Court's gradual turnabout from *Thornhill* to *Vogt*. In *Milk Wagon Drivers Union v. Meadowmoor*, the Court upheld a broad injunction against picketing because of the history of violence in that specific labor relationship.[94] "[I]t could justifiably be concluded that the momentum of fear generated by past violence would survive even though future picketing might be wholly peaceful,"

88. 310 U.S. at 94.

89. 310 U.S. at 95 n.6.

90. *Id.*

91. 310 U.S. at 97, citing Schneider v. State, 308 U.S. 147, 162–65 (1939); Hague v. C.I.O., 307 U.S. 496, 516 (1939); Lovell v. Griffin, 303 U.S. 444, 451 (1938).

92. 29 U.S.C. Sec. 101, *et seq.*

93. 354 U.S. 284 (1957).

94. 312 U.S. 287 (1941).

the Court had stated in *Milk Wagon*.[95] The Court showed no interest in entertaining a challenge to the injunction on behalf of hypothetical, "wholly peaceful" picketers. "Soon, however, the Court came to realize that the broad pronouncements, but not the specific holding, of *Thornhill* had to yield "to the impact of facts unforeseen," or at least not sufficiently appreciated," Frankfurter explained.[96] Thus in a succession of decisions culminating in *Vogt* itself, the Court took more and more interest in the specific conduct at which the injunctions were aimed, and less and less interest in hypothetical conduct as to which the injunctions might be applied.

With McCarthy's asinine, nationally televised performance in the Army hearings of 1954 and his ensuing censure by the Senate six months later, the sun was finally starting to set on the anticommunist movement. When, in 1961, Frankfurter's opinion for the Court finally upheld the constitutionality of the registration requirements of the McCarran Act,[97] the political atmosphere had cooled considerably. But Frankfurter continued to press for his views on justiciability, with an eye toward the coming civil rights movement. Indeed, the last victory for Frankfurter in the justiciability area came in 1961 in *Poe v. Ullman*, the second Connecticut contraceptives case.[98]

Two married women in Connecticut brought separate actions in state court for declarations to the effect that the state's anticontraceptives law was unconstitutional. One, "Pauline Poe," was twenty-six years old and had given birth to three children who suffered from multiple congenital abnormalities. Each died shortly after birth. The other, "Jane Doe," was twenty-five years old and had recently undergone a dangerous pregnancy—two weeks of unconsciousness and nine weeks of acute sickness, leaving her with partial paralysis. Another pregnancy would again threaten her life. Both women consulted one Dr. Buxton, "an obstetrician and gynecologist of eminence," whose opinion was that they should be instructed in the use of contraceptives.[99] Connecticut law, however, made it a crime to "use[] any drug, medicinal article or instrument for the purpose of preventing conception."[100] The Connecticut Supreme Court of Errors upheld demurrers to each of the actions.

The Court voted 5–4 to dismiss the appeals. Frankfurter wrote for a plurality composed of himself, Earl Warren, Tom Clark, and Charles Whittaker. William Brennan provided the swing vote but only concurred in the judgment. Frankfurter's opinion began by noting that the appeals might well be dismissed for ripeness problems under *United Public Workers v. Mitchell*. After all, the

95. 312 U.S. at 294.
96. 354 U.S. at 289.
97. Communist Party of the United States v. SACB, 367 U.S. 1.
98. 367 U.S. 497 (1961).
99. 367 U.S. at 498.
100. Conn. Gen. Stat. Rev. Sec. 53–32 (1958).

complaints did not allege that the state's attorney had specifically threatened to prosecute these plaintiffs, but only that he had announced his general intention to "prosecute any offenses against Connecticut law."[101] Yet Frankfurter abruptly turned away from the ripeness issue and embarked on a discussion of justiciability generally. The fact that the eighty-two-year-old statute had only been enforced once, and even then only in a test case, deprived the litigation "of the immediacy which is an indispensable condition of constitutional adjudication," Frankfurter wrote. "This Court cannot be umpire to debates concerning harmless, empty shadows."[102]

One could be forgiven for failing to appreciate the distinction between Frankfurter's "ripeness" and "justiciability" analyses. Both seemed to turn on little more than the lack of immediacy in the threat of prosecution. Moreover, Frankfurter made it clear that the dismissals were *not* mandated by Article III. "The restriction of our jurisdiction to cases and controversies within the meaning of Article III of the Constitution . . . is not the sole limitation on the exercise of our appellate powers, especially in cases raising constitutional questions," he stated.[103] Citing Justice Brandeis's paean to judicial restraint in *Ashwander*, Frankfurter asserted that the system worked best when courts rendered opinions only at the behest of truly adversary parties locked in a battle with immediate earthly consequences. In closing, Frankfurter acknowledged the Delphic quality of justiciability doctrine:

> Justiciability is of course not a legal concept with a fixed content or susceptible of scientific verification. Its utilization is the resultant of many subtle pressures, including the appropriateness of the issues for decision by this Court and the actual hardship to the litigants of denying them the relief sought. Both these factors justify withholding adjudication of the constitutional issue raised under the circumstances and in the manner in which they are now before the Court.[104]

Why did Frankfurter not rest the dismissals on the ripeness doctrine as explicated in *United Mine Workers v. Mitchell*? Perhaps it was to avoid invoking Article III, upon which Justice Reed's *Mitchell* opinion had quite clearly relied. This is the greatest mystery surrounding Frankfurter's justiciability jurisprudence: why did he invoke Article III in some cases and not in others? In *Coleman* and *McGrath* he clearly situated at least the core of standing and justiciability in the Constitution. In *Poe* and *Baker*, however, he assiduously avoided invoking Article III. There appears to be no algorithm to explain when Frankfurter would find a justiciability problem to be rooted in the Constitution and when he would not.

101. 367 U.S. at 501.
102. 367 U.S. at 508.
103. 367 U.S. at 502–03 (citation omitted).
104. 367 U.S. at 508–09.

There was probably a strategic element to Frankfurter's justiciability approach. Frankfurter almost certainly had provided the inspiration for Bickel's theory of the "passive virtues," which argued that the Supreme Court should use the standing, mootness, and ripeness doctrines to duck cases when the circumstances prevented a principled decision. Frankfurter himself repeatedly stressed the need for flexibility in justiciability doctrine. It would only make sense for Frankfurter to have wanted the standing doctrine, and justiciability more generally, to have the free-floating quality of prudential rules. At the same time, however, Frankfurter's justiciability opinions often conveyed the sense of a court claiming that its hands were tied, that it was powerless to reach the merits. This impression would have been difficult to achieve if all the constraints were transparently self-imposed. Frankfurter therefore deliberately maintained an opaqueness in the distinction between the portion of justiciability that was compelled by Article III and the portion that was self-imposed. Perhaps in his mind relatively little of the doctrine was actually compelled by Article III, yet the fuzziness of the line permitted the Court to ditch sensitive cases while maintaining a pious front.

6. BRENNAN, CIVIL RIGHTS, AND THE "PERSONAL STAKE" GAMBIT

The next term, his last before a stroke forced him to retire, Felix Frankfurter suffered one of his most stinging defeats. In *Baker v. Carr*,[1] the landmark decision that opened the door to "one man, one vote," the Court all but overruled Frankfurter's majority opinion in *Colegrove v. Green*. Not only did *Baker* play a pivotal role in the judicial protection of the civil rights movement, but it marked the ascendancy of Justice William Brennan to a position of power within the Warren Court. Less known is that some of the language from Brennan's opinion in *Baker* laid the seeds for the conservative counterrevolution in justiciability law in the 1970s and 1980s.

* * *

William Joseph Brennan, Jr., was born on April 24, 1906, to William Joseph Brennan, Sr., and the former Agnes McDermott, in Newark, New Jersey. He was their second child, but the first male, and Brennan Sr. was a stern taskmaster. An Irish immigrant who originally worked as a coal heaver in a brewery, he eventually became Newark's most successful reformer, initially in organized labor, and later (after having been beaten bloody by the police during a labor dispute) as the police commissioner. It was he who decided that Brennan Jr., upon graduation from the University of Pennsylvania, would attend the Harvard Law School.

As a law student Brennan was a hard worker, a "prodigious note-taker," but not at the top of his class. He missed out on being chosen for the *Harvard Law Review*, the honor reserved for the highest achievers, and was also passed over for a position as a student adviser, which was the second tier. He did manage to be named to the Harvard Legal Aid Bureau, the third-tier honor, and in that capacity argued many cases on behalf of indigent clients. His legal aid experience, along with his decade of labor law practice at Pitney, Hardin & Ward of Newark, helped prepare him for his appointment to the Superior Court (a trial court) in 1949. He was elevated to the New Jersey Supreme Court in 1951.

In 1956, Republican Dwight Eisenhower faced a reelection battle against the man he had defeated four years earlier, liberal Democrat Adlai Stevenson. An election now assumed to have been a walkover was actually, at one point, a nail-biter. Shortly after the California primary, Eisenhower underwent major abdominal surgery. With the qualifications of Vice President Richard Nixon suddenly under the microscope, Eisenhower realized he had a fight on his hands.

1. 369 U.S. 186 (1962).

On September 7, Sherman Minton announced his resignation from the Court for health reasons. Eisenhower now had a Supreme Court appointment with which to appease various electoral constituencies. One, interestingly, was the Association of State Court Judges, which bitterly complained that no state court judge had been elevated to the U.S. Supreme Court since Benjamin Cardozo. If the state court judges had been the only squeaky wheel—or at least the largest one—Eisenhower's choice probably would have been Arthur Vanderbilt, the esteemed chief justice of the New Jersey Supreme Court. Vanderbilt had campaigned prominently to make adjudication in the New Jersey courts more efficient, with fewer trials and faster times to trial. Eisenhower, ever the administrator, appreciated that. But there was a far more powerful constituency nipping at Ike's heels—the Catholic Church. Francis Cardinal Spellman met with Eisenhower to lobby him for a Catholic appointment. Spellman reminded Ike that, counting his first two Supreme Court appointments (Earl Warren and John Marshall Harlan), the last six appointments to the Court had been Protestants. When Minton resigned, Eisenhower decided that his replacement had to be a Catholic and a sitting state court judge.

Attorney General Herbert Brownell and his second-in-command, William Rogers, discussed the vacancy. Hadn't Brennan, an associate justice on the New Jersey Supreme Court, been the man who had subbed for an ailing Vanderbilt as a speaker at a judicial administration conference not long before? Rogers asked. Yes, replied Brownell, and Brennan had been impressive in stressing the need for greater efficiencies in adjudication. He seemed to be in the Vanderbilt mold. That he was a Democrat didn't matter to Ike—what did matter was that he really be a practicing Catholic. After verifying this fact through Cardinal Spellman (who had never heard of Brennan and had to investigate through his parish priest), Brownell called Brennan and asked him to come to Washington to meet the president. After a twenty-minute conversation with Eisenhower about hats and his army experience, Brennan had the nomination.

Eisenhower and Brownell thought they were getting a political moderate, if not a conservative, who would emphasize judicial efficiency. Ike was under the distinct misimpression that Brennan had been "Vanderbilt's boy," which presumably meant someone with Vanderbilt's establishment views and judicial sensibilities. Brownell had only scratched the surface of Brennan's record. There were Brennan opinions indicating a solicitude for civil rights and for criminal procedure rights. There were also some extrajudicial remarks in which Brennan labeled some anticommunist investigations as "witch hunts." Overall, however, Brennan's brief tenure on the New Jersey Supreme Court had presented him with issues generally dissimilar to those facing the U.S. Supreme Court, and his jurisprudence on free speech and assembly, equal protection, and federalism were largely unformed. Although Brownell had not done his due diligence, it is not entirely clear how much difference it would have made. In any event,

"Brennan would have the honor of becoming the second of what Eisenhower called his two biggest mistakes."[2]

But it wasn't so much the fact that Brennan himself was incorrigibly liberal. It was his genius in engineering majorities on the Court in service of that liberalism that filled Eisenhower with remorse. Brennan had inherited the political deftness of his father. He became a maestro in making a key concession to win a critical vote, or to keep that vote from wandering into dissent. He rarely made strident, ideological statements for posterity's sake, or for their cathartic value. Instead, Brennan's opinion-writing was generally strategic. Every statement or passage had a carefully calculated purpose—to parry a thrust from a dissent, to win a swing vote, to lay the foundation for a future case. If money and favor were the currency of ward politics, opinion writing was the currency of politics in the rarified intellectual environment of the Supreme Court. Brennan became the most influential member of the Court during his tenure.

If the Court were going to fully vindicate civil rights, Brennan realized, there would have to be some liberalization of the Brandeis/Frankfurter constitutional avoidance regime. An early move in this direction was *United States v. Raines*, handed down in early 1960.[3] An integral part of Jim Crow was, through a combination of clever devices and outright intimidation, to render the Negro right to vote a purely formal construct. The Civil Rights Act of 1957 stated that all citizens "shall be entitled and allowed to vote . . . without distinction of race, color, or previous condition of servitude," irrespective of any state law to the contrary. In the twilight of the Eisenhower administration, the Department of Justice sued under this provision for an injunction to stop the Board of Registrars of Terrell County, Georgia, from discriminating against Blacks attempting to register to vote. The registrars challenged the constitutionality of the law: if it were read for all it was worth, they argued, it purported to prohibit purely private acts against Blacks trying to vote. That, continued the argument, would exceed Congress's powers under the Fifteenth Amendment. In other words, the registrars argued that the law was overbroad. It might have been constitutionally authorized insofar as it reached the acts of county officials, but not to the degree that it reached the acts of private persons. The district judge agreed, and dismissed the federal government's complaint.

Justice Brennan's opinion for the Court reversed without reaching the constitutional question. The complaint wasn't brought against any private persons, only against county officials. When and if the Department of Justice ever tried to sue private parties under the statute, it would be time enough to consider the provision's theoretical reach. Brennan could tersely have said that, under the usual practice, a court only considers whether a law violates the constitution as it

2. James MacGregor Burns, Packing the Court: The Rise of Judicial Power and the Coming Crisis of the Supreme Court 186 (Penguin Press 2009).

3. 362 U.S. 17.

has actually been applied to the person before the court, and not as it might hypothetically be applied to others who might be very differently situated. *Thornhill*, the case in which the Court struck down the antipicketing law despite the absence of any real facts, was exceptional because it involved the First Amendment. But Brennan passed over this minimalist approach in favor of something more expansive.

"The very foundation of the power of the federal courts to declare Acts of Congress unconstitutional lies in the power and duty of those courts to decide cases and controversies properly before them," Brennan started. He was channeling Frankfurter perfectly. "The delicate power of pronouncing an Act of Congress unconstitutional is not to be exercised with reference to hypothetical cases thus imagined," Brennan continued. When a court reaches a constitutional question prematurely, it denies other courts the ability to "save" the statute by interpreting it in such a way that it would not violate the constitution. So far, it was an opinion that could have been written by Frankfurter himself.

Brennan then acknowledged that there were exceptions to the general rule that federal courts consider only those matters strictly before them. One was the *Thornhill* situation, where a law threatened free speech so widely that limiting analysis to the peculiar facts of the immediate case would leave a shroud of uncertainty over other people who wished to engage in similar speech but feared punishment. The First Amendment might not protect the precise speech involved in the case, but if the law being challenged clearly applied to other types of speech that *would* be protected, reaching the issue now would prevent other people from being caught between the horns of a cruel dilemma: obey the law in question and forego what one believes to be constitutionally protected speech, or engage in the speech and run the risk of being punished for it.

But the *Thornhill* "First Amendment overbreadth" scenario was only one of six exceptions that Brennan's opinion identified. Another was the situation where the claimant before the court sought to invoke rights belonging to someone else. To represent this situation, Brennan cited *Barrows v. Jackson*,[4] a case decided just three years before *Brown v. Board of Education*. A White landowner in Los Angeles sold her house to the highest bidder. The problem was that the highest bidder was Black, and there was a racially restrictive covenant running with the land. Another landowner in the neighborhood then sued the seller for damages for breach of the covenant. A few years earlier, the Supreme Court had decided the landmark case of *Shelley v. Kraemer*, in which it held that racially restrictive covenants could not be enforced against Black would-be buyers.[5] In *Barrows*, however, the defendant seller was White; allowing damages for her breach of the covenant would not violate her right to equal protection of the laws.

4. 346 U.S. 249 (1953).
5. 334 U.S. 1 (1948).

Yet, in an opinion signed by Minton and obviously engineered by Frankfurter, the Court permitted the seller to defend the damages action by asserting the equal protection rights of non-Caucasians. If damages were allowed in this case, future sellers would either refuse to sell to Negroes, or they would demand higher prices in order to cover their liability for breaching the covenant. Under the unique circumstances of the case, and because it would otherwise be difficult for Negroes to invalidate such obviously illegal covenants on an individual basis, the Court effectively permitted the seller in *Barrows* to act as the representative of a class constituted by all non-Caucasians who might someday wish to buy homes in neighborhoods with racially restrictive covenants. Frankfurter, ever concerned to limit White backlash against judicial invalidation of segregation, thought it would be safer to rule in favor of Negroes indirectly. After all, the nominal winner here was a White person who simply wanted top dollar for her house, not a Black person, and not even a White Negro sympathizer. The *Barrows* opinion explicitly attempted to limit the holding to the "peculiar circumstances of this case."

In his *Raines* opinion, however, Brennan portrayed *Barrows* as something more than one peculiar case. He held it out as an example of one of six types of exceptions to the rule against considering only matters strictly before the court. By detailing and systematizing these exceptions, Brennan reified them. In fact, several of them had precedential foundations, but Frankfurter through his treatises had marginalized them. In *Raines*, even as Brennan refused to listen to the registrars' hypothetical scenario, he set the stage for future cases in which the court could entertain hypotheticals. Brennan's list of six exceptions in *Barrows* was almost the mirror image of Brandeis' list of seven decision-avoidance canons in *Ashwander*.

Another one of Brennan's exceptions was exemplified by *NAACP v. Button*, a 1963 decision that involved Virginia's attempt to derail the NAACP's (National Association for the Advancement of Colored People) litigation campaign by using its power to regulate the legal profession.[6] Virginia law had long prohibited the solicitation of legal business by a "runner" or "capper," but in 1956 the legislature for the first time expanded the definition of "runner" or "capper" to include anyone working for an organization that was not itself a party to the litigation and had no pecuniary right or liability in the matter. The NAACP sued in federal district court for an injunction prohibiting Virginia from enforcing this new provision, arguing (among other things) that it violated the First Amendment as it applied against the states through the Fourteenth Amendment.

The state, following the Brandeis/Frankfurter playbook of constitutional decision avoidance, urged the Court to construe the new statutory provision narrowly so as to minimize the scope of any constitutional holding. The Virginia Supreme

6. 371 U.S. 415 (1963).

Court had held that a certain subset of the NAACP's activities violated the statute in question; the state wanted the constitutional question limited to those enumerated activities. But the subset of activities was defined only vaguely, and Justice Brennan, writing for a 5–4 majority, refused to circumscribe the constitutional question on that basis. "If the line drawn by the [state court] between the permitted and prohibited activities of the NAACP . . . is an ambiguous one, we will not presume that the statute curtails constitutionally protected activity as little as possible," Brennan wrote. "For standards of permissible statutory vagueness are strict in the area of free expression."[7] He then invoked the First Amendment overbreadth doctrine, professing the same kind of indifference to the precise facts of the case at bar as Justice Frank Murphy had expressed in *Thornhill*: "[T]he instant decree may be invalid if it prohibits privileged exercises of First Amendment rights whether or not the record discloses the petitioner has engaged in privileged conduct. For in appraising a statute's inhibitory effect upon such rights, this Court has not hesitated to take into account possible applications of the statute in other factual contexts besides that at bar."[8] Frankfurter's replacement, Arthur Goldberg, provided the crucial fifth vote for Brennan's majority opinion. Frankfurter, having left the Court the previous term, could only watch from the sidelines as Brennan, his former student, undermined his constitutional avoidance jurisprudence. "I always encouraged my students to think for themselves," Frankfurter groused, "but Brennan goes too far."[9]

Two years later, Brennan again invoked the First Amendment overbreadth doctrine in a civil rights case from the South, *Dombrowski v. Pfister*.[10] Dr. James Dombrowski was the executive director of the Southern Conference Educational Fund, Inc., which was being prosecuted in Louisiana under two criminal statutes —the Louisiana Subversive Activities and Communist Control Law and the Communist Propaganda Control Law. Dombrowski and his fellow activists sued in federal court for an injunction stopping these prosecutions on the ground that the statutes were facially overbroad. They also claimed the prosecutions were being brought in bad faith, not to obtain convictions, but merely to harass the plaintiffs and intimidate them from continuing their advocacy on behalf of Negro rights. The three-judge district court refused to reach the merits of the plaintiffs' constitutional challenge on the ground that the state courts should be permitted a first opportunity to construe the reach of the statutes.

Writing for a 5–2 majority, Justice Brennan looked to cement the federal equity power as a force for civil rights in the South. He began the core of his

7. 371 U.S. at 432.

8. *Id.*

9. Burns, Packing the Court, *supra* note 2 of this chapter.

10. 380 U.S. 479 (1965).

opinion with a sweeping characterization of *Ex Parte Young*, the rate regulation case in which Justice David Brewer had celebrated the federal equity power as a force for property rights in the face of the regulatory state. "In *Ex Parte Young*, the fountainhead of federal injunctions against state prosecutions, the Court characterized the power and its proper exercise in broad terms," Brennan wrote.[11] Such injunctions should be available whenever state officers threaten judicial proceedings brought under an unconstitutional state law. Certainly Dombrowski's case fit that description. The type of antisubversive statutes involved in his case had been declared unconstitutional in other cases. But there were cases after *Ex Parte Young* in which the Supreme Court had cut back substantially, if not entirely, on the rule that federal injunctions were available to protect federal constitutional rights against threatened state prosecutions.

Prominent among these decisions was a 1943 case, *Douglas v. City of Jeannette*, in which Jehovah's Witnesses were denied an injunction to stop prosecutions under a local ordinance prohibiting door-to-door solicitation without a license.[12] The ordinance was indeed unconstitutional as applied to the Witnesses' conduct,[13] but the Court—without mentioning *Ex Parte Young*—held that a federal court may not bar enforcement of state criminal law in the absence of "great and immediate" irreparable injury. Well-settled law required the applicant for any kind of injunction to demonstrate simple irreparable injury—that is, the inadequacy of money damages in that situation—but the *Douglas* Court now discovered a much more strenuous requirement where the proposed injunction would block the state from prosecuting under its criminal law. Chief Justice Harlan Fiske Stone was the author of the *Douglas* opinion, but Frankfurter's influence is unmistakable. *Douglas* was part of Frankfurter's attempt to stop federal judges from interfering with state policy implementation. One could scarcely imagine a more different notion of equity than Brewer had adumbrated in *Young*. Equity went from the handmaiden of vested rights to the handmaiden of federalism, from a God-given remedy for God-given rights to an instrument for the technical accommodation of state and federal interests.

Having decided that the plaintiffs in *Dombrowski* were entitled to their injunction, Brennan faced a dilemma. Should he mount a frontal attack on *Douglas*'s intertwining of equity and federalism? Or should he finesse the issue by distinguishing *Douglas*? He chose the latter. Rather than challenge the nearly insurmountable requirement of "great and immediate" irreparable injury, Brennan carved out an exception for cases involving First Amendment overbreadth. *Douglas* involved a challenge to the solicitation license ordinance *as it had been specifically applied to the Jehovah's Witnesses*; surely the law was constitutionally sound in most other contexts. By contrast, Brennan argued, the antisubversive

11. 380 U.S. at 483.
12. 319 U.S. 157.
13. Murdock v. Pennsylvania, 319 U.S. 105 (1943).

statutes were facially overbroad—that is, unconstitutional in so many of their applications that the Court deemed them unenforceable unless and until given an acceptable limiting interpretation. If the plaintiffs in *Dombrowski* were not permitted to obtain a blanket injunction against the enforcement of these overbroad statutes, their only alternative would be to challenge the statutes on a case-by-case basis, each time they were prosecuted. This would be unacceptable in the free expression area, Brennan asserted, because of the likelihood of self-censorship. (This, along with *New York Times v. Sullivan*,[14] was one of the cases in which the Court popularized the phrase "chilling effect.") Such self-censorship was an injury not only to the individual, but to society, which depended on the free flow of ideas to keep a self-governing citizenry well informed. "For free expression—of transcendent value to all society, and not merely to those exercising their rights—might be the loser," he wrote.[15] With *Dombrowski*, Brennan believed he was installing First Amendment overbreadth as an exception to two doctrines—the rule generally prohibiting constitutional challenges based on hypothetical facts, and the rule prohibiting federal injunctions against state criminal prosecutions. But in doing so, he had expressly acquiesced in the doctrines themselves.

By the early 1970s, both of Brennan's achievements in *Dombrowski* had been all but erased. In *Younger v. Harris*,[16] decided in 1971, the Court refused to permit an injunction against a state criminal prosecution under circumstances virtually indistinguishable from those in *Dombrowski*. Justice Hugo Black's majority opinion in *Younger* marginalized *Dombrowski*'s First Amendment overbreadth exception to the general requirement of "great and immediate" irreparable injury by holding, entirely implausibly, that the reasoning of *Dombrowski* itself was limited to situations in which the prosecutions were undertaken in bad faith and for purposes of harassment. Then, in 1973, Justice Byron White's opinion for the Court in *Broadrick v. Oklahoma* severely curtailed *Dombrowski*'s overbreadth exception to the rule against considering constitutional challenges based on hypothetical facts, saying that from that point forward, the law had to be not only overbroad, but "substantially" so—a standard that, unsurprisingly, proved virtually impossible to meet.

The most obvious cause of *Dombrowski*'s demise was changes in Court personnel. In *Younger*, Justices Hugo Black and Potter Stewart were in the majority, voting to marginalize *Dombrowski*; although both of them were on the Court when *Dombrowski* was decided, neither of them participated. Joining them were Harlan, a *Dombrowski* dissenter, and new Nixon appointees Warren Burger and Harry Blackmun, who now occupied the seats previously held by Earl Warren

14. 376 U.S. 254 (1964).
15. 380 U.S. at 486.
16. 401 U.S. 37 (1971).

and Arthur Goldberg.[17] In *Broadrick*, four of the five justices in the majority were Nixon appointees—Burger, Blackmun, Lewis Powell, and William Rehnquist. Another possible factor in *Dombrowski*'s decline was changes in the White establishment's perceptions of race relations. When civil rights activists were engaging in sit-ins and voter registration, that was one thing; when the race riots in Watts were nationally televised in 1965, some White establishment figures, including Black, felt that public order had become the most compelling priority. These two factors may well have sealed *Dombrowski*'s fate.

But it remained true that Brennan's opinion had made it easier for the Court to retreat. Owen Fiss, a former Brennan clerk who went on to become a professor at Yale, later wondered aloud whether Brennan's decision to forego a frontal attack on the Frankfurterian citadel of federalism and constitutional avoidance had doomed the opinion in the long run.[18] Neither Black's opinion for the Court in *Younger* nor White's opinion for the Court in *Broadrick* faced the task of rehabilitating the federalism and constitutional avoidance orthodoxies, for Brennan himself had left them undisturbed. They merely had to repeat those orthodoxies and portray *Dombrowski* as a factual outlier. Indeed, in *Broadrick*, White repeatedly used Brennan's Frankfurterian discussion of general standing rules against him.

Perhaps Brennan's most fateful move in the area of judicial restraint, however, came in *Baker v. Carr*, in 1962. The case is justly famous as a huge victory for the voting rights movement; as a crushing defeat for Frankfurter; and as the authoritative modern statement of the so-called "political question" doctrine. Upon his retirement, Earl Warren referred to *Baker* and the voting rights cases following it as the most important line of cases decided during his tenure. But the lasting effect of Brennan's opinion in *Baker* extended well beyond voting rights and the somewhat obscure political question doctrine, to the much more critical doctrine of standing to sue. Standing was not a major issue in *Baker*, yet a few words in Brennan's opinion exerted enormous influence over the course of standing doctrine, and over the course of public interest litigation for the next fifty years.

* * *

In the summer of 1960, a Harvard philosophy graduate student named Robert Moses became too distracted by the excitement of student sit-ins in the South to continue his studies. In August, nine months before the Freedom Riders would make the route famous, Moses boarded an Atlanta Greyhound bus destined for Mississippi. As the bus approached Anniston, Alabama, Moses quietly moved to a back seat. Moses was looking for students to attend a conference of the newly

17. Goldberg's seat was taken by Lyndon Johnson appointee Abe Fortas in October 1965. Fortas, disgraced by his unethical behavior, resigned the seat in 1969 and was eventually replaced by Blackmun.

18. Owen M. Fiss, *Dombrowski*, 86 YALE L. J. 1103 (1977).

formed Student Nonviolent Coordinating Committee (SNCC). His bus ride took him to see SNCC founder Ella Baker's contacts all over the South, but it was his stop in Cleveland, Mississippi, that changed everything, because it was in Cleveland that Moses met Amzie Moore.[19]

Moore was a World War II veteran and gas station owner who for several years had been working to get Negroes registered to vote. It was fine for SNCC to recruit youth from Mississippi to take part in sit-ins and other demonstrations, he told Moses, but they were missing the bigger picture. SNCC should be *sending* students to Mississippi to register voters under the protection of the new civil rights laws. The Freedom Rides were a good thing, but "they didn't go to the heart of what troubled Mississippi: Jim Crow politics."[20] Moore had a concrete plan. "Amzie thinks he can lay his hands on a bus if we can gas it up," Moses wrote Jane Stembridge, a key volunteer back in the SNCC office. "The idea is to tackle the 2nd and 3rd Congressional Districts, about 25 counties in all . . . . The main thrust is to take place next summer . . . . Nobody [is] starry eyed, these are nasty jobs but we're going to find some nasty people to do them . . . ."[21] Stembridge could barely contain herself. "I cannot believe your letters . . . . I got so excited that things almost happened to my kidneys. This VOTER REGISTRATION project is IT!"[22] Stembridge spread the word around SNCC and immediately began scrounging up funds to print up 200,000 copies of the Mississippi constitution, which would be necessary if their recruits were going to pass the literacy tests.

Moses would soon be experiencing what he would later call the "living" Constitution in rural Mississippi, while in Washington, D.C., the Justice Department began work on what Moses would call, with slight bemusement, the "adjudicated" Constitution. John Doar had practically become a one-man workforce for voting rights in the Eisenhower Justice Department. Doar was a private practitioner in Wisconsin when fellow Princeton alum Harold Tyler, chief of the Civil Rights Division, tracked him down and offered him the first assistant's position. No politically connected Republican in 1960 had expressed any interest in the job, so Tyler fished Doar out of his modest courthouse practice to help step up enforcement of the 1957 and 1960 Civil Rights Acts.[23] Doar developed a practice of taking matters into his own hands. When the Civil Rights Division asked the FBI to investigate complaints that White farmers in Hayward County, Tennessee, were systematically evicting Negro sharecroppers who tried to register, the

19. *See* Robert P. Moses, *An Earned Insurgency: Quality Education as a Constitutional Right*, 79 HARV. EDUC. REV. 370, 371 (Summer 2009).

20. *Id.* at 373, citing C. M. PAYNE, I'VE GOT THE LIGHT OF FREEDOM: THE ORGANIZING TRADITION AND THE MISSISSIPPI FREEDOM STRUGGLE 105 (Univ. of Calif. Press 1995).

21. TAYLOR BRANCH, PARTING THE WATERS: AMERICA IN THE KING YEARS 1954–63 at 330–31 (Simon & Schuster 1988).

22. *Id.* at 331.

23. *Id.*

bureau's agents dragged their feet and ignored credible evidence substantiating the complaint. The Midwesterner Doar, who had only been in D.C. a few weeks, immediately violated etiquette by going to Hayward County himself, driving out into the back country, and attending church meetings. The first night, he found himself in front of a congregation of sharecroppers who had tried to register to vote. When he asked whether any of them had received notices of eviction, almost every hand went up. "It was a moment of shock that Doar never forgot," wrote Taylor Branch in the first installment of his magisterial account of the civil rights movement, *Parting the Waters*. "Staring into all those faces, he doubted that the drive to prevent Negro voting could be so widespread, until he collected fifty affidavits from sharecroppers who had saved their written eviction notices and were willing to testify."[24] Doar returned to D.C. with a new perspective on things, "learning more from a few days on his own than he had gleaned from thousands of pages of memos."

At precisely 11 a.m. on October 19, 1960, eighty demonstrators requested service in eight different segregated establishments in Atlanta. Their purpose was to be arrested and put in jail. Only one of the demonstrators was not a student—the Rev. Martin Luther King, Jr. King was among those refused service at a snack bar at Rich's, the city's largest department store. When company officials declined to have them arrested at the snack bar, the demonstrators decamped to the Magnolia Room, the store's most elegant restaurant, where they were arrested under a state antitrespass law. Several days later, the mayor, seeking to avoid further demonstrations by either Negroes or Klansmen, ordered the prisoners released that Monday morning. But other forces were at work. Jail officials notified King's lawyers that a judge in neighboring DeKalb County had issued a bench warrant ordering them not to release King. The previous May, King had been convicted of a misdemeanor offense: driving on his Alabama license some three months after moving to Georgia. At the time, Judge Oscar Mitchell had given King a suspended sentence, and now he wanted to hold a hearing on whether the trespass at Rich's department store violated the terms of the suspension. The nearly two hundred King supporters crowded into Judge Mitchell's courtroom were shocked when the judge revoked King's probation and ordered him to serve four months of hard labor on a state road gang, starting immediately.

When King was suddenly transported with no notice from the DeKalb county jail to the maximum-security prison at Reidsville, those within the movement feared the worst. No one knew what might happen next. King's wife Coretta, six months pregnant with their third child, was nearly hysterical. She called Harris Wofford, who was the aide in the John Kennedy for President campaign closest to the civil rights movement. In fact, Wofford was virtually alone in the Kennedy

24. *Id.* at 334.

campaign in wanting to voice support for King and the civil rights movement; everyone else was mortified by the prospect of alienating segregationists and losing the South. Wofford got through to Sargent Shriver, who was with the candidate in Chicago. Even if Kennedy wouldn't make a public statement in King's favor, couldn't he at least call Coretta and wish her well? Wofford asked. Just that small gesture would "reverberate all through the Negro community in the United States," he pleaded.

Shriver relented, took the phone number of King's residence, and stuck it in his pocket, waiting for the right moment. Finally, after the senator excused himself from his clutch of aides, saying he did not feel well, Shriver alone followed him into the bedroom and suggested that he give Mrs. King a call. Kennedy sat up wearily on the bed. "What the hell," he said. "That's a decent thing to do. Why not? Get her on the phone."[25] The conversation was not even two minutes and could only be described as banal. "I know this must be very hard for you," Kennedy told Mrs. King. "I understand you are expecting a baby, and I just wanted you to know that I was thinking about you and Dr. King. If there is anything I can do to help, please feel free to call on me." "I certainly appreciate your concern," she responded. "I would appreciate anything you could do to help." With that, the call ended. Kennedy was on his way back to the airport.

Hours later, Judge Mitchell changed his mind and ordered King released on $2,000 bond. But it wasn't John Kennedy's call to Coretta Scott King that changed his mind. Robert Kennedy, the candidate's younger brother and a lawyer, had called Judge Mitchell from a phone booth in New York and expressed his opinion that "any decent American judge would release King on bond by sundown." When reporters confronted campaign officials with the story, the officials were so incredulous that they laughed it off. Calling a judge to influence him in a pending case was so clear a violation of legal ethics that no one could take it seriously. That night, Bobby called campaign aide John Seigenthaler for a routine check-in. "Guess what that crazy judge says in Georgia?" Seighenthaler snorted. "He says you called him about King not getting bail." There was a long pause. "Did he say that?" Kennedy asked. "Yes. But don't worry, I put out a denial," Seigenthaler reassured him. Another long pause. "Well, you better . . . retract it," Kennedy replied. He admitted that he had lost his temper thinking about this backwater judge "screwing up my brother's campaign and making the country look ridiculous before the world."[26]

The cumulative effect of the two phone calls caused a "phenomenal 'sea change' within the Negro electorate," wrote Branch. Rev. Martin Luther King, Sr., known as "Daddy King," had been supporting Nixon, the Republican, but he

25. *Id.* at 362.
26. *Id.* at 367.

now did an immediate and public about-face while addressing an impromptu mass at Ebenezer Baptist Church:

> I had expected to vote against Senator Kennedy because of his religion. But now he can be my President, Catholic or whatever he is. It took courage to call my daughter-in-law at a time like this. He has the moral courage to stand up for what he knows is right. I've got all my votes and I've got a suitcase, and I'm going to take them up there and dump them in his lap.[27]

With only days left before the election, the campaign's civil rights office quickly moved to capitalize on developments. The plan was to print a pamphlet for mass distribution in Negro churches on the last Sunday before the election. They would establish a "dummy committee" of preachers to protect the Kennedy campaign from being identified as the source of the literature. The pamphlet would contain nothing more than statements by the King family and Negro preachers about Senator Kennedy's call to Mrs. King. It would be headlined, "'No Comment' Nixon Versus a Candidate with a Heart, Senator Kennedy." The pamphlet, printed on cheap blue paper, became known as "the blue bomb," and the civil rights office of the campaign was staking everything on it.

The results were spectacular. No single factor ever decides an election, but Kennedy's margin among Black voters fairly jumped off the page. In 1956, Blacks had voted 60–40 in favor of Ike and the Republicans; in 1960, they voted Democratic by 70–30. "This 30 percent shift accounted for more votes than Kennedy's victory margins in a number of key states, including Michigan, New Jersey, Pennsylvania, Illinois, and the Carolinas," Branch wrote. The day after the election, the chair of the national Republican Party declared that "they had taken the Negro vote too much for granted." An inconsolable Eisenhower blamed the loss on "a couple of phone calls" by the Kennedy brothers.[28]

Newly installed as attorney general, Robert Kennedy asked Doar to stay on in the Civil Rights Division. Doar's summaries of the voting rights cases he was then litigating helped Bob Kennedy reach the conclusion that voting rights "were the strongest political and moral opportunity for the Justice Department in the field of civil rights."[29] "I want to move on voting," he told Doar. It made sense. Establishment Whites were not as squeamish about registering Negro voters as they were about confrontational direct action. Moreover, building Negro political power was ultimately the best way of securing meaningful representation, and

---

27. *Id.* at 366. Later, in private, Senator Kennedy mused about Daddy King's statement admitting his anti-Catholic sentiment. "That was a hell of a bigoted statement, wasn't it?" he told Harris Wofford. "Imagine Martin Luther King having a bigot for a father?" He grinned and added, "Well, we all have fathers, don't we?" *Id.* at 370.

28. *Id.* at 374–75.

29. *Id.* at 387.

social and economic progress, for the Negro community. And, perhaps best of all, the Negro community had now demonstrated that it would reward even Democrats at the polls if they supported civil rights; the more thoroughly enfranchised the Negro community became, the larger the reward.

Within the movement, direct action still beckoned. The Congress of Racial Equality (CORE) planned a set of "Freedom Rides" on Greyhound and Trailways buses throughout the South, challenging the states to comply with the Supreme Court's recent decision in *Boynton v. Virginia* (holding that the Interstate Commerce Act banned segregation in interstate common carrier facilities).[30] During this first series of Freedom Rides, running from May 4 to May 26 in 1961, student groups from CORE endured one segregationist mob after another, being beaten, dragged, kidnapped, and starved, but never defeated. They raised the profile of the civil rights movement nationally and internationally. But the public relations value of the Freedom Rides declined significantly after the first ride. By late May, White establishment opinion had turned away from this form of direct action. Even the *New York Times* came out against the continuation of the rides. And Bob Kennedy, never enthusiastic about the Freedom Rides to begin with, now went public with his opposition to further rides.

The Attorney General was determined to help turn the civil rights movement toward voter registration. The Justice Department stepped up efforts to create a well-financed, tax-exempt organization to register Negro voters in the South. Kennedy himself intervened with the IRS to obtain a tax exemption for the new Voter Education Project (VEP). On June 16, a delegation from the Freedom Ride Coordinating Committee met with Attorney General Kennedy in the hope of securing more federal protection for future Freedom Rides. Instead, they got a lecture. The Freedom Rides were no longer productive, Kennedy told them. They had a choice: the jails could be filled with Freedom Riders, or they could be filled with segregationists trying to obstruct voter registration. The delegates did not appreciate Kennedy's patronizing manner, but he had a point.[31]

Bob Kennedy now put on a full-court press to convince SNCC that they should turn away from direct action and toward voter registration. He invited the Black entertainer Harry Belafonte to his home on Hickory Hill to get Belafonte to push the students in that direction. Belafonte offered $10,000 of his own money to get them going. Kennedy gave an interview to the *New York Times*, telling the paper that the Rev. King and other movement leaders had decided to focus on voting, and that the Justice Department would give full protection to those attempting to register voters. At the end of July, the heads of the major civil rights organizations convened with the Attorney General's immediate subordinates in New York, with the Justice Department representatives pushing Kennedy's voter

30. 364 U.S. 454 (1960).
31. *Id.* at 480.

registration argument. It was a tough slog, as Branch recounted, but ultimately successful:

> [James] Farmer, just out of jail in Mississippi, had to be convinced that he was not abandoning CORE's entire purpose at its moment of glory. Roy Wilkins had to be convinced that the NAACP would not appear to be abandoning its banner of school desegregation. . . . Nevertheless, a month later these same people were back in the Fifth Avenue offices of the Taconic Foundation, this time with "working papers." They divided the territory of the South and resolved acute differences over the proportional allocation of funds. They recruited the Field Foundation and the Stern Fund to supplement the Taconic Foundation's money. They searched for administrators and conduits who were acceptable to all the various grantees, grantors, and intermediaries. . . . Within another month, foundation executives translated the deals into fuzzy language, and lawyers checked organizational flow charts against the tax code.
>
> The Voter Education Project was created essentially by a forced march in the opposite direction from the Freedom Rides, in spirit if not in purpose. To accomplish the march that same summer of 1961, with the Freedom Rides still going on, was a tribute to the willfulness of the Kennedy Justice Department. . . .[32]

As news of the SNCC voter registration drive spread by local radio, Bob Moses headed to McComb, Mississippi. McComb was in Pike County, just east of Highway 55. It was chosen because it was, relatively speaking, more densely populated and cosmopolitan than Amite County to the west and Walthall County to the east. But these were heady days, and Moses allowed himself to be talked into going outside of McComb, as he later recalled:

> Mrs. Schoby came with her sister and asked if we would go with them and their brother to Liberty, across the county line in Amite. Webb Owens, "Super Cool Daddy," stashed his cane in front of him on both hands, leaned forward just a little bit, opened his "fish eye" as wide as he could, and stared in stone silence: McComb was one thing, Amite was another. I agreed to go. On our way back from the Liberty courthouse on August 15, the Mississippi highway patrol stopped our car and arrested me. I put in a call to John Doar, a connection that made a difference. I lucked out, being connected collect like I did.[33]

In order to get around in the rural spaces of Amite County, Moses had to borrow a car and make a lot of sleeping arrangements. On August 15, he and the first three Amite County volunteers drove to the county courthouse in Liberty

32. *Id.* at 481–82.

33. Moses, *supra* note 19 of this chapter, at 374.

and went to the office of the registrar. What did they think they were doing there? the registrar asked. The three volunteers stood speechless. Moses spoke up from behind: "They would like to try to register to vote." After asking Moses what his interest was in the matter, the dubious registrar slowly retrieved some forms and gave them to the volunteers. As curious county officials came by to see for themselves the Negroes who were asking to register, the volunteers painstakingly completed their forms and turned them in. Moses knew they would be rejected, but they considered it a victory that they were permitted to fill out the forms at all. Six hours later, they left the courthouse and started off for McComb.

They were being followed. A highway patrolman from the registrar's office tailed them for ten miles along Highway 24 and stayed with them as they took every side road they could find. Finally he pulled them over and ordered them to follow him into McComb, where Moses was arrested and booked for interfering with an officer in the discharge of his duties. It was then that Moses made his collect call to Doar. The justice of the peace, evidently unnerved by Moses' Justice Department connection, offered to suspend his sentence if Moses would agree to pay court costs of five dollars—essentially compensation "for pulling the judge away from his supper," as Branch put it. But Moses refused the offer, quietly explaining that it was part of an unjust prosecution, and he spent the next two nights in jail. An NAACP lawyer eventually paid the $50 fine in full and Moses was released.[34]

By the time Moses had gotten back to Amite, word had spread. The voting project was being discussed at meetings of the White Citizens Council. Moses was now having trouble getting Amite Negroes to attend registration classes. Finally, two weeks after the first attempt, a farmer named Curtis Dawson agreed to try to register, and an "old man known only as Preacher Knox jumped up to join him."[35] The next morning, August 29, they set off for the courthouse, but the sidewalk was blocked by three young White men. The leader of the posse was Billy Jack Caston, well known to Amite Negroes as the mercurial and violent son-in-law of segregationist leader E. H. Hurst, and the cousin of the Amite sheriff. Caston asked where they thought they were going; Moses said they were going to try to register. Caston then launched a savage attack on Moses that, as Taylor Branch chronicled, very nearly martyred him:

> . . . Moses felt himself separating from his body as he staggered on the sidewalk. He floated about ten feet up in the air so that he could watch the attack on himself comfortably. His fears became as remote as Caston's grunts, and time slowed down so that he could hear Preacher Knox running away on the sidewalk before he saw Caston slapping and shaking him. In peaceful surrender, he saw Caston hit him again behind the right temple, saw himself

34. Branch, *supra* note 21 of this chapter, at 494–95.
35. *Id.* at 497.

> sink to his knees, saw Caston drive his face to the pavement with a crushing blow to the top of the head. Through waves of concussion, he distinctly heard Curtis Dawson pleading with Caston to stop the beating.
>
> His first thoughts, upon hearing the feet of his attackers depart were that he could function in spite of his wounds and that it was urgently important to reach the courthouse. "We've got to go on to the registrar," he said, as Dawson struggled to overcome his horror at the sight of the blood flowing down from the gashes in Moses' head. "We can't let something like this stop us," said Moses. "That's the whole point."
>
> The county registrar reserved a practiced, well-what-have-we-got-here look for Negro customers, but it vanished in a gasp at the sight of Moses, whose bloody head and shirt combined with his serene, quiet voice to give him a presence as eerie as Banquo's ghost. The registrar gamely sought refuge in bursts of businesslike indifference, excessive politeness, and put-upon impatience, before all his bureaucratic poses collapsed under the weight of his nerves. He said he was closing the office and asked the three Negroes to leave.[36]

After receiving nine stitches in three separate head wounds, Moses was taken to a mass meeting at the Masonic Temple. Following the fiery oratory of others, Moses rose reluctantly to recount what had happened earlier in the day at the Liberty courthouse. Speaking in an almost inaudible voice to a stunned crowd, he announced that he intended to return to the courthouse the next day to swear out a complaint against Billy Jack Caston for criminal assault. Moses thought it imperative for him to act as if he and other Negroes had the same legal rights as all Whites in Mississippi. The jury, surrounded by an angry White mob, acquitted Caston in no time flat, but the more notable fact was that the conscience-stricken prosecutor went forward with the case knowing full well that it would imperil Moses' well-being and his own legal career in Amite County.[37]

Moses' first month in Mississippi ended with no registered Negro voters in Amite and very few new ones in Pike County. But many were now standing with him. Already his name "was acquiring a Christlike ring within SNCC," where the story was repeated that he had clasped his hands and looked heavenward during the Caston assault, saying "Forgive them." The story was apocryphal, but "[a]mong the legendary Freedom Riders, Moses himself was a budding legend," Branch wrote.[38] Enough so that when Doar later flew to Mississippi and met the man whose collect call he had taken after the first registration attempt in Liberty, he developed the highest regard for Moses' credibility and character. Doar, and

---

36. *Id.* at 497–98.
37. *Id.* at 498–99.
38. *Id.* at 500.

the Justice Department, were now acutely aware of what was happening on the ground in Mississippi. Although the department often could not provide Negroes in the voter registration movement as much protection as they wanted or needed, it gave them what Moses called a "crawl space" to get things started.[39] On August 29, 1962—the first anniversary of Billy Jack Caston's assault on Bob Moses, and five months after the Supreme Court's decision in *Baker v. Carr*—the Justice Department filed suit on behalf of the United States against the state of Mississippi, challenging its entire system of voter registration. The "adjudicated" Constitution and the "living" Constitution were starting, just starting, to come together.

* * *

The lead plaintiff in *Baker v. Carr* was Charles Baker, a Republican who lived in Shelby County, Tennessee. He claimed that the state legislature's persistent failure to enact any kind of reapportionment unconstitutionally diluted his vote. The last apportionment in Tennessee had taken place in 1901. By 1961, the population of Baker's district was roughly ten times the population of the sparsest rural districts in the state. The most populous state senate district had roughly five times as many people as the least populous senate district; the densest house district had about eighteen times as many people as the sparsest. Baker sued the Tennessee Secretary of State, Joe Carr, and other state officials for an injunction prohibiting them from conducting any further elections until there had been a reapportionment. Baker and his fellow plaintiffs, who were qualified voters in various other districts, sued as individuals and as representatives of "all other voters in the State of Tennessee." The complaint alleged that the plaintiffs had suffered "a debasement of their votes by virtue of the incorrect, arbitrary, obsolete and unconstitutional apportionment of the General Assembly." That malapportionment prevented the Tennessee Legislature from "being a body representative of the people of the State of Tennessee," was "contrary to the basic principle of representative government," and, most grandly, was "contrary to the philosophy of government in the United States and all Anglo-Saxon jurisprudence . . . ."[40]

The justices sparred over the legal meaning of these allegations. Frankfurter said they amounted to little more than a claim that Tennessee had violated the so-called Guarantee Clause of the federal constitution, which states: "The United States shall guarantee to every State in this Union a Republican form of government . . . ."[41] Frankfurter's opinion in *Colegrove* had found the Guarantee Clause to be "nonjusticiable," meaning unenforceable by the judiciary. In his majority opinion in *Baker*, Brennan acknowledged that the plaintiffs' Guarantee Clause claim was judicially unenforceable, but he insisted that the plaintiffs' principal

39. Moses, *supra* note 19 of this chapter, at 374.
40. 369 U.S. 274 (Frankfurter, J., dissenting).
41. U.S. Const., Art. 4, Sec. 4.

claim was under the Equal Protection Clause—and, in that capacity, enforceable. Frankfurter in turn acknowledged that the plaintiffs had styled their complaint as one under the Equal Protection Clause but insisted that "[i]t is, in effect, a Guarantee Clause claim masquerading under a different label."[42] But Warren, Black, and William O. Douglas were solidly with Brennan, who then carefully cultivated Potter Stewart to secure a majority. Brennan now had the votes to "dispel[] the fog" of *Colegrove*,[43] remove the political question doctrine as an impediment to judicially ordered reapportionment, and open the door to "one person, one vote." It would be difficult to overstate the impact of *Baker v. Carr* (and its famous progeny, *Reynolds v. Sims*[44]) on voting rights in America.

At the same time, Brennan's *Baker* opinion made an impact on the doctrine of standing, cutting in the other direction. One of the defendants' arguments had been that the plaintiffs lacked standing to sue. It was not one of their major arguments, and relatively little of the briefing had been devoted to it. Almost certainly what the defendants meant was that the plaintiffs' claim was what would today be called a "generalized grievance"—one belonging generally to the polity rather than to identifiable individuals. As we have seen, this was the line of precedents involving challenges to legislative action, such as *Fairchild* and *Frothingham*. Under these precedents, in order to establish that the plaintiffs had standing, Brennan needed to establish that the plaintiffs' claims in *Baker* were not in effect generalized grievances. The problem was that the Court had never said *precisely* what it was about the claims in *Fairchild* and *Frothingham* that had made them nonjusticiable; it had never defined what it meant for something to be a generalized grievance.[45] In *Fairchild*, the Court had made it clear that one's citizenship did not, in itself, give him standing to challenge any sort of government illegality. In *Frothingham*, the Court made it equally clear that one's status as a taxpayer did not, by itself, give her standing to challenge any sort of government expenditure. In each of these cases, the Court had found a lack of standing because of an insufficiently tight relationship between the claim and the claimant. But the Court never positively explained what made for a sufficient relationship.

Brennan had some choices available to him in explaining this relationship. One was not to explain it at all—he could have simply rested on the many voter cases in which the Court had assumed, without deciding, that the plaintiffs had standing to sue.[46] This would have been the most prudent course, as the briefs

42. 369 U.S. 297 (Frankfurter, J., dissenting).

43. Memorandum of William J. Brennan addressed to Chief Justice Warren and Justices Black and Douglas, Jan. 27, 1962 (Earl Warren Papers, Container 480, Library of Congress).

44. 377 U.S. 533 (1964).

45. *See* Mark Gabel, *Generalized Grievances and Judicial Discretion*, 58 HASTINGS L. J. 1331 (2007).

46. *See* cases cited at 369 U.S. at 206 fn. 26.

said little about standing. Another possibility would be to assert (as he would claim in the mid-1970s) that "personal stake" was merely a proxy for the sharpness of adversary presentation and sufficiency of litigating initiative critical to the adjudicative process. On this theory, if a plaintiff had a good-faith belief that he possessed a personal stake in the outcome of the controversy, this would suffice for standing. A third possibility (as one of his future law clerks, William A. Fletcher, later advocated[47]) would have been to say that a plaintiff's claim is *not* a "generalized grievance" so long as he has alleged the violation of a vested legal right belonging to him. On this interpretation, the plaintiff in *Fairchild* had no vested legal right not to have the Suffrage Amendment ratified; the plaintiff in *Frothingham* had no vested legal right not to have Congress subsidize infant mortality research by the states; the plaintiff in *Ex Parte Levitt* had no vested legal right that Hugo Black not be seated on the Supreme Court; and so on. By contrast, the plaintiffs in *Baker* clearly *did* have a vested legal right not to have the state arbitrarily dilute the strength of their votes. This approach would have had the virtue of unifying the Court's standing jurisprudence. Both challenges to legislative action and challenges to administrative agency action would then be judged by the same criterion for the purposes of standing analysis: has the plaintiff suffered a legal wrong? It also would have had the not inconsiderable virtue of bringing standing jurisprudence in line with the vested rights approach of John Marshall. But Brennan chose a different approach.

"Have the appellants alleged such a *personal stake in the outcome of the controversy* as to assure that concrete adverseness which sharpens the presentation of issues upon which the court so largely depends for illumination of difficult constitutional questions?" wrote Brennan. "This is the gist of the question of standing."[48] Brennan cited no authority for this assertion. The Court had never before referred to standing as a question of "personal stake in the outcome," and had certainly never before attempted to reduce the standing doctrine to a single sentence. On the contrary, Justice Frankfurter's statements in prior cases had insisted that the doctrine was too subtle, too finely nuanced to be domesticated as a proposition of black-letter law. Brennan's "personal stake" formulation represented a synthesis of dicta from prior cases.[49] In one case, for example, Justice Black had concluded that the plaintiffs had standing to sue because "they have been injured as individuals."[50] In the Child Labor Amendment case, the Court upheld the standing of senators to sue, saying that they had a "plain, direct, and

47. William A. Fletcher, *The Structure of Standing*, 98 YALE L. J. 221 (1988).

48. 369 U.S. at 204 (emphasis added).

49. Justice Brennan may also have been influenced by Solicitor General (and Harvard Law professor) Archibald Cox's Brief for the United States as Amicus Curiae in Support of Appellants, which used very similar language.

50. Colegrove v. Green, 328 U.S. 549, 568 (Black, J., dissenting).

adequate interest in maintaining the effectiveness of their votes."[51] Finally, Justice Brennan consulted *Marbury v. Madison*: "The very essence of civil liberty certainly consists in the right of every individual to claim the protection of the laws, whenever he receives an injury."[52]

If Brennan was going to try to capture the standing doctrine in a single verbal formulation, he may have felt that he had no choice but to use something like the "personal stake" standard. The Court in *Sanders Brothers* had held that the plaintiff needed to show "substantial impairment of a private interest" rather than violation of a "legal right." Subsequent to *Sanders Brothers*, several justices, including Douglas, had said that Congress had broad discretion to authorize judicial review of agency action, but that any plaintiff had to have a private interest of some sort. Moreover, Kenneth Culp Davis, the doyen of administrative law scholars, had written in his highly respected treatise that each plaintiff, while not required to demonstrate "legal injury," was required to show that he was "adversely affected in fact."[53] On the other hand, these statements were all made in the context of challenges to agency action, and *Baker* was not an agency case.

The precedents on the "generalized grievance" track could also been seen as requiring some kind of personal stake on the plaintiffs' part. The plaintiffs in *Fairchild* who feared that women might be permitted to vote in other states where women did not hold suffrage presumably were not motivated to sue by fear that their votes would be diluted. They rather transparently sued out of an ideological commitment to the notion that women ought not be allowed to vote. Mrs. Frothingham, the woman who could not abide the federal government funding infant mortality research by the states, was presumably not worried about the indeterminable number of pennies that the program cost her in additional tax liability per year. She apparently held a fervent belief in a certain version of federalism. Neither had anything to gain but the satisfaction that one gains from the political tide turning one's way. The plaintiffs in *Baker*, on the other hand, had something selfish to gain from their challenge of reapportionment. Surely ideology was an important, perhaps indispensable, motivating factor behind the lawsuit. But there was also something undeniably selfish about it. If the prayed-for reapportionment were granted, the plaintiffs' political power would be greatly enhanced. The comparison of *Baker* to *Fairchild* and *Frothingham* is complicated by the fact that *Baker* was styled as a class action, but it is not difficult to see the narrowly selfish interest in *Baker* that is missing from the other two cases.

Adoption of the "personal stake" formulation for standing, then, got Justice Brennan where he wanted to go in the immediate case. Whether or not it was compelled by precedent, it was convenient here. But endorsement of the

51. 369 U.S. at 208, quoting Coleman v. Miller, 307 U.S. 433, 438 (1939).
52. 369 U.S. at 208, quoting Marbury v. Madison, 1 Cranch 137, 163 (1803).
53. Kenneth Culp Davis, Administrative Law Treatise, Sec. 22.02 (1958).

"personal stake" standard had unanticipated intellectual consequences. It divided self-interested plaintiffs from ideologically driven plaintiffs and recognized standing only in the former. Mere concerned bystanders, motivated only by altruism, need not apply. One cannot help but think that Brennan, the liberal lion, did not have this in mind. In a footnote, Justice Brennan observed that the plaintiffs purported to sue on behalf of "all other voters" in Tennessee. "This may be read to assert a claim that voters in counties allegedly over-represented in the General Assembly also have standing to complain," Brennan remarked. "But it is not necessary to decide that question in this case."[54] It is possible that Brennan believed in a process of self-government in which all voters had an indivisible stake, and therefore that even those whose votes were illegally *inflated* had a "personal stake" in the integrity of the process. It is possible that he intended to announce in an appropriate future case that some subset of litigation purely in pursuit of the "public interest" would fulfill the "personal stake" requirement. As we shall see in the next chapter, however, that is not how other justices came to perceive it.

Somewhat surprisingly, the Court did not return to the question of standing for the next six years, when it decided *Flast v. Cohen*[55] in 1968.[56] *Flast* was the Warren Court's lone effort to defang the standing doctrine and thereby render it harmless toward the public law litigation that the Court was then encouraging through its decisions on equal protection and procedural due process. But tactical errors and a lack of follow-through doomed the effort.

The plaintiffs in *Flast* claimed that federal funds were being used to finance "instruction in reading, arithmetic and other subjects and for guidance in religious and sectarian schools."[57] These expenditures violated the Establishment Clause, the plaintiffs argued, and they prayed for a judicial declaration either that these expenditures were not authorized by the relevant congressional appropriations statute or, if Congress had authorized the expenditures, it had done so unconstitutionally. A three-judge district court was convened to decide the standing question. It dismissed the complaint on standing grounds, and the plaintiffs appealed directly to the Supreme Court.

Chief Justice Warren's opinion for the Court began by taking *Frothingham* head-on. Although the Court had accepted jurisdiction in three taxpayer suits

---

54. 369 U.S. 205 fn. 24.

55. 392 U.S. 83 (1968).

56. It may be significant that there was no true "liberal" majority on the Warren Court until 1967, when Thurgood Marshall was appointed. Arthur Goldberg's replacement of Felix Frankfurter in 1962 would have created such a liberal majority but for Hugo Black's turn to the right around that time. *See* MORTON J. HORWITZ, THE WARREN COURT AND THE PURSUIT OF JUSTICE (1999).

57. 392 U.S. at 87.

prior to *Frothingham* without passing on the standing question,[58] it had since treated *Frothingham* as an absolute barrier to taxpayer suits. Was it really an absolute barrier? Warren asked. The government argued that *Frothingham* announced a constitutional rule, compelled by Article III limits on jurisdiction, and, more generally, separation of powers. The plaintiffs, on the other hand, argued that *Frothingham* represented a prudential doctrine of self-restraint on the Court's part. Warren found a textual analysis of the *Frothingham* opinion inconclusive: it "can be read to support either position."[59]

Unable to determine the scope and status of the *Frothingham* doctrine by analysis of the opinion, Warren turned to a general examination of the concept of justiciability. He characterized justiciability as "the term of art" used to describe the principles underlying the "case or controversy" requirement of Article III. In turn, he identified two such principles:

> Embodied in the words "cases" and "controversies" are two complementary but somewhat different limitations. In part those words limit the business of federal courts to questions presented in an adversary context and in a form historically viewed as capable of resolution through the judicial process. And in part those words define the role assigned to the judiciary in a tripartite allocation of power to assure that the federal courts will not intrude into areas committed to the other branches of government.[60]

In other words, the "case or controversy" requirement has two functions. One is procedural—to limit litigation to forms that courts are competent to deal with. The other is political—to check the powers of the federal judiciary and keep them separate from the powers of the other two branches. One possible way to realize these functions would be to stick closely to the practices of English common law courts at the time of the Founding. Although it is far from clear that the argument is correct, one might claim that such well-established practices had been proven to ensure both judicial administrability and compatibility with legislative sovereignty. Indeed, Justice Frankfurter had implied as much in his lengthy *Joint Anti-Fascist Committee* excursus on justiciability. Chief Justice Warren obviously recognized Frankfurter's historical thesis as a threat to the continued development of public law litigation in federal courts. He attempted to make short work of Frankfurter's thesis by citing the advisory opinions doctrine. "The power of English judges to deliver advisory opinions was well established at the time the Constitution was drafted," Warren wrote.[61] "Yet," he continued, "the oldest and most consistent thread in the federal law of

---

58. 392 U.S. at 91 n.5.

59. 392 U.S. at 93. He did note, however, that the weight of academic commentary favored the view that it was a prudential rule. *See* 392 U.S. 92 n.6.

60. 392 U.S. at 95.

61. 392 U.S. 96.

justiciability is that the federal court will not give advisory opinions."[62] Thus the advisory opinion could not be explained by mere history, Warren concluded, but only by reference to the two functional principles underlying Article III that Warren had previously identified. The citation of a single anomalous practice by English courts had hardly demolished Frankfurter's argument, but Warren evidently viewed it as sufficient to shift the battleground from history to policy.

The question was now joined. How could the Court view a taxpayer action like *Frothingham* or *Flast* as consistent with the notion of separation of powers (the second principle that Warren had identified with justiciability)? The government's position in *Flast* was that the lawsuit presented the federal courts with nothing more than a political disagreement with how taxpayer monies should be spent. "[T]he resolution of such disagreements is committed to other branches of the Federal Government and not to the judiciary," the government argued.[63] In essence, the government's position was that the lawsuit presented a political question.

Chief Justice Warren seized on this implied characterization of the problem. The question before the Court was whether the plaintiffs had standing, not whether the subject matter of the litigation presented a nonjusticiable political question. For the first time, the Supreme Court was drawing a bright line between one justiciability doctrine and another:

> The fundamental aspect of standing is that it focuses on the party seeking to get his complaint before a federal court and not on the issues he wishes to have adjudicated. The "gist of the question of standing" is whether the party seeking relief has "alleged such a personal stake in the outcome of the controversy as to assure that concrete adverseness which sharpens the presentation of issues upon which the court so largely depends for illumination of difficult constitutional questions. *Baker v. Carr.*" In other words, when standing is placed in issue in a case, the question is whether the person whose standing is challenged is a proper party to request an adjudication of a particular issue and not whether the issue itself is justiciable. Thus, a party may have standing in a particular case, but the federal court may nevertheless decline to pass on the merits of the case because, for example, it presents a political question. . . . The question whether a particular person is a proper party to maintain the action does not, by its own force, raise separation of powers problems related to improper judicial interference in areas committed to other branches of the Federal Government. Such problems arise, if at all, only from the substantive issues the individual seeks to have adjudicated.[64]

62. *Id.*
63. 392 U.S. at 98.
64. 392 U.S. at 99–101.

This is an extraordinarily important passage. To begin with, it established for the first time that standing is a matter of the "who" rather than the "what." Previous cases had generally failed to maintain this distinction. Second, the opinion accepted the "personal stake" test of *Baker v. Carr* as the barometer of whether a given plaintiff was an appropriate person to sue. This effectively cemented the distinction between self-interested and altruistic plaintiffs as the dividing line between plaintiffs with and without standing. Third, the opinion sought to dissociate standing from separation of powers considerations, as opposed to the political question and advisory opinion doctrines. Separation of powers was impacted by the "what" (subject matter) and "how" (adversary form) of federal court litigation, but not by the "who," Chief Justice Warren asserted. Finally, because a taxpayer "may or may not have the requisite personal stake in the outcome, depending upon the circumstances of the particular case," there could be no absolute bar to taxpayer suits. The only remaining question was, under what circumstances could such suits be maintained?

It was here that Chief Justice Warren propounded his famous "logical nexus" test. A taxpayer would only be granted standing to sue in federal court when there was a sufficient "logical nexus between the status asserted and the claim sought to be adjudicated."[65] This test yielded two requirements for taxpayer plaintiffs. First, "a taxpayer will be a proper party to allege the unconstitutionality only of exercises of congressional power under the taxing and spending clause of Art. I, Section 8, of the Constitution."[66] This limitation on taxpayer standing had the virtue of distinguishing *Doremus,* in which the plaintiff had attacked the "incidental expenditure of tax funds in the administration of an essentially regulatory statute."[67] Second, the taxpayer plaintiff had to allege that the expenditure of tax monies violated "specific constitutional limitations imposed upon the . . . taxing and spending power, and not simply that the enactment is generally beyond the powers delegated to Congress by Art. I, Section 8."[68] This second limitation on taxpayer standing served to distinguish *Frothingham,* in which the plaintiff had challenged the legislation as exceeding Congress's enumerated powers.[69] The *Flast* majority had carefully crafted this dual limitation on taxpayer standing to avoid the formal overruling of *Doremus* and *Frothingham.*

At the same time, the dual limitation had been painstakingly contoured to admit the case at bar. The *Flast* plaintiffs were challenging an aid-to-schools program that had been enacted pursuant to the taxing and spending clause of

65. 392 U.S. at 102.

66. *Id.*

67. *Id.*

68. 392 U.S. at 103.

69. Although it should be noted that the plaintiff in *Frothingham* also challenged the legislation under the Tenth Amendment—a fact that Chief Justice Warren conveniently ignored.

Art. I, Section 8. Furthermore, they had alleged that the program violated the Establishment Clause, which (according to the Court) was meant to place a specific limit on Congress's taxing and spending powers. It was not simply a claim that Congress generally lacked the authority to pass this type of legislation. Chief Justice Warren declined to speculate about what other provisions in the Bill of Rights might also represent specific limits on the taxing and spending power: "Whether the Constitution contains other specific limitations can be determined only in the context of future cases."[70] Warren's refusal to name other constitutional provisions under which taxpayer plaintiffs could sue was undoubtedly influenced by the positions of Justices Stewart and Abe Fortas, who in separate concurrences explicitly stated that their votes were premised on the understanding that taxpayer suits in federal court were limited to challenges under the Establishment Clause.[71] (Justice Douglas would have gone the opposite direction and overruled *Frothingham* altogether.[72])

Justice Harlan's dissent exposed the intellectual defects of the majority's "logical nexus" test. The problem, in short, was that nothing in the test served to ferret out any possible "personal stake" that the plaintiff might have in the controversy. Reviewing the majority's dual limitation on taxpayer standing, Harlan commented:

> The difficulties with these criteria are many and severe, but it is enough for the moment to emphasize that they are not in any sense a measurement of any plaintiff's interest in the outcome of any suit. . . .
>
> It is surely clear that a plaintiff's interest in the outcome of a suit in which he challenges the constitutionality of a federal expenditure is not made greater or smaller by the unconnected fact that the expenditure is, or is not, "incidental" to an "essentially regulatory" program. . . .
>
> The Court's second criterion is similarly unrelated to its standard for the determination of standing. The intensity of a plaintiff's interest in a suit is not measured, even obliquely, by the fact that the constitutional provision under which he claims is, or is not, a "specific limitation" upon Congress' spending powers.[73]

Turning to his own analysis, Harlan began by dividing plaintiffs into two categories: Hohfeldian and non-Hohfeldian.[74] A Hohfeldian plaintiff was one who held "the personal and proprietary interests of the traditional plaintiff,"

70. 392 U.S. at 105.

71. 392 U.S. at 114 (Stewart, J., concurring); 392 U.S. at 115 (Fortas, J., concurring).

72. 392 U.S. at 107 (Douglas, J., concurring).

73. 392 U.S. at 120–22 (Harlan, J., dissenting).

74. 392 U.S. at 119 and n.5 (Harlan, J., dissenting). Harlan borrowed the phraseology from Professor Stanley Jaffe, who had coined it in tribute to the ideas of Professor Wesley N. Hohfeld.

while a non-Hohfeldian plaintiff was one who held "the representative and public interests of the plaintiff in a public action."[75] To put it most simply, a Hohfeldian plaintiff is one who sues in pursuit of his personal self-interest, while a non-Hohfeldian plaintiff is one who sues out of altruistic motives. Like the *Flast* majority, Harlan was unwilling to find that Article III absolutely prohibited lawsuits by non-Hohfeldian plaintiffs, whether taxpayers or otherwise. The Court's long-standing tolerance of actions by "private attorneys general" made it too difficult for Harlan to sustain such an absolute ban.[76] Thus, as with the majority, the question became one of how to ascertain *which* non-Hohfeldian plaintiffs ought to be granted standing. Because he had already laid bare the incoherence of the majority's test for identifying such plaintiffs, Harlan offered his own. "This Court has previously held that individual litigants have standing to represent the public interest, despite their lack of economic or other personal interests, if Congress has appropriately authorized such suits," Harlan wrote. "I would adhere to that principle."[77] The courts should wait for the most majoritarian branch of government to approve this subspecies of lawsuits, which so "strain the judicial function and press to the limit judicial authority."[78]

* * *

The greatest twist in standing doctrine was yet to come. In 1970, in the companion cases of *Data Processing Assn. v. Camp*[79] and *Barlow v. Collins*,[80] the Court upheld standing to challenge administrative action in cases where the plaintiffs could not have met the "legal interest" test of *Edward Hines* and its progeny. Without confronting any of the cases in that line of authority by name, Justice Douglas's *tour de force* majority opinion curtly stated that the "legal interest" test "goes to the merits" and not to the question of standing. Instead, he asserted, the question of standing consists of asking whether the plaintiff has alleged "injury-in-fact." So long as the plaintiff properly alleged that the agency action caused him real-world harm, it was irrelevant to the standing inquiry whether that action also invaded some protected legal interest held by the plaintiff. Douglas' "injury-in-fact" test immediately derived from the "personal stake" formulation of *Baker v. Carr* (by way of *Flast v. Cohen*) and, more remotely, from *Sanders Brothers*.[81] If a plaintiff had suffered real-world injury, he perforce had a personal stake in the outcome of a lawsuit. The common law might or might not have supplied him

75. 392 U.S. at 119 (Harlan, J., dissenting).

76. *See generally* Evan Caminker, *The Constitutionality of Qui Tam Actions*, 99 Yale L. J. 341 (1989).

77. 392 U.S. at 131 (Harlan, J., dissenting).

78. 392 U.S. at 130 (Harlan, J., dissenting).

79. 397 U.S. 150 (1970).

80. 397 U.S. 159 (1970).

81. As well as from Ken Davis's scholarship. *See* Kenneth Culp Davis, Administrative Law Treatise, Sec. 22.02 (1958).

with a remedy; he might or might not have suffered a deprivation of liberty or property. None of this was relevant under the "injury-in-fact" test. He was personally injured ("aggrieved") by agency action, and thus Congress had entitled him to a remedy.

For the first time, the Court had unified the test for standing to sue. "Injury-in-fact" was now required of all plaintiffs, whether challenging legislative or agency action. But did this change actually increase access to federal court, as the Court's liberals believed? On the agency side, the effect was mixed. Regulated parties could now challenge agency action to protect a competitive advantage that the previous regulatory regime had given them. Their inability to show that the common law would have protected that competitive advantage no longer disqualified them from suing. On the other hand, the "injury-in-fact" requirement significantly limited Congress' ability to authorize the intended beneficiaries of statutes to challenge agency action. So long as the Court interpreted "injury-in-fact" as requiring harm to the plaintiff's *selfish* interests, those who had lobbied for the legislation out of altruistic motives (say, environmentalists) were largely excluded from suing for judicial review. After *Camp*, the courts would have the final say on standing in agency cases. Even if Congress authorized "any aggrieved person" to sue, that person would have to demonstrate that the agency action caused him "injury-in-fact"—a matter for the courts to decide. The legal scholar Cass Sunstein has referred to "injury-in-fact" as "pre-legal injury," meaning that judges are left to use their own personal values to decide what constitutes "harm," as opposed to allowing legislatures to make that determination.[82]

There was more. In addition to "injury-in-fact," the *Camp* majority set forth another requirement for those wishing to challenge agency action. The plaintiff also had to "arguably fall[] within the zone of interests" meant to be protected by the statute. This "zone of interests" inquiry was not, like the injury-in-fact inquiry, mandated by the "case or controversy" requirement of Article III. The Court was adopting it as a prudential matter. The plaintiff in *Camp* easily satisfied it, as the Court determined that the enabling statute was meant to protect those who, like the plaintiff, suffered some kind of competitive injury.[83]

Justice Brennan, joined by Justice White, dissented from the majority's adoption of the "zone of interests" test as a supplement to the "injury-in-fact" test in cases challenging agency action. Brennan was happy to see "injury-in-fact" replace the *Edward Hines* "legal right" or "legal interest" test, as it meant that his "personal stake" formulation from *Baker* was being carried forward. But he was

---

82. Cass Sunstein, *Standing and the Privatization of Public Law*, 88 Colum. L. Rev. 1432, 1451–60. Sunstein points out that "there is no prepolitical or prelegal way to decide who is a bystander" for purposes of standing analysis, *id.* at 1436 n. 18.

83. The Court followed *Assn. of Data Processors v. Camp* in *Arnold Tours v. Camp*, 400 U.S. 45 (1970), and *Investment Company Institute v. Camp*, 401 U.S. 617 (1971), both of which also involved claims of competitive injury.

genuinely puzzled by this additional "zone of interests" requirement. Was it not effectively the same thing as the "legal right" test that had just been discarded? Under both the "zone of interests" test and the "legal right" test, the Court was asking whether the plaintiff was entitled to some kind of judicial remedy against the challenged agency action. Whether the protected interest was inferred from the utterances of common law judges or legislators, the very process of inference was a matter pertaining to the merits and not to the threshold inquiry of standing. "The Court's approach does too little to guard against the possibility that judges will use standing to slam the courthouse door against plaintiffs who are entitled to full consideration of their claims on the merits," Brennan complained.[84]

Brennan had miscalculated. It was not Douglas' "zone of interests" test that would end up slamming the courthouse door. It was the "injury-in-fact" requirement, channeled through Brennan's own "personal stake" formulation, that ended up posing a formidable obstacle to civil rights, civil liberties, and other public interest plaintiffs. By 1970, the major social and constitutional issues of the day had revealed themselves to be, on some level, claims of group or collective rights. Race and gender equality, abortion, school busing, the environment, even the legality of the Vietnam War, were all intelligible as issues where a group of people claimed to suffer a collective harm because of illegal government conduct. Whether or not "group rights" has any coherence as an intellectual concept, surely the perception among judges, lawyers, and the general public was that groups of people were making certain claims to rights. As a matter of litigation practicality, it was clear that courts had to have the capacity to deal with such claims of collective harm and/or collective rights, as exemplified by the explosion in federal court practice with class actions. And yet the "injury-in-fact" test, undergirded by the more general idea of "personal stake," moved the federal courts in precisely the opposite direction. Here was a norm that viewed plaintiffs exclusively as individuals rather than as members of larger groups. The injury-in-fact test required that a plaintiff in federal court allege a harm to himself as an individual, not merely as a member of a group that has suffered some collective harm. The test was designed to harness self-interest as a source of locomotion for the litigation process, not altruism or abstract political ideals. This being true, one can only wonder why Justice Brennan thought that the next two decades of standing cases would come out any differently than they did.

84. 397 U.S. at 178 (opinion of Brennan, J.).

7. THE TRIUMPH OF SELF-INTEREST

From the time of the decisions in *Camp* and *Barlow* in 1970 until his retirement in 1990, William Brennan lost the vast majority of battles he fought in the standing and other justiciability cases. The subject matter of those cases ranged from the environment, through welfare rights and the legality of the Vietnam War, to discriminatory police practices and affirmative action in higher education. Of course, the composition of the Court changed substantially in the first Nixon administration, with Warren Burger replacing Earl Warren, Harry Blackmun replacing Abe Fortas, Lewis Powell replacing Hugo Black, and William Rehnquist replacing John Harlan. Not all of these changes were seismic; Brennan was eventually able to cultivate Blackmun as a reliable ally in the justiciability cases, and Rehnquist was not drastically more conservative than Harlan had been in that area. But many of Brennan's defeats came in 5–4 or 6–3 decisions, where one or two more votes would have made the difference.

The tables began to turn on Brennan in *Sierra Club v. Morton*, a 1972 case involving proposed development in the Mineral King Valley, nestled in the Sierra Nevadas on the California side.[1] Mineral King had once been the site of extensive mining activity but long since had become a mecca for campers and conservationists. Emblematic of the consumerism of the post-war period, the U.S. Forest Service solicited bids from private developers for a ski resort that would double as a recreation area in the summer. The high bidder was Walt Disney Enterprises, Inc., which proposed a complex of motels, restaurants, swimming pools, parking lots, ski lifts, ski trails, and a railway. To provide electricity to the resort, there would be a high-voltage power line cutting through Sequoia National Park. Finally, to get people to the resort, the State of California proposed a twenty-mile long highway, also cutting through the park. In January 1969, the Forest Service approved this plan, over the longstanding and repeated objections of the Sierra Club and other conservationists.

In June 1969, the Sierra Club sued the Secretary of the Interior and the Forest Service for an injunction prohibiting them from issuing final permits necessary for development of Mineral King. The complaint in federal district court in San Francisco described the plaintiff, Sierra Club, as a membership corporation with a "special interest in the conservation and the sound maintenance of the national parks, game refuges and forests of the country."[2] The district court granted the injunction, but the Court of Appeals for the Ninth Circuit reversed, finding that

1. 405 U.S. 727.
2. 405 U.S. at 730.

the Sierra Club lacked standing to sue. In the Ninth Circuit's view, the complaint failed to allege that individual members of the Sierra Club would be personally affected by the proposed development, other than that they would find it "personally displeasing or distasteful."

With new members Powell and Rehnquist sitting on the sidelines—they had been confirmed too late to participate in the decision—the Court agreed 4–3 that the Sierra Club lacked standing. Writing for the majority, Justice Potter Stewart confirmed that, following *Camp* and *Barlow*, the question was whether the Sierra Club properly alleged that it had suffered "injury-in-fact." In *Camp* and *Barlow*, the plaintiffs had suffered economic injury—loss of the competitive advantage they enjoyed under the prior regulatory regime. Clearly, economic injury constituted injury-in-fact. Indeed, any kind of property or liberty interest traditionally protected at common law qualified as injury-in-fact. Here, however, the plaintiffs claimed what Stewart characterized as "aesthetic and environmental" injury. The complaint alleged that the development "would destroy or otherwise adversely affect the scenery, natural and historic objects and wildlife of the park and would impair the enjoyment of the park for future generations." Whether that sort of noneconomic injury qualified as injury-in-fact was a question of first impression.

Perhaps surprisingly, the majority accepted this allegation as injury-in-fact with no resistance whatsoever. Stewart approvingly noted a trend of recent cases in the U.S. Court of Appeals for the District of Columbia Circuit in which noneconomic harm had been held sufficient to sustain a challenge to agency action. "Aesthetic and environmental well-being, like economic well-being, are important ingredients of the quality of life in our society," wrote Stewart. But there was a problem in this case: the Sierra Club had failed to allege that any of its individual members used, or would use, Mineral King. Aesthetic injury might qualify as "injury-in-fact," but only if suffered by the plaintiff. "[B]roadening the categories of injury that may be alleged in support of standing is a different matter from abandoning the requirement that the party seeking review must himself have suffered an injury," according to Stewart. Justice Byron White, who joined Stewart's majority opinion, was reported to have said privately, "Why didn't the Sierra Club have one goddamn member walk through the park and then there would have been standing to sue."[3]

The dissenters were thrown off balance, partly by the loss of the usually liberal Thurgood Marshall to the majority, partly by the fact that Stewart's opinion had hoisted William O. Douglas and William Brennan on their collective petard. "Injury-in-fact" was Douglas' literary work, derived from "personal stake," penned by Brennan. Stewart had done nothing more than give those terms their

---

3. Bob Woodward & Scott Armstrong, The Brethren: Inside the Supreme Court 164 fn. * (Simon & Schuster 1979).

ordinary meaning in common parlance. Whatever might qualify as injury-in-fact, the plaintiff had to suffer it personally. Douglas, the lover of the outdoors who fled back to Yakima, Washington, as soon as each Supreme Court term came to an end, wrote a florid and emotional—some would say over-the-top—dissent. He proposed that the law of standing be modified to allow environmental issues to be litigated "in the name of the inanimate object about to be despoiled, defaced, or invaded by roads and bulldozers and where injury is the subject of public outrage."[4] "This suit would therefore be more properly labeled as Mineral King v. Morton," wrote Douglas. But, aside from its superficial implausibility, Douglas' proposal solved nothing. Even if inanimate objects were given standing to sue, a person or persons would still have to institute the lawsuit on their behalf—but *which* person or persons? All Douglas's proposal did was to postpone the question. Even Brennan could not bring himself to join Douglas's dissent, instead joining Blackmun's.

"If this were an ordinary case, I would join the [majority] opinion and the Court's judgment and be quite content," began Blackmun, foregoing any frontal attack. But the environment was not an ordinary problem. Striking a highly pragmatic tone that he would bring to the justiciability area for the remainder of his tenure on the Court, Blackmun chided the majority for taking the doctrine too seriously. "Must our law be so rigid and our procedural concepts so inflexible that we render ourselves helpless when the existing methods and the traditional concepts do not quite fit and do not prove to be entirely adequate for new issues?" he asked.[5] Blackmun was ready to try a new approach, which had recently been proposed by two prominent federal courts of appeals. In a case called *Citizens Committee for the Hudson Valley v. Volpe*,[6] the influential Second Circuit had found that a citizens' environmental protection organization had standing to challenge federal agency action "as responsible representatives of the public." Where agency action is alleged to have harmed the public interest, the court reasoned, appropriate representatives of the public interest have standing to challenge it in federal court, so long as Congress has seen fit to authorize the litigation. (The Second Circuit's opinion in *Volpe* made no mention of the new "injury-in-fact" test that had been handed down by the Supreme Court in *Camp* and *Barlow* only six weeks before.) Shortly after *Volpe* was handed down, David Bazelon, the liberal powerhouse chief judge of the District of Columbia Circuit, delivered his opinion in *Environmental Defense Fund v. Hardin*.[7] There, several pro-environment groups including the Sierra Club sued to challenge the Secretary of Agriculture's refusal to stop the interstate shipment of the pesticide

4. 405 U.S. at 741 (Douglas, J., dissenting), citing Christopher Stone, *Should Trees Have Standing?—Toward Legal Rights for Natural Objects*, 45 S. Cal. L. Rev. 450 (1972).

5. 405 U.S. at 755–56 (Blackmun, J., dissenting).

6. 425 F.2d 97, 105 (2d Cir., 1970).

7. 428 F.2d 1093 (D.C. Cir., 1970).

DDT, which had been found to have harmful effects on humans and animals. Bazelon's opinion dutifully cited the new "injury-in-fact" test, but made no real attempt to engage it intellectually. People who unwillingly consume DDT residue have standing to sue, he asserted uncontroversially. The problem was, these plaintiff organizations had not alleged that their individual members actually had consumed or would consume DDT residue. Bazelon then went on to find standing on the same theory advanced by the *Volpe* court: "Consumers of regulated products and services have standing to protect the public interest in the proper administration of a regulatory system enacted for their benefit."[8] Furthermore, Bazelon asserted, those consumers did not have to sue in their own name—they could be represented by organizations like the Environmental Defense Fund and the Sierra Club. "[T]he consumers' interest in environmental protection may properly be represented by a membership association with an organizational interest in the problem."

Although he cited neither *Volpe* nor *Hardin*, Justice Blackmun (joined by Justice Brennan) appeared to have something similar in mind. "I would permit an imaginative expansion of our traditional concepts of standing" in order to enable a bona fide environmental organization like the Sierra Club to litigate environmental issues, he wrote. Without saying it, Blackmun was endorsing the following reasoning: where the public is injured, the public has standing to sue for redress. Environmental degradation was a paradigm form of public injury. The *Volpe* and *Hardin* decisions operated on the same reasoning. Justice Stewart's majority opinion rejected this reasoning for lack of a principled stopping place. "[I]f any group with a bona fide 'special interest' could initiate such litigation, it is difficult to perceive why any individual citizen with the same bona fide special interest would not also be entitled to do so," Stewart wrote. Blackmun's response provided Stewart with little comfort. He had suggested that there should be no fear of opening a "Pandora's Box," for "the courts will exercise appropriate restraints just as they have exercised them in the past."[9]

In the end, there was something seemingly irreconcilable about the Stewart and Blackmun views. They were based on different conceptions of the proper occasions for judicial review. Stewart closed his opinion with a quote from Tocqueville: "[B]y leaving it to private interest to censure the law, and by intimately uniting the trial of the law with the trial of an individual, legislation is protected from wanton assaults and from the daily aggressions of party spirit."[10] Presumably what Tocqueville meant was that, without something like a "personal stake" requirement, the losing party in the legislature could always appeal to the courts. If private interest is required to sue, then the eligible pool of plaintiffs shrinks considerably, and in some cases there is no pool at all. The legislative

8. 428 F.2d at 1097.
9. 405 U.S. at 758 (Blackmun, J., dissenting).
10. 405 U.S. at 740.

process is left completely intact. Blackmun, by contrast, closed his opinion with John Donne: "No man is an Iland, intire of itself . . . And therefore never send to know for whom the bell tolls; it tolls for thee." Whatever validity a public-private distinction might have at the poles, surely it broke down at the margins. In the case of residual pesticide toxins transmitted by countless different vehicles, or the degradation of lands regarded as public treasures, what did it really mean to insist upon the presence of a "private interest"? Such a notion was virtually incoherent.

A scant three weeks after *Sierra Club* was announced, a group formed by five law students in Washington, D.C., filed suit in federal district court against the United States, requesting an injunction that would in effect have prohibited the nation's railroads from levying a 2.5 percent surcharge that the railroads claimed was necessary to avert financial collapse.[11] The student group called itself Students Challenging Regulatory Agency Procedures (SCRAP) and teamed up with more established environmental groups for litigation purposes. They alleged that the surcharge would discourage use of recyclable materials and thereby promote use of new raw materials, in turn harming the environment by increasing mining, logging, and other "extractive" activities. The complaint further alleged that individual members of the plaintiff organizations were forced to pay more for finished products, suffered impairment in the use of forests and streams because of unnecessary destruction of timber and extraction of raw materials, and the accumulation of otherwise recyclable materials. For its part, the railroad pointed out that the surcharge was nondiscriminatory, and therefore would not have a disproportionate impact on recyclables. The three-judge panel issued the requested injunction.

The students had done their homework on the standing issue. Their complaint assiduously adhered to the pleading template that Justice Stewart had in effect laid out in *Sierra Club*. The trouble with the Sierra Club's complaint was not that "aesthetic" or "environmental" injury was metaphysically too squishy or epistemologically too uncertain. The problem was that the Sierra Club had failed to allege that the injury, however squishy or uncertain, extended to at least some of its individual members. SCRAP and its fellow plaintiff organizations were careful to avoid that mistake. "[T]hey point specifically to the allegations that their members used the forests, streams, mountains, and other resources in the Washington metropolitan area for camping, hiking, fishing, and sightseeing, and that this use was disturbed by the adverse environmental impact caused by the nonuse of recyclable goods brought about by a rate increase on those commodities," wrote Stewart approvingly.[12] The student plaintiffs had passed their first exam, as it were.

---

11. United States v. Students Challenging Regulatory Agency Procedures (SCRAP), 412 U.S. 669 (1973).

12. 412 U.S. at 685.

There was a second, and intellectually more challenging, exam that awaited them. The complaint effectively alleged that the surcharge had an adverse environmental impact on all natural resources nationwide. "Rather than a limited group of persons who used a picturesque valley in California," Stewart noted, "all persons who utilize the scenic resources of the country, and indeed all who breathe its air, could claim [similar] harm." If one were to read *Fairchild* and *Frothingham* as having denied standing on the theory that the claimed injuries were too widely shared, it was certainly plausible that the plaintiffs in SCRAP had a similar problem. Yet Justice Stewart made surprisingly quick work of the generalized grievance argument. "[S]tanding is not to be denied simply because many people suffer the same injury," he stated firmly. "To deny standing to persons who are in fact injured simply because many others are also injured, would mean that the most injurious and widespread Government actions could be questioned by nobody. We cannot accept that conclusion."[13] Stewart had not mentioned, much less analyzed, a single one of the cases in the *Fairchild/Frothingham* line.

The plaintiffs in *SCRAP* ultimately succumbed to a finding that the district court lacked jurisdiction under the relevant environmental statute to issue the injunction. This holding left undisturbed the Court's finding that they had standing to sue. But the enduring effect of *SCRAP* may have come from Justice White's dissent. "The majority acknowledges that these allegations reflect an 'attenuated line of causation,' but is willing to suspend its judgment in the dim hope that proof at trial will in some unexplained way flesh them out and establish the necessary nexus between" the plaintiffs and the complained-of surcharges, White wrote. "To me, the alleged injuries are so remote, speculative, and insubstantial in fact that they fail to confer standing." Responding on behalf of the majority, Justice Stewart conceded that "pleadings must be something more than an ingenious academic exercise in the conceivable," but he insisted that such was not the case with SCRAP and its fellow plaintiffs. "We cannot say on these pleadings that the [plaintiffs] could not prove their allegations...."[14]

White's point about the "attenuated line of causation" had not prevailed in *SCRAP*, but it would soon become the law. It was not enough that a plaintiff allege that he suffers an injury-in-fact; the plaintiff also had to allege that, if not for the defendant's offending conduct, the plaintiff would not have suffered the injury. In other words, the plaintiff had to show that the defendant's allegedly illegal behavior was the legal cause of the plaintiff's injury. One's instinct might be that this requirement of causation, normally associated with the common law of torts, is out of place in the law of federal court jurisdiction. In fact, however, it flowed directly from Justice Brennan's "personal stake" formulation.

13. 412 U.S. at 687–88.
14. 412 U.S. 689–90.

Suppose that a plaintiff properly alleges an injury-in-fact, but that the injury has nothing to do with the defendant's allegedly offending conduct—it has an entirely different cause. How can it then be said that the plaintiff has a personal stake in the outcome of *this* controversy between him and *this* defendant? He has no stake in the outcome of this controversy at all, because his real fight is with someone else.

The same point could, and would, be made concerning the relationship between the claimed injury and the relief requested by the plaintiff. In order for the "personal stake" requirement to be met, there had to be a direct relationship between injury and relief. The Court said as much the very next term in *Linda R.S. v. Richard D.*[15] An unmarried mother in Texas wanted the father to pay child support, but he refused. She had no legal leverage over him, as the Texas courts had consistently interpreted the criminal child support statute to apply only to the parents of legitimate children. She then sued in federal district court for an order that would have prohibited Texas prosecutors from discriminating between parents of legitimate and illegitimate children in seeking child support payments, but the three-judge panel dismissed her complaint for want of standing.

The Supreme Court affirmed the dismissal, 5–4. Justice Thurgood Marshall wrote for the majority, finding that the relationship between the alleged injury and the requested relief was too attenuated to support standing. If the plaintiff had won on the merits, the best she could have done would be to obtain an order requiring the local prosecutor to secure a criminal conviction of the deadbeat dad. Justice Marshall noted that this would not have been a matter of civil contempt, in which case payment of the delinquent child support would have earned the father his release. A criminal conviction would produce a fixed jail term punishing his past behavior, whether or not he eventually came around and made good. Thus, Marshall concluded, "[t]he prospect that prosecution will, at least in the future, result in payment of support can, at best, be termed only speculative."[16] In later cases, the Court would refer to this as the "redressability" requirement of standing: the plaintiff must properly allege that the relief she requests will "redress" her alleged injury. For if the relief would not redress that injury, then it could not be said that the plaintiff had a "personal stake in the outcome of this controversy." Her injury would remain unredressed whether she won or lost the litigation. In *Linda R.S.*, Justice Marshall and the majority held that this was the plaintiff's precise problem.

Justices White and Douglas, dissenting, found this conclusion odd. "I had always thought our civilization has assumed that the threat of penal sanctions had something more than a 'speculative' effect on a person's conduct," he wrote.[17]

15. 410 U.S. 614 (1973).
16. 410 U.S. at 618.
17. 410 U.S. at 621 (White, J., dissenting).

Although it was true, as Marshall had pointed out, that the length of a criminal sentence would be formally unaffected by the payment of delinquent child support, surely there were ways to finesse this. The prosecutor could bring charges and offer to drop them if delinquent payments were made. If this did not work, the prosecutor could go to trial, secure a conviction, and then offer to drop the entire thing if payments were made. Perhaps the father would prefer a jail term over making payments, but that was no more speculative than whether the subject of *any* injunction would rather obey than go to jail. Justices Blackmun and Brennan dissented separately.

On the surface, Marshall's vote with the majority is surprising, but a second look suggests an explanation. After oral argument was held in *Linda R.S.*, the Court handed down *Gomez v. Perez*, a civil case in which the Court ruled that Texas' discrimination between legitimate and illegitimate children in support obligations violated the Equal Protection Clause.[18] *Gomez* now made it possible for the mother in *Linda R.S.* to sue the father directly, without the aid of the criminal law. Indeed, Blackmun and Brennan dissented in *Linda R.S.* because they thought the case was moot in light of *Gomez*. Marshall therefore could rest assured that the mother in the immediate litigation was probably going to get her support payments even if the Court held she did not have standing to sue for criminal prosecution. Why not, then, vote with Blackmun and Brennan to dismiss the case as moot? Marshall was evidently uncomfortable with the idea that private individuals could ever have standing to force criminal prosecutions. "[I]n American jurisprudence, at least, a private citizen lacks a judicially cognizable interest in the prosecution or nonprosecution of another," he wrote.[19] In the aftermath of the racial rioting of the late 1960s and the White law-and-order backlash of the early 1970s, Marshall may well have thought that such standing would often be invoked to force prosecutions against racial minorities. Though he generally supported a broad conception of standing, Marshall believed he could limit *Linda R.S.* to cases in which people were suing to force criminal prosecutions. But he was mistaken, and he now joined his liberal colleagues, Brennan and Douglas, as each having written a key opinion that would help set the stage for the coming crackdown on left-progressive public interest litigation in federal court.

The new "causation" and "redressability" requirements took center stage in a pair of mid-1970s cases. In *Warth v. Seldin*,[20] a group of plaintiffs sued the town of Penfield, a suburb of Rochester, New York, for allegedly using its zoning ordinance to exclude low- and middle-income families from the town. The plaintiffs further alleged that this exclusion had dramatic racial effects, as Puerto Ricans and Blacks were disproportionately represented among these low- and

18. 409 U.S. 535 (1973).
19. 410 U.S. at 617.
20. 422 U.S. 490 (1975).

middle-income families. There were effectively three groups of plaintiffs. The first consisted of people who wanted to live in Penfield but could not find affordable housing there. The second group consisted of Rochester residents who claimed that Penfield's exclusion of low- and middle-income housing forced Rochester to provide more such housing. In order to encourage more affordable housing within its city limits, Rochester had to provide developers with tax breaks, which in turn occasioned a higher property tax burden on existing Rochester landowners, including plaintiffs. The third group of plaintiffs was a pair of pro-housing organizations, one an industry association and the other a public interest group. Both organizations alleged that they wished to be involved in affordable housing developments in Penfield. The complaint requested that the court enjoin future enforcement of the existing zoning ordinance in Penfield and develop a new ordinance to alleviate the effects of the existing one.

The Court held, 5–4, that all three groups of plaintiffs lacked standing. The four Nixon appointees, joined by Potter Stewart, comprised the majority. Justice Powell stated that the first group of plaintiffs, people desiring to buy housing in Penfield, failed both the causation and redressability tests. Doubtless the zoning ordinance had contributed to higher housing prices in Penfield, Powell acknowledged, but how could anyone really know whether the zoning ordinance was the critical difference between the plaintiffs being able to afford Penfield housing and plaintiffs being unable to afford it? The causal link between the defendant's conduct and the plaintiffs' injury was too speculative. "Petitioners must allege facts from which it could be reasonably inferred that, absent the respondent's restrictive zoning practices, there is a substantial probability that they would have been able to purchase or lease in Penfield," Powell asserted.[21] Moreover, the plaintiffs had to allege facts establishing a likelihood that a change in the ordinance would permit plaintiffs to buy or lease in Penfield. (In this case, establishing "causation" would presumably also establish "redressability," but in other cases, the two analyses might diverge.) Powell hinted that the result might well have been different if a specific development project or projects had been proposed and shot down by the zoning ordinance.

With respect to the Rochester residents who were complaining of an increased tax burden, the Court switched doctrinal gears. The problem with these plaintiffs was not that they lacked injury-in-fact—increased taxes surely qualified. Perhaps the majority could have found the causal chain too attenuated, but it did not. Instead, Justice Powell focused on the question of whose rights these plaintiffs were asserting. As Justice Brennan had acknowledged in *Dombrowski*, the usual rule is that plaintiffs may only assert their own legal rights and not the rights of others. There were exceptions, such as in the First Amendment overbreadth cases and in cases where the right-holders might have difficulty asserting their

21. 422 U.S. at 504.

own rights in court. But here, the plaintiffs who wanted to live in Penfield could assert their own equal protection rights, so long as they did it in a sufficiently concrete factual setting. The plaintiffs complaining of increased taxes were unable to point to the violation of any legal right belonging to them. Justice Powell and the majority were unwilling to let them assert anyone else's rights in this litigation.

The Court treated the standing of the two organizational plaintiffs separately. Metro-Act was an association made up of individuals, some of whom lived in Penfield. The Penfield members of Metro-Act alleged that the exclusionary zoning ordinance deprived them of the "social benefits of living in an integrated community."[22] Justice Powell found that this did not qualify as "injury-in-fact." True, the Court found this same allegation to constitute sufficient injury to support standing in a previous case, *Trafficante v. Metropolitan Life Ins. Co.*, but in that case the plaintiffs were suing under a federal statute that explicitly authorized litigation to protect such a right.[23] In *Warth*, the plaintiffs were not suing pursuant to any statute. Powell and the majority apparently viewed alleged harms as falling into three categories as far as standing is concerned: (1) harms that always qualify as injury-in-fact (such as deprivations of liberty or property interests protected at common law); (2) harms that qualify as injury-in-fact if Congress recognizes them, but not otherwise (such as denial of an opportunity to live in an integrated community, and perhaps harms to aesthetic or environmental well-being); and (3) harms that never qualify as injury-in-fact, even if Congress attempts to recognize them (such as the idealistic harm suffered by every citizen whenever his government breaks the law in any way).

Finally, with respect to the homebuilders' association plaintiff, the Court again switched gears and found their claim unripe. If any of these developers had a live project proposal whose viability was threatened by the zoning ordinance, the case might be ripe for adjudication, but that was not the case. Thus all three categories of plaintiffs in *Warth* were found not to present a justiciable case.

The Court reinforced the new causation and redressability requirements the next term, in *Simon v. Eastern Kentucky Welfare Rights Organization*.[24] In 1969, the Internal Revenue Service issued Revenue Ruling 69-545, which had the effect of announcing a relaxation in the standards for the amount of indigent patient care required of hospitals in order to maintain their "charitable" tax-exempt status. Organizations representing indigents across the country sued the IRS in federal district court, claiming that Ruling 69-545 was illegal for various reasons. They requested an injunction that would have required the IRS to withdraw the charitable status of hospitals that did not provide a larger amount of indigent patient care. The complaint alleged that individual members of

22. 422 U.S. at 512.
23. 409 U.S. 205 (1972).
24. 426 U.S. 26 (1976).

the plaintiff organizations had been denied care at various hospitals because of their inability to pay.

With the newest justice, John Paul Stevens, on the sidelines, the Court voted 6–2 that the plaintiffs lacked standing to sue. Justice Powell again wrote for the majority. As was the case with the plaintiffs in *Warth* who wanted to live in Penfield, the *Simon* plaintiffs had properly alleged injury-in-fact—denial of hospital services. But were those denials really attributable to Ruling 69-545, or were they attributable to the independent conduct of the hospitals? "It is purely speculative whether the denials of service specified in the complaint fairly can be traced to petitioners' 'encouragement' or instead result from decisions made by the hospitals without regard to the tax implications," Powell wrote.[25] Only about 4 percent of private hospital revenues nationwide came from private philanthropy, he noted. For the same reason, it was highly uncertain whether conditioning tax-exempt status on a greater amount of indigent services would actually increase the provision of such services. "[I]t is just as plausible that the hospitals to which respondents may apply for service would elect to forego favorable tax treatment to avoid the undetermined financial drain" of greater indigent services, Powell stated.[26] In finding that the plaintiffs had failed the "causation" and "redressability" prongs of the standing requirement, Powell repeatedly invoked Brennan's "personal stake" formulation from *Baker v. Carr.*

Brennan's frustration level was reaching a new high. In *Sierra Club, Simon,* and *Warth,* he detected an unwelcome trend. The new conservative majority on the Court was selectively imposing heightened pleading requirements in cases whose subject matter they considered more appropriate for resolution by the political process. Environmental and distributive justice cases seemed to fall within this category—were there others? "We may properly wonder where the Court, armed with its 'fatally speculative pleadings' tool, will strike next," Brennan wrote. Would the Court now also require that remedies for race discrimination come from the political process? "[W]ill minority schoolchildren now have to plead and show that" tax breaks for discriminatory private schools are a cause of "white flight" from the public schools?[27] These heightened pleading standards were improper because they required plaintiffs to effectively prove "causation"—generally an element of the merits—at the preliminary stage of the litigation, Brennan insisted.

He also believed the conservatives were distorting the "personal stake" requirement. Brennan denied that the new "causation" and "redressability" requirements had anything to do with his language in *Baker,* which was simply that the plaintiff allege "a personal stake sufficient to create concrete adverseness

---

25. 426 U.S. at 42–43.
26. *Id.* at 43.
27. 426 U.S. at 63 (Brennan, J., dissenting).

meeting minimal conditions for Art. III justiciability."[28] In Brennan's eyes, "personal stake in the outcome of the controversy" did not necessarily denote selfishness. What constituted a "personal stake" was not necessarily to be viewed from the standpoint of society, or from the standpoint of judges. It was instead what lawyers and judges referred to as a "subjective" question—that is, if a plaintiff sincerely felt sufficient "personal stake" in a matter to drive him to litigation, and if that zeal to litigate created a truly antagonistic relationship between him and the defendant, such that both sides would have incentive to marshal the best arguments that could be mustered on behalf of their respective positions, then the "case or controversy" requirement of Art. III was satisfied. To Brennan, it was ridiculous to say that the members of the Sierra Club lacked a "personal stake" in the preservation of Mineral King, even if none of them planned to go there. Why would they take it all the way to the Supreme Court if they felt no such personal stake? Similarly, it was absurd to say that these indigents had no personal stake in whether the IRS was vigilant or lax in requiring hospitals to provide indigent care to maintain their tax-exempt status. Clearly they had an interest in seeing that the IRS limit tax favors to hospitals that served the poor, as set forth in the Internal Revenue Code. On the surface, at least, Brennan's mid-1970s interpretation of "personal stake" as a subjective concept looked like a case of revisionism.

For the liberals on the Court, what made it worse was that the conservatives were deploying the standing doctrine in other ways as well. In 1974, the Court found a lack of standing in a pair of cases challenging aspects of the Vietnam War, or, at least, the conduct of national defense. In *Schlesinger v. Reservists to Stop the War*, a group of present and former reservists challenged the practice of allowing sitting members of Congress to serve in the military reserves.[29] They claimed that it violated Art. I, Section 6 of the Constitution, which states:

> No Senator or Representative shall, during the Time for which he was elected, be appointed to any Civil office under the Authority of the United States, which shall have been created, or the Emoluments whereof shall have been encreased during such time; and no Person holding any Office under the United States, shall be a member of either House during his Continuance in Office.

The plaintiffs claimed that some members of Congress had received reserve commissions while in office, and that others had already been reservists when they assumed seats in Congress. Both of these types of cases violated Art. I, Section 6, they argued. In *United States v. Richardson*, the taxpayer plaintiff had made repeated unsuccessful attempts to obtain detailed information about the

---

28. 426 U.S. at 56 (Brennan, J., dissenting).
29. 418 U.S. 208 (1974).

expenditures of the Central Intelligence Agency (CIA).[30] He argued that the statute permitting the CIA to get away with these nondisclosures violated the Statements and Accounts Clause of Art. I, Section 9, of the Constitution. He claimed that, without this detailed information, he could not intelligently exercise his obligations as a member of the electorate.

The Court, in opinions by Chief Justice Warren Burger, rejected standing to sue in both cases. Citing the taxpayer standing decisions in *Frothingham* and *Flast,* Burger characterized William Richardson's claim as a "generalized grievance," unsuitable as a platform for judicial review. He gave two reasons.[31] First, "the impact on [Richardson] is plainly undifferentiated and 'common to all members of the public.'" In other words, the injury was too widely shared.[32] Second, Richardson failed to allege that, "as a taxpayer, he is in danger of suffering any particular concrete injury...."[33] His claimed injury—insufficient information to make intelligent voting decisions—was too abstract for federal court adjudication. One might legitimately ask what logical relationship exists between the "concreteness" or "abstractness" of an injury on the one hand and whether that injury is "generalized" or "specific" on the other, but there is no evidence that Burger gave any thought to the relationship.

If Burger's explanation for why the claimed injury constituted a "generalized grievance" was less than intellectually satisfying, perhaps the true rationale lay in the opinion's next passage. "It can be argued that if respondent is not permitted to litigate this issue, no one can do so," Burger acknowledged. The absence of any suitable plaintiff suggested that "the subject matter is committed to the surveillance of Congress, and ultimately to the political process." Burger was suggesting, without holding, that individual lawsuits to enforce the Statements and Accounts Clause presented a nonjusticiable political question. "Any other conclusion," he wrote, "would mean that the Founding Fathers intended to set up something in the nature of an Athenian democracy or a New England town meeting to oversee the conduct of the National Government by means of lawsuits in federal courts."[34]

---

30. 418 U.S. 166 (1974).

31. Citing the citizen standing decision in *Ex Parte Levitt,* Burger actually gave a third reason that Richardson's claim amounted to a nonjusticiable "generalized grievance"—that he failed to allege sufficiently "direct" injury. As he further explained this idea, however, it became clear that the injury was not direct because it was too widely shared with other members of the public. Analytically, then, it collapsed back into Burger's first reason.

32. Chief Justice Burger did not acknowledge, must less explain, how his statement could be squared with the majority opinion in *SCRAP,* which stated plainly that standing is not to be denied simply because many people suffer the same injury.

33. 418 U.S. at 176–77.

34. 418 U.S. at 179.

This passage revealed something important about the Court's approach. As a response to what the Nixon appointees saw as unwarranted meddling with the political process by the Warren Court, the Court was now relying on a free-floating principle of separation of powers to short-circuit lawsuits that technically fell within the jurisdiction of the federal courts. If citizens disagree with the actions of their elected officials, they should vote them out of office. Burger now stretched this truism to say that, if citizens felt their elected officials were violating the law, they should vote them out of office, and that this was sometimes their only recourse. "Slow, cumbersome, and unresponsive though the traditional electoral process may be thought at times," he said, "our system provides for changing members of the political branches when dissatisfied citizens convince a sufficient number of their fellow electors that elected representatives are delinquent in performing duties committed to them."[35] This concept of the self-correcting polity had no obvious limits. Taken to its logical end, it would conclude that courts exist exclusively to settle disputes in private dealing, not to check government power against the citizenry. It would recall the early republican notion that, because democratic government truly represents the people's will, it is conceptually *impossible* for government to harm the people. The people cannot harm themselves.

In his concurring opinion, Justice Powell took a more nuanced view. He agreed with Burger that separation of powers concerns should lead the federal courts to tread lightly in cases where plaintiffs were suing solely in their capacity as citizens or taxpayers. This subset of public interest litigation posed the greatest threat to democratic self-government. Powell's view thus contained its own well-demarcated limit; Burger's view, taken to its logical end, threatened to wipe out constitutionally and congressionally authorized federal jurisdiction in all lawsuits against government officials. Powell, like Burger, endorsed the basic notion that democratic political process had to be given preference over judicial process as a remedy for governmental wrongs. Unlike Burger, however, Powell recognized that the political system could not always be counted on to correct its own malfunctions. Powell acknowledged that *Baker v. Carr*, for one, strained his theory of judicial restraint. But he found room for it: "[Baker] was perhaps a necessary response to the manifest distortion of democratic principles practiced by malapportioned legislatures and to abuses of the political system so pervasive as to undermine democratic processes."[36] *Richardson*, on the other hand, was nothing like *Baker v. Carr*; one could hardly say that the failure of the CIA to disclose its expenditures with great specificity was the product of pervasive systemic failure in the democratic process.

---

35. *Id.*

36. 418 U.S. at 195 fn. 17 (Powell, J., concurring). In support of this statement, Justice Powell could have cited both footnote 4 of *Carolene Products* and John Hart Ely's famous book, DEMOCRACY AND DISTRUST (Harvard U. Press 1980).

Chief Justice Burger's opinion in *Schlesinger* largely parroted his *Richardson* opinion. He did, however, include an important passage that effectively responded to a gambit in Justice Brennan's dissent, which covered both *Schlesinger* and *Richardson*. In that dissent, Brennan explicitly proposed a "subjective" test to measure the presence or absence of "injury-in-fact." "The 'standing' of a plaintiff . . . is established, in my view, by his good-faith allegation" that the defendant's conduct has caused him injury-in-fact, Brennan wrote.[37] So long as he also alleged the violation of a legally protected right, a plaintiff's sincere allegation that he suffered what he perceived to be harm would suffice for standing. This mind-dependent view of injury-in-fact, of course, is not at all how the conservatives regarded it.[38] They assumed injury-in-fact was to be determined by an "objective" test, which meant judges would say what injuries were "cognizable." Brennan again revisited his "personal stake" formulation in *Baker*: the gist of standing is whether the plaintiff has "alleged such a personal stake in the outcome of the controversy as to assure that concrete adverseness which sharpens the presentation of issues upon which the court so largely depends for illumination of difficult constitutional questions."[39] Some plaintiffs' lawyers, pointing to this full passage, argued that their clients should be deemed to have standing so long as they demonstrated a strong and consistent commitment to the subject matter of the litigation, as where a long-standing environmental protection organization like the Sierra Club or Friends of the Earth sued to challenge government actions that threatened the environment. Indeed, the district court in *Schlesinger* accepted a similar argument in finding standing. If such organizations truly *perceived* a stake in the outcome of the controversy—no matter whether a judge would say they have such a stake—then the "adverseness" required for the sharp presentation of issues and argumentation in litigation would exist. If the only reason for the "personal stake" requirement was as a proxy for sharp adversary presentation, then it was satisfied by a subjective, good-faith belief in such a stake by the plaintiff.

Whether or not it was his conscious object, Burger included a passage in his opinion that had the effect of cutting off Brennan's proposal in its incipiency. "We have no doubt about the sincerity of respondents' stated objectives and the depth of their commitment to them," he conceded. But, quoting Felix Frankfurter's opinion in *Doremus*, he insisted that the essence of standing "is not a question of motivation but of possession of the requisite . . . interest that is, or is threatened to be, injured by the unconstitutional conduct."[40] Brennan and the district court had tried to cast "personal stake" and "injury-in-fact" as functional concepts

37. 418 U.S. at 235 (Brennan, J., dissenting).

38. Indeed, it is not even clear that his liberal colleagues viewed it that way, as none of them joined his dissent.

39. *Id.* at 237, quoting Baker v. Carr, 369 U.S. at 204.

40. 418 U.S. at 225–26, quoting Doremus v. Bd. of Education, 342 U.S. at 435.

rather than legalistic ones. What was really important for the functioning of federal courts, Brennan now tried to say, was not the "personal stake" or the "injury" itself—it was the litigating initiative that they tended to carry with them. So long as that initiative was present, the concerns of Art. III were satisfied. But Burger and the majority were having none of it. It was not a question of the policy underlying Art. III, but rather the letter of it. Litigation in which the plaintiff could demonstrate no personal stake or direct injury did not constitute a "case or controversy." These functional policy concerns may have been at the bottom of the adoption of the "case or controversy" requirement, but the courts' jurisdiction depended on the satisfaction of formal Art. III requisites, not impressionistic assessments of policy norms.[41]

* * *

Brennan worried openly about where these cases might be leading. Although the standing decisions of the early 1970s concerned welfare rights, the environment, and the Vietnam War, it seemed inevitable that the Court would eventually use the standing doctrine to restrict the federal judiciary's future involvement in the drive for racial justice. His fears materialized in the affirmative action cases of the 1970s and 1980s, but with a twist.

Alex Bickel, a Yale constitutional law scholar and Frankfurter protégé, had written that the Supreme Court ought to employ the standing, mootness, and ripeness doctrines in service of something he called "the passive virtues."[42] Drawing on the insight of his Yale constitutional law colleague Charles Lund Black, Jr., Bickel noted that the nonlawyer population had a pronounced tendency to regard judicial decisions holding government action "not unconstitutional" as placing an imprimatur of "constitutionality" on the action in question. If, for example, the Supreme Court were to hold that a particular affirmative

41. This line of standing decisions was analyzed and critiqued in a large number of law review articles. The most influential were William A. Fletcher, *The Structure of Standing*, 98 Yale L. J. 221 (1988) (arguing that standing should be seen as a question of whether the underlying law creates a right on behalf of the plaintiff, and demonstrating how most standing decisions can be understood in this way); and Cass Sunstein, *Standing and the Privatization of Public Law*, 88 Colum. L. Rev. 1432, 1477–79 (1988). Fletcher's penetrating argument has the distinct virtue of fulfilling *Marbury*'s injunction that rights must have remedies. Other influential articles include Susan Bandes, *The Idea of a Case*, 42 Stan. L. Rev. 227 (1990) (criticizing these and other decisions for failing to develop an idea of an Article III "case," and endorsing a public law model of adjudication); Gene R. Nichol, *Rethinking Standing*, 72 Calif. L. Rev. 68 (1984) (criticizing the Court's application of the injury requirement); Steven L. Winter, *The Metaphor of Standing and the Problem of Self-Governance*, 40 Stan. L. Rev. 71 (1988); Edward Hartnett, *The Standing of the United States: How Criminal Prosecutions Show that Standing Doctrine Is Looking for Answers in All the Wrong Places*, 97 Mich. L. Rev. 2239 (1999).

42. *See* Alexander M. Bickel, The Least Dangerous Branch: The Supreme Court at the Bar of Politics (2d ed. 1986).

action program did not violate the Constitution, a considerable portion of the public would view it as a statement that affirmative action at some level is constitutionally mandated, or at least constitutionally "protected." Viewed through the lens of *Marbury*, of course, this way of thinking is completely foreign; in John Marshall's contemplation, the Court has merely found that the Constitution places no obstacle in the way of enforcing the legislature's enactment. The mere statement that an enactment is "not unconstitutional" does not necessarily express any sentiment about its desirability or place in the constellation of American public values. In modern Supreme Court practice, however, the judgment that a challenged government action is "not unconstitutional" is invariably accompanied by an opinion that, at a minimum, explains why the action is "rationally related" to a "legitimate governmental interest." In the tradition of judicial literary overkill, the opinion usually goes well beyond this minimum, celebrating the government's historical involvement in the subject matter area in question and emphasizing the seriousness of the social or economic problem being addressed. Laypersons could be excused for failing to appreciate that the Court was expressing no opinion about the underlying value of the enactment. This *de facto* imprimatur on legislation found "not unconstitutional" was particularly troubling where the states were acting as "social laboratories." If a few states enacted socially experimental legislation found "not unconstitutional," the imprimatur effect might prematurely extinguish public debate about the wisdom of the legislation. Social experimentation required time for "percolation" in the political process.

Bickel suggested that the federal courts use the justiciability doctrines to avoid the imprimatur effect. Instead of ruling a socially experimental or otherwise controversial government practice "not unconstitutional" on the merits, a court should find that there was no standing to sue, or that the dispute was already over (moot) or prematurely brought (unripe). These dispositions would permit the challenged practices to continue but would have no imprimatur effect. The social experimentation could go on. The public debate could continue.

Whether the relationship was coincidental or causal, the Court followed the Bickelian template in two pairs of affirmative action cases. In 1973, the Court granted review in a case called *DeFunis v. Odegaard*.[43] Marco DeFunis was a White male seeking admission to the University of Washington School of Law. When his application was denied, he sued the school for violating his right to equal protection. The law school had admitted minority candidates ahead of him who had inferior qualifications, DeFunis alleged. The state courts ordered DeFunis admitted during the pendency of the litigation. This meant that, by the time the case reached the U.S. Supreme Court, DeFunis was in his final semester of law school.

43. 416 U.S. 312.

The Court's liberals wanted to hear the merits of the case and rule against DeFunis with the aim of generally validating affirmative action programs in higher education. But they were only four—Powell held the swing vote—and he was holding out for something more nuanced. He agreed with the liberals that institutions of higher education ought to be able to take race into account, as a temporary measure, to even the playing field for future generations. At the same time, he agreed with the conservatives that no innocent individual ought to be made to bear a disproportionately large share of the cost of such measures. Whether Powell wanted to give the political process time to better acclimate itself to race-conscious remedies, whether he was searching for a better litigation vehicle to expound his nuanced position, whether he was simply buying time to refine his position, or whether he simply thought the case nonjusticiable, Powell voted with the conservatives to punt.

In a *per curiam* (unsigned) opinion, the Court held that the case was moot and therefore no longer constituted a "case or controversy" within the meaning of Art. III. As with the obvious collusion in *Fletcher v. Peck*, the Court had been well aware of the mootness issue in *DeFunis* when it granted certiorari. Indeed, the Court ordered special briefing on the mootness question, in response to which the university denied mootness, insisting that DeFunis would have to petition the faculty to continue his studies if he were to lose in the Supreme Court. But at oral argument, the university changed its tune. The school's lawyer now admitted that DeFunis would be allowed to finish and get his degree no matter who finally prevailed in the litigation. That was all the conservatives and Powell needed to hear. DeFunis no longer had a "personal stake in the outcome of the controversy." His injury had been remedied by the preliminary injunction permitting him to enroll and proceed toward a degree. Clearly he had an ideological zeal to vindicate himself and his opposition to affirmative action, but that was insufficient to satisfy Art. III.

In dissent, Brennan (joined by Douglas, White, and Marshall) insisted that the case was not moot. DeFunis might get sick or flunk a class in his last semester—then he would have to seek readmission, Brennan wrote. It was a weak argument. Even if DeFunis were forced to seek readmission for some reason, he would not be competing against any specific group of applicants. He would never again bump up against the law school's race-conscious admissions scheme. Interestingly, Brennan and the liberals did not deploy an argument that probably ought to have carried the day: DeFunis had a personal stake in winning the litigation to erase the stigma of having been admitted by a court order that had never been fully vindicated. That stigma, from DeFunis's standpoint, was the result of discrimination on the basis of his race. Although freedom from "stigma" might not have been a liberty or property interest protected at common law, after *Brown v. Board of Education*, it could hardly be denied that stigma growing out of state-sponsored race discrimination was a judicially cognizable harm.

Four years later, the Court granted certiorari in *Bakke v. Regents of the University of California*.[44] Powell was now ready to explicate his Solomonic solution. The Court held, 5–4, that Allan Bakke, a White male, had to be admitted to the medical school at the University of California, Davis. At the same time, the Court held 5–4 that race could be used as a "plus" in admissions in order to remedy past discrimination. Powell was the swing vote both times. His separate opinion acknowledged that the attainment of diversity in a student body was a legitimate state interest. The Davis medical school, however, had set aside sixteen seats out of one hundred in the entering class for applicants of color. Powell found that this scheme was not narrowly tailored to the objective of a diverse student body. He pointed approvingly to the Harvard College affirmative action program, which used race as only a single factor in admissions. "This kind of program treats each applicant as an individual in the admissions process," Powell wrote. "The applicant who loses out on the last available seat to another candidate receiving a 'plus' on the basis of ethnic background will not have been foreclosed from all consideration for that seat simply because he was not the right color or had the wrong surname."[45] Never mind that the respective races of the two applicants would be the decisive factor in some cases; that could never be conclusively proven in any given case. The virtue of Powell's scheme was its opaqueness. It smoothed the sharp emotional edge off affirmative action.

In perfecting this masterpiece of political statesmanship, Powell waved away accusations of judicial activism. Some of the *amici curiae* (those filing "friend of the court" briefs) had argued that Bakke lacked standing to sue. Under *Warth v. Seldin* and *Linda R.S.*, Bakke had to demonstrate that a favorable ruling would be likely to redress his injury. Yet according to the trial court Bakke failed to show that he would have been admitted if even in the absence of the special program.[46] In a footnote, Powell slipped past the redressability problem by quietly switching to a different form of injury. "The constitutional element of standing is plaintiff's demonstration of any injury to himself that is likely to be redressed by favorable decision of his claim," wrote Powell.[47] "The trial court found such an injury, apart from failure to be admitted, in the University's decision not to permit Bakke to compete for all 100 places in the class, simply because of his race." It was a colossal stretch.[48] People do not apply to medical school with the object of competing for each seat in the class—they apply to get admitted.

---

44. 438 U.S. 265 (1978).

45. 438 U.S. at 318 (opinion of Powell, J.).

46. 438 U.S. at 409 (opinion of Stevens, J.).

47. 438 U.S. at 280–81 n. 14 (opinion of Powell, J.).

48. The noted constitutional scholar Richard Fallon wrote that in *Bakke* the Court "chose to overlook a difficult standing problem." See Richard H. Fallon, Jr. & Paul C. Weiler, *Firefighters v. Stotts: Conflicting Models of Racial Justice*, 1984 Supreme Court Rev. 1.

Presumably someone who gets a seat does not care whether he was permitted to compete for any other seat in the class, and by the same token, someone who walks away without a seat cares only that he did not get one. The fact that he was not permitted to compete for a certain subset of the seats might provide him with an opening to argue that he has been unfairly or illegally treated, but his subjective motivation was to obtain any seat, not to compete for all of them. It did not matter to Powell. By 1978, he was ready to administer his salve to the wounds of a nation riven by the fight over affirmative action, and no technical deficiency would hold him back.[49]

* * *

By the mid-1970s, Brennan's fears had materialized. In many cases, the passive resistance employed by the civil rights movement had given way to more militant demands for Black empowerment, alienating some White sympathizers and strengthening the resolve of conservatives to strike back through zealous law enforcement. Moreover, racial unrest had ceased to be a regional matter. Watts burned in the summer of 1965; Detroit burned in the summer of 1967. Both were largely reactions to perceived racist treatment of Blacks by law enforcement.[50] These conflicts arose across the country, albeit less spectacularly, through the late 1960s and early 1970s. As resulting litigation began to bubble up through the system, the Supreme Court began to use the "case or controversy" doctrines, in conjunction with considerations of federalism, to limit federal judicial involvement in cases alleging systemic race discrimination in the local administration of criminal justice.

The cases, although separated by a few years, effectively made up a trilogy, involving three localities—Cairo, Illinois; Philadelphia; and Los Angeles. In *O'Shea v. Littleton*,[51] seventeen Black plaintiffs sued in federal district court, alleging that the police, prosecutor, and criminal court judges of Alexander County had engaged in a set of practices intended to defeat a civil rights campaign in Cairo. The campaign had begun in the early 1960s and had gradually developed into an economic boycott of bigoted local merchants. The complaint alleged, among other things, that the county magistrate and judge engaged in three

---

49. Powell also abjured the approach of Justice Stevens, who would have held only that the university's special admissions program violated Title VI, the statute that prohibits race discrimination in programs receiving federal funding. Because such a statutory holding would have dictated affirmance of the state court's order to admit Bakke, it would have rendered Powell's entire constitutional analysis unnecessary. Disposition of federal litigation on statutory grounds to avoid unnecessary constitutional questions was, of course, one of Brandeis's cardinal propositions in *Ashwander*.

50. On the Watts riots, see GERALD HORNE, FIRE THIS TIME: THE WATTS UPRISING AND THE 1960s (Univ. of Va. Press 1995). On the Detroit riots, see SIDNEY FINE, VIOLENCE IN THE MODEL CITY: THE CAVANAGH ADMINISTRATION, RACE RELATIONS, AND THE DETROIT RIOT OF 1967 (Univ. of Mich. Press 1989).

51. 414 U.S. 488 (1974).

systematic practices: (1) setting bond in criminal cases according to an "unofficial bond schedule," without regard to the individual facts of cases or the circumstances of the person seeking bond; (2) setting more severe sentences and creating more severe detention conditions for Black defendants than for White defendants; and (3) charging jury fees of defendants in certain cases. The federal appellate court ruled that their lawsuit could go forward and that, should they prevail at trial, the district court should fashion appropriate relief, which might consist of something like requiring the county magistrate and judge to file periodic reports on their bail and sentencing activity.

The Supreme Court, speaking through Justice White, reversed on the ground that the plaintiffs failed to present an actual "case or controversy." As in *Sierra Club*, the Court pointed out that none of the plaintiffs alleged that he personally had suffered any of the alleged injuries. It was true, White acknowledged, that during oral argument plaintiffs' counsel asserted that some of them had in fact been victimized by the alleged discriminatory practices during bail and sentencing proceedings. But they were not seeking damages for those past injuries—they were seeking an injunction to prevent future injuries. "[H]ere the prospect of future injury rests on the likelihood that [plaintiffs] will again be arrested for and charged with violations of the criminal law and will again be subjected to bond proceedings, trial, or sentencing before [defendants]," White wrote, labeling this "speculation and conjecture." In reality, it was anything but speculative: the plaintiffs made it abundantly clear that they were intent on continuing their nonviolent campaign to achieve equal rights, which included some civil disobedience. It was as if the Court was saying that, if the plaintiffs chose to engage in civil disobedience, they would simply have to take their chances that the judicial system would ultimately treat them fairly. If they did not want law enforcement to discriminate against them, then they should not give law enforcement any reason to come into contact with them. "We assume that [plaintiffs] will conduct their activities within the law and so avoid prosecution and conviction as well as exposure to the challenged course of conduct said to be followed by petitioners," stated the Court.[52] For "case or controversy" and federalism reasons, the federal courts would not step in to assure that local officials would treat the plaintiffs according to law—no matter what the history between them.

In the summer of 1970, the Black Panthers declared war on police officers nationwide. On August 31, 1970—one week before the Panthers were scheduled to convene a "People's Revolutionary Convention" at Temple University—the Philadelphia Police Department raided the Panthers' offices. Officers strip-searched the arrestees in front of news cameras that broadcast the images worldwide. The police commissioner was the famously mercurial and complex Frank Rizzo, a larger-than-life figure whose tough, hands-on leadership would soon

52. 414 U.S. at 497.

thereafter elevate him to the office of mayor. Rizzo had not ordered the raid; on the contrary, he helped to prevent a violent confrontation over it. Nonetheless, he had a rocky relationship with the city's African-American community, being accused of racially targeting certain activities in that community.

Even before the raid of the Panther offices, a lawsuit had been filed in federal court, requesting systemic court remedies for what it characterized as systemic race discrimination in Philadelphia law enforcement. The lead plaintiff was Wilson Goode, a Black community activist who years later would defeat Frank Rizzo twice in mayoral elections. Immediately following the raid, twenty-one individuals and four organizations filed another suit in federal court. The organizations were the Council of Organizations on Philadelphia Police Accountability and Responsibility (COPPAR) (itself an amalgamation of thirty-two community groups); the Southern Christian Leadership Conference; the Black Panthers; and the Young Lords Party, a Hispanic group. Both lawsuits were brought as class actions against Rizzo, the city's managing director, and the city's police commissioner. The plaintiffs claimed to represent all Philadelphia residents and, more to the point, all Black residents of Philadelphia. The district court heard 250 witnesses over 21 days of hearings, covering more than 40 law enforcement incidents, each of which "might alone have been the piece de resistance of a short, separate trial."[53] Finally, the district court ordered the defendants to "submit to [the district court] for its approval a comprehensive program for improving the handling of citizen complaints alleging police misconduct,"[54] and the court of appeals affirmed.

The Supreme Court, speaking through Justice William Rehnquist, reversed, calling the district court's injunction "an unwarranted intrusion by the federal judiciary into the discretionary authority committed to them by state and local law to perform their official functions."[55] Thus federalism was an integral part of the Court's rationale; primary responsibility for law enforcement has always been state and local. But Rehnquist was just getting started. Another problem was the highly unorthodox structure of the litigation. The *Goode* case was made up of incidents involving two Highway Patrol officers who were not named defendants. Three of these incidents were judged to have involved violations of constitutional rights. The *COPPAR* case was made up of twenty-eight incidents, sixteen of which involved the constitutional violations by police officers. Rehnquist and the majority detected a "central paradox" that permeated the district court's legal conclusions: "Individual police officers not named as parties to the action were found to have violated the constitutional rights of particular individuals, only a few of whom were parties plaintiff."[56] The causal connection

53. Rizzo v. Goode, 423 U.S. 362, 367 (1976).
54. *See* COPPAR v. Rizzo, 357 F. Supp. 1289 (1973).
55. 423 U.S. at 366.
56. 423 U.S. at 371.

between the named plaintiffs and the named defendants was too attenuated. "In sum," concluded Rehnquist, "the genesis of this lawsuit—a heated dispute between individual citizens and certain policemen—has evolved into an attempt by the federal judiciary to resolve a 'controversy' between the entire citizenry of Philadelphia and the [defendants] over what steps might . . . [prevent] future police misconduct."[57] Citing *O'Shea v. Littleton*, the Court professed "serious doubts" whether, on that factual record, there was an Art. III case or controversy. The *Goode* and *COPPAR* cases boiled down to little more than a question of "what one of a small, unnamed minority of policemen might to do [plaintiffs] in the future because of that unknown policeman's perception of departmental disciplinary procedures."[58] In the end, the Court made it clear that the alleged failure of the police department to respond effectively to violations of constitutional rights was a matter for the political process, not the federal judiciary, to address.

Among other things, *Rizzo v. Goode* could sensibly be interpreted as the repudiation of David Brewer's view of the federal equity power.[59] Brewer and Rufus Peckham had not hesitated to use the equity power to protect property rights even in the most far-reaching cases. Their consciences were completely clear—equity was a God-given remedy for the protection of God-given rights. Considerations of federalism gave them no pause. The state's very highest law enforcement officer, the attorney general, could be dragged before a federal court and ultimately held in contempt for merely trying to enforce the state's criminal laws, all in the name of protecting constitutional property rights. But as Protestant idealism had ebbed away from federal jurisprudence and was replaced by scientific pragmatism (and, ultimately, by a credo of legislative and police power primacy), the justificatory foundation for equity withered away as well. To justices like Rehnquist, raised in the intellectual nursery of Brandeis, Frankfurter, and Robert Jackson, the broad use of federal equity power was presumptively illegitimate. God and natural rights simply did not enter the equation. "Property" was whatever the states said it was, not what federal judges in their theological meditations imagined it to be.[60] For Rehnquist and most of the other Nixon appointees (Blackmun was an exception), the natural rights philosophy had no more legitimacy in the area of civil rights than it did in the area of property rights. If individuals could prove discrimination in their interactions with law enforcement, they could get money damages. Equity was not available to ensure that government would never discriminate against them. An injunction, particularly against a state or local official, was an *extraordinary* remedy; race discrimination,

57. *Id.*

58. 423 U.S. at 372.

59. I do not mean to suggest that if Brewer had been on the Court in 1976 he would have voted with the liberals in *Rizzo*, only that his view of equity was inconsistent with the majority's.

60. *See* Pruneyard Shopping Center v. Robins, 447 U.S. 74 (1980).

however unlawful, was not an extraordinary occurrence. "There was no showing that the behavior of the Philadelphia police was different in kind or degree from that which exists elsewhere," Rehnquist shrugged. Instead, the problems were "fairly typical of [those] afflicting police departments in major urban areas."[61] Rehnquist scoffed at the plaintiffs' claim that the citizenry had a "'right' to be protected from unconstitutional exercises of police power."[62] The "federal courts must be constantly mindful of the 'special delicacy of the adjustment to be preserved between federal equitable power and State administration of its own law.'"[63] Interestingly, Blackmun's dissent, joined by Brennan and Marshall, did not object to the majority opinion on any broad basis, but only at the margins.

* * *

The final, and most bitterly contested, installment of the Court's "local law enforcement" trilogy was still to come. Justice Thurgood Marshall, in an unusually emotional dissent, recited the facts:

> [Plaintiff] Adolph Lyons is a 24-year-old Negro male who resides in Los Angeles. According to the uncontradicted evidence, at about 2 a.m. on October 6, 1976, Lyons was pulled over to the curb by two officers of the Los Angeles Police Department (LAPD) for a traffic infraction because one of his taillights was burned out. The officers greeted him with drawn revolvers as he exited from the car. Lyons was told to face his car and spread his legs. He did so. He was then ordered to clasp his hands and put them on top of his head. He again complied. After one of the officers completed a patdown search, Lyons dropped his hands, but was ordered to place them back above his head, and one of the officers grabbed Lyons' hands and slammed them into his head. Lyons complained about the pain caused by the ring of keys he was holding in his hand. Within 5 to 10 seconds, the officer began to choke Lyons by applying a forearm against his throat. As Lyons struggled for air, the officer handcuffed him, but continued to apply the chokehold until he blacked out. When Lyons regained consciousness, he was lying face down on the ground, choking, gasping for air, and spitting up blood and dirt. He had urinated and defecated. He was issued a traffic citation and released.[64]

The police department had instructed its officers that use of this type of chokehold did not constitute "deadly force," and therefore could be used to control arrestees even when they posed no threat of harm to the arresting officers.[65]

---

61. 423 U.S. at 375.

62. 423 U.S. at 377.

63. *Id.* at 378.

64. City of Los Angeles v. Lyons, 461 U.S. 95, 114–15 (1983) (Marshall, J., dissenting).

65. There were actually two different kinds of holds employed by the LAPD. One was referred to as a "bar arm" hold and the other a "carotid artery" hold. It was not clear which was used on Lyons.

Lyons sued in federal district court, asking for money damages and an injunction prohibiting the LAPD from using the chokehold in nondeadly threat situations. By the time the district court issued the requested injunction (the case had already been up on appeal once), ten arrestees had been killed by use of the chokehold. After the court of appeals stayed the injunction pending appeal, four more had died. Before the LAPD adopted a voluntary moratorium on use of the chokehold in nondeadly threat situations, still two more had died, for a total of sixteen. Twelve of them were Black men.

No one disputed Lyons' right to go forward on his claim for money damages. But the Supreme Court held that Lyons did not have standing to sue for an injunction. "That Lyons may have been illegally choked by the police on October 6, 1976 . . . does nothing to establish a real and immediate threat that he would again be stopped for a traffic violation . . . by an officer or officers who would illegally choke him into unconsciousness without any provocation or resistance on his part," wrote Justice Byron White for a 5–4 majority.[66] In order to have standing, Lyons would have to allege that he was certain to be stopped by the police again, and that "*all police officers in Los Angeles always choke any citizen with whom they happen to have an encounter*," or at least that the city authorizes such behavior, White continued.[67] It was tantamount to saying that the federal courts were powerless to issue injunctions against local police misconduct, for no one could possibly make such allegations with that degree of certainty.

The *Lyons* majority, consisting of White, Burger, Powell, Rehnquist, and Reagan-appointee Sandra Day O'Connor, fully intended this result. If the LAPD was violating individuals' constitutional rights, then they could all sue and obtain damages.[68] When the municipality tired of defending such lawsuits and paying out large damage awards, it presumably would alter its policies to reduce or eliminate its liability. It was unfortunate that some arrestees would have to be injured or killed before municipalities would react to their liability exposure, but the Court's conservatives were resolved that the federal courts could not and would not take over the management of local police departments. In the 1960s and 1970s, federal district judges throughout the country had taken over state prisons, mental hospitals, and public school districts, often appointing so-called "special masters" who dictated the operational details of these institutions for years, sometimes decades. These "structural reform" cases had provoked charges

---

66. 461 U.S. at 105.

67. 461 U.S. at 105–06.

68. Though even this avenue of redress was limited, at least in federal court, by the series of decisions beginning with *Monell v. Dept. of Social Services*, 436 U.S. 658 (1978), holding that an individual may not sue a municipality under 42 U.S.C. Section 1983—the main federal civil rights law—unless he or she proves that the injury was caused by a municipal "custom or policy," and not merely the unauthorized behavior of rogue officers.

of "government by judiciary." The Court's conservatives would do their best to roll back this state of affairs, and certainly would not let it spread to other areas. The "case or controversy" doctrine, in conjunction with federalism, became one of their most potent tools for rolling back "government by judiciary." The paradigm "case or controversy" had a bilateral party structure, a clear and discrete event at the center of the argument, and a one-shot, self-contained remedy.[69] As litigation moved away from these traditional features, it strained the proper function of the federal courts and became less legitimate. When the party structure became amorphous and polycentric, the disputed events multiple and tenuously linked, and the remedy managerial and ongoing, the courts had lost their way. These matters were no longer within the "judicial power" of Art. III. They were matters for the state courts, or better yet, the political process. From this perspective, it can be understood why the Court's conservative majority would refuse adjudication in *O'Shea* and *Rizzo*, which could readily be described as amalgamations of discrete events. But it was surprising, and alarming, for the Court to view *Lyons* in this vein, given its outward appearance as a simple case of police brutality against a readily identifiable individual.

69. *See* Abram Chayes, *The Role of the Judge in Public Law Litigation*, 89 HARV. L. REV. 1281 (1976).

8. SCALIA, THE ENVIRONMENT, AND THE MODERN STANDING DOCTRINE

By the 1970s, the slogan of judicial restraint—once the battle cry of Progressives and New Dealers—was firmly associated with conservatives. Just as the Court of David Brewer, Rufus Peckham, and George Sutherland had aggressively used federal equity to protect vested property rights, the Court of Earl Warren, William Brennan, and William O. Douglas had aggressively used federal equity to protect civil rights and civil liberties. Each time the backlash took the form of a rhetorical attack not on the substance of the rights being protected, but on the "activist" manner in which the courts behaved. Yet in the historical evaluation of these attacks it is impossible to fully disentangle the propriety of judicial review from the legitimacy of the rights being protected. In the abstract, all exertions of judicial review bump up against majoritarian prerogative, while acts of judicial restraint necessarily entail the potential sacrifice of rights. Neither choice is inherently liberal or conservative, despicable or praiseworthy. The evaluation of any act of judicial review is largely inextricable from its context, which includes matters internal to the law (rules) and matters exogenous to the law (tradition, judicial culture, social culture, politics, exigent circumstances). A contemporary case in point is Antonin Scalia.

* * *

In 1983, as a young judge on the D.C. Circuit, Scalia published a law review article called "The Doctrine of Standing as an Essential Element of the Separation of Powers."[1] In it, he laid bare many of his beliefs about the relationship among the three branches of the federal government. "My thesis is that the judicial doctrine of standing is a crucial and inseparable element of [the separation of powers principle], whose disregard will inevitably produce—as it has during the past few decades—an overjudicialization of the processes of self-governance," he stated.[2] In support of his thesis, he cited David Horowitz's 1977 book, *The Courts and Social Policy*, which argued that courts should stick to umpiring disputes between individuals and stay away from cases calling for reform of government practices because of the high risk of judicial error in such litigation. The federal courts had insinuated themselves into the People's business, and if the impropriety of that wasn't enough, they were incompetent at it, too. Standing was, and should be, a key tool in reversing this folly.

---

1. 17 Suffolk L. Rev. 881 (1983).
2. *Id.*

Scalia's article began with a short history of standing. Although he conceded it was difficult to trace the law of standing directly to the text of Article III, it could readily be traced to *Marbury*. The courts were empowered to expound on the law only to the degree it was necessary to resolve concrete claims of right by individuals. This foundational rationale underlying *Marbury* clearly implied something like the modern law of standing, which ensured a tight relationship between harms to individuals and the process of judicial review. To illustrate this, Scalia challenged his reader to contrast the rationale of *Marbury* with the opening paragraph of the 1971 D.C. Circuit decision that "began the judiciary's long love affair with environmental litigation":

> These cases are only the beginning of what promises to become a flood of new litigation—litigation seeking judicial assistance in protecting our natural environment. Several recently enacted statutes attest to the commitment of the government to control, at long last, the destructive engine of material "progress." But it remains to be seen whether the promise of this legislation will become a reality. Therein lies the judicial role. In these cases, we must for the first time interpret the broadest and perhaps most important of the recent statutes: the National Environmental Policy Act of 1969 (NEPA). We must assess claims that one of the agencies charged with its administration has failed to live up to the congressional mandate. Our duty, in short, is to see that important legislative purposes, heralded in the halls of Congress, are not lost or misdirected in the vast hallways of the federal bureaucracy.[3]

The writer of these doctrinaire words was J. Skelly Wright, originally one of the judicial heroes of the civil rights movement as a district judge in the South, and later one of the liberal lions on the D.C. Circuit. Wright had just the sort of reputation as a "judicial activist" that Scalia loved to mock. In fact, Wright was fairly deferential to agencies in most areas of administrative law.[4] But when it came to the environment, Wright was a flat-out activist. He had written the D.C. Circuit opinions ruling for the plaintiffs in *SCRAP v. United States* (which the Supreme Court affirmed) and *Sierra Club v. Morton* (reversed). His signature environmental decision, *People Against Nuclear Power (PANE) v. Metropolitan Edison Co.*, grew out of the March 1979 reactor core meltdown at Three Mile Island on the Susquehanna River just south of Harrisburg, Pennsylvania. In September 1981, the Nuclear Regulatory Commission voted to permit one of the reactors at Three Mile Island to reopen, rejecting PANE's argument that the community would suffer serious psychological problems. Writing for a 2–1 panel majority, Skelly Wright overruled the commission, insisting that the National

---

3. *Id.* at 884, quoting Calvert Cliffs Coordinating Comm'n v. Atomic Energy Comm'n, 449 F.2d 1109 (D.C. Cir. 1971).

4. *See* Arthur Selwyn Miller, A "Capacity for Outrage": The Judicial Odyssey of J. Skelly Wright ch. 4 (Greenwood 1984).

Environmental Policy Act (NEPA) required the commission to consider "post-traumatic anxieties, accompanied by physical effects and caused by fears of recurring catastrophe."[5] The Supreme Court promptly and unanimously reversed; even Wright's dear friend Brennan could not bring himself to vote for affirmance.

In his article, Scalia traced this overactive judicial review of agency action back to the courts' interpretation of Section 702 of the Administrative Procedure Act of 1947 (APA). Section 702 stated that "any person suffering legal wrong because of any agency action, or adversely affected or aggrieved by such action within the meaning of any relevant statute, shall be entitled to judicial review thereof."[6] The first clause was an obvious reference to the *Edward Hines* rule requiring that those who seek judicial review of administrative action demonstrate the violation of some vested legal right. Clearly, such a violation of legal right would continue to be sufficient for judicial review after 1947. But it would no longer be necessary; the second clause now made judicial review available to any person "adversely affected or aggrieved by [agency action] within the meaning of any relevant statute."

But what precisely did this second clause mean? There were at least two possible interpretations. One (favored by Scalia) was that the clause merely codified decisions like *Sanders Brothers*, the 1940 decision permitting judicial review of an FCC decision by a plaintiff who had no legal injury, but only competitive or economic injury. Recall that the judicial review provision of the Federal Communications Act had authorized an appeal to the D.C. Circuit by any person "aggrieved or whose interests are adversely affected by any decision" granting or denying a license application. The *Sanders Brothers* Court construed that language to include those who were *damnum absque injuria*—harmed without suffering legal injury. In Scalia's view, the second clause of Section 702 of the APA merely confirmed that Congress did not mean to repudiate decisions like *Sanders Brothers*, which expansively interpreted judicial review provisions in existing enabling statutes. If any given statute authorized judicial review by way of language like "any person aggrieved," or "any party in interest," or "a person holding a substantial interest," then the second clause of Section 702 authorized suit by someone who had suffered economic but not legal injury.

That interpretation was a far cry from the construction that later prevailed in the *Data Processing* litigation: any aggrieved person may sue so long as they suffer "injury-in-fact" and fall within some "zone of interests" meant to be protected by the enabling statute, even if that enabling statute contained no judicial review provision using the words "any person aggrieved" or reasonable facsimile. In his 1983 article, Scalia argued that the *Data Processing* interpretation was

5. 678 F.2d 222, 228 (D.C. Cir. 1982).
6. 5 U.S.C. Sec. 702.

incorrect as a matter of legislative intent. He quoted the statements of then attorney general Tom Clark and Senator Pat McCarran to the effect that Section 702 "reflects existing law." (Ironically, *Justice* Scalia would presumably reject *Judge* Scalia's proffer of such legislative history to guide interpretation of the statutory text.)[7] More importantly, however, the *Data Processing* interpretation had admitted judicial review to places where it never belonged. "It is difficult to exaggerate the effect which this interpretation . . . has had upon the ability of the courts to review administrative action," he lamented.[8] As proof, he pointed to the *SCRAP* litigation, in which the Supreme Court had affirmed Skelly Wright's decision permitting standing on the basis of a highly attenuated causal chain. Scalia ridiculed the decision as permitting a generalized grievance, saying that it was tantamount to recognizing standing in "all who breathe [the country's] air."[9] *SCRAP* could not have happened if not for the misbegotten *Data Processing* interpretation of Section 702.

For Scalia, the relationship of the individual to the government action in question was intimately related to separation of powers. "When an individual who is the *very* object of a law's requirement or prohibition seeks to challenge it, he always has standing," he wrote. "That is the classic case of the law bearing down upon the individual himself, and the court will not pause to inquire whether the grievance is a 'generalized' one."[10] But challenges to agency action in the post–*Data Processing* era were less and less likely to fit this description. Instead, they frequently involved plaintiffs "complaining of an agency's unlawful *failure* to impose a requirement or prohibition upon *someone else*."[11] In these cases, judicial involvement was highly suspect because the schema strayed too far from the traditional paradigm. First, these cases involved agency inaction rather than action. Agencies are entitled to exercise their discretion not to move forward with enforcement for practical reasons unrelated to the law. Second, Scalia apparently believed that judicial review should be less available for those who suffer secondary, or unintended, effects of agency decisions than those who suffer primary, or intended, effects.[12] This belief may derive from a more general philosophy, namely that judicial review of agency decisions should generally be available to regulated parties and generally unavailable to intended beneficiaries of the

7. And, to be fair, Scalia acknowledged in a footnote that some members of Congress apparently intended for Section 702 to expand judicial review. *See* 17 Suffolk L. Rev. at 888 n.35.

8. *Id.* at 889.

9. *Id.* at 890.

10. *Id.* at 894.

11. *Id.*

12. *See* Lujan v. Defenders of Wildlife, 504 U.S. 555, 562 (1992) ("when the plaintiff is not himself the object of the government action or inaction he challenges, standing is not precluded, but it is ordinarily 'substantially more difficult' to establish").

enabling statute. In any event, one who complains of an agency's decision not to go after someone else has a long way to go in answering Scalia's gut test for standing: "What's it to you?"[13]

Scalia's principal rationale for limiting standing in agency review cases applied especially strongly in environmental litigation. The doctrine of standing is meant to keep courts to their unique and limited role, which is to protect the vested legal rights of minorities from overreaching legislative or executive action. William Marbury, a member of the vanquished Federalist minority, could call upon the courts to protect his judicial commission against an obnoxious new Republican majority bent on stealing it. That was precisely what courts were meant for. What courts were *not* good for, Scalia continued, was telling the elected branches how best to serve the interests of the majority. Yet this, in his view, was often what happened when the courts engaged in judicial review of agency action in environmental cases. Congress would enact a statute aimed at protecting the environment on behalf of the entire nation and then charge an expert agency with the enforcement of that statute. Environmental public interest groups might disagree with the methods or pace of that enforcement, culminating in litigation to force the agency's hand. In Scalia's view, such judicial review was nothing more than the least majoritarian, least electorally accountable branch second-guessing how the agency should best serve the interests of the majority. The courts' "greatest success in such an enterprise—ensuring strict enforcement of the environmental laws, not to protect particular minorities, but for the benefit of all the people—met with approval in the classrooms of Cambridge and New Haven, but not in the factories of Detroit and the mines of West Virginia."[14]

Scalia's theory of standing doctrine—as protection against courts telling majorities how best to pursue their own interests—resonated the most deeply in the environmental cases, where it was obvious that all citizens were similarly vulnerable. But it extended to other areas as well. Scalia ridiculed the *Flast* decision permitting standing to challenge congressional expenditures allegedly violating the Establishment Clause. What singular minority was meant to be protected by the Establishment Clause? No such minority existed. All citizens, no matter what faith or nonfaith they profess, are protected by that prohibition against governmental endorsement of any particular church. How, then, ought the majority to protect itself against such endorsement, with its attendant danger of religious tyranny? Scalia would say the majoritarian branches must be given full discretion to decide on this methodology. The same would go for *Richardson v. United States*, the case in which the plaintiff challenged the CIA's refusal to disclose its expenditures, allegedly in violation of the Statements and

13. *Id.* at 882.
14. Scalia, *supra* note 264 at 897.

Accounts Clause. The Statements and Accounts Clause exists to protect the entire citizenry against undue secrecy in government, and to ensure that all the members of the electorate have sufficient information to exercise their franchise. The majority knows best how to protect these interests. It does not need "aristocratic" federal judges to tell it how.

* * *

In 1920, Antonino and Maria Scalia took their children, Salvatore Eugene and Carmela, from their village of Sommatino on the island of Sicily, and set sail for America.[15] Coming through Ellis Island, the family settled in Trenton, New Jersey, where the Scalias had friends among the other Sicilian immigrants. Already ensconced in Trenton were the Panaros—Pasquale, Maria, and their children, the eldest being Catherine. On August 19, 1929, Salvatore Eugene Scalia and Catherine Panaro were married.

It would be almost seven years until Salvatore and Catherine had their only child, Antonin. In the meantime, Salvatore had embarked on an academic career, working on a doctorate in Romance Languages at Columbia. He taught Italian, French, and Spanish, and he particularly became an expert on Dante. He was hired as an instructor in the Romance Languages department at Brooklyn College in 1939, and, after earning his Ph.D. in 1950, he was promoted to assistant professor.

Salvatore Eugene Scalia was an unremittingly serious man. In his spare time, he did scholarship, studied opera, and collected Italian lyrics and sheet music. He had no time for any kind of sports, games, or joking around. And he had the highest of expectations for his only child. According to Scalia biographer Joan Biskupic, if Antonin brought home a grade of A, the father asked why it was not an A-plus. "That's fine Nino," he would say, "but maybe next time you could do this better." In a 2008 interview, Biskupic recalled Salvatore's reputation as a "severe" man and asked the Justice whether it was true. "Yes," Scalia said, shaking his head. "He was severe. He was demanding."[16] The father was equally a man of integrity and impeccable comportment. "Brains are like muscles—you can hire them by the hour," he told young Nino. "The only thing that's not for sale is character." From his father, Antonin learned "to value the words of a text and appreciate cast-iron rules akin to those found in Dante's orderly universe of sin and suffering," wrote Biskupic.[17]

If Salvatore and his side of the family were taciturn and reticent, the Panaros were charismatic and outgoing. Catherine's father Pasquale was a bon vivant and jack-of-all-trades, mixing in with other immigrants and becoming a leader in the

---

15. This entire biographical sketch has been lifted from JOAN BISKUPIC, AMERICAN ORIGINAL: THE LIFE AND CONSTITUTION OF SUPREME COURT JUSTICE ANTONIN SCALIA (Farrar, Straus 2009).

16. *Id.* at 15.

17. *Id.* at 17.

Order of the Sons of Italy, a network for newly arrived Italians. Her mother Maria was the anchor of the family, eventually acquiring property and becoming a shrewd businesswoman. Her brother Vincent became a lawyer and ran for office. From the Panaro clan, wrote Biskupic, Antonin "picked up a knack for levity and the good timing of a storyteller, along with a sense of showmanship and the gestures of comical exaggeration."[18]

Young Scalia was an excellent student, earning a scholarship to Xavier High, an all-boys Jesuit school on Sixteenth Street in lower Manhattan. At Xavier, all students participated in junior ROTC, wearing uniforms replete with insignia indicating rank, saluting all in positions of authority. "Four years there established Antonin's academic prowess, entrenched his regard for Catholicism, and reinforced his rule-oriented nature," Biskupic observed.[19] Scalia graduated first in his class and was named valedictorian. He won a Naval ROTC scholarship and wanted to use it at Princeton. But Princeton, clubby even by Ivy League standards, turned him down. "I was an Italian boy from Queens, not quite the Princeton type," Scalia told Biskupic.

He enrolled at Georgetown instead and thrived there. He was active in drama and debate. He was president of the Mask and Bauble theater club and played the fiddler and a member of the jury in *The Devil and Daniel Webster*, the Faust adaptation in which a New Hampshire farmer sells his soul to the devil and is defended by the famous American lawyer. He majored in history and graduated as valedictorian in 1957. In an interview with Biskupic, Scalia recounted the culmination of his history major, which was a comprehensive set of oral exams:

> I went before a panel of three professors who quizzed you[.] The chairman of the panel [was] a lovely man, a wonderful man, and he's giving me these questions. And I'm knocking them out of the ballpark and I'm feeling really good. Then he says, "Very good, Mr. Scalia. I have one last question: If you look back over all the history that you've studied here over the last four years. If you had to pick one event that you thought was the most significant, what would it be?"
>
> And I'm thinking, there's no wrong answer to this . . . I don't remember what I even answered, maybe the Battle of Waterloo, maybe the Battle of the Solomon Islands . . . . And he shook his head sadly and said, "No, Mr. Scalia. The Incarnation, Mr. Scalia." It was the last lesson I learned at Georgetown: not to separate your religious life from your intellectual life. They're not separate.[20]

18. *Id.*
19. *Id.* at 21.
20. *Id.* at 25.

The next stop for Scalia was Harvard Law School. Again he was a top student, making the *Harvard Law Review* and sharing a small office with fellow editor Frank Michelman, who would later clerk for Brennan and play a key role in drafting *Baker v. Carr* prior to joining the Harvard faculty. As was typical of law review editors, Scalia and Michelman spent many late nights editing, largely displacing their study time. Michelman, who would end up well on the left of the political and jurisprudential spectrum, could recall nothing about his time with Scalia that would presage the future arch-conservative and *agent provocateur*. "He recalled Scalia as convivial," wrote Biskupic. Michelman said he never would have predicted that his classmate would prove to be "such a gifted and colorful prose stylist, whose opinions would grab attention, in part, for their occasional bouts of vituperation. I did not see that coming."[21]

Scalia befriended many important people at Harvard, including future Massachusetts governor and presidential nominee Michael Dukakis, future U.S. Senator Paul Sarbanes, and future Eighth Circuit Judge Richard Arnold. But the most important person he met was on a blind date. Maureen McCarthy, daughter of a self-made physician and a self-sacrificing homemaker, was matriculating at Radcliffe. She had grown up in the suburbs, where Catholics were rare; some of the neighborhood children had been forbidden from playing with her because of her faith. She was an English major, but loved politics, and had recently become disillusioned with what she saw as the excessive "social welfare" orientation of the Democratic Party. "This was not how I was raised," she told Biskupic. "It was that you work hard and make your way." She was enthusiastic about staying home to raise a large family. Antonin and Maureen hit it off instantly and before long were married. Looking back, Justice Scalia marveled at his good fortune. "How often can you get a Radcliffe graduate to settle down and devote her life to raising nine kids?"[22]

After graduation, Scalia was persuaded to join the establishment firm of Jones, Day, in Cleveland. His practice was a success, and he was about to be made a partner before abruptly swerving to a faculty position at the University of Virginia Law School, where he became an expert in administrative law. He had always intended to follow in his father's academic footsteps. But the Panaro side of him was too restless for the ivory tower. Before long he had taken what he thought would be a brief stint as general counsel of the Office of Telecommunications Policy in the Nixon administration, where he helped crack down on the Corporation for Public Broadcasting, which the administration believed had gone too far toward "liberal causes." He was ready to return to his faculty position at Virginia in spring 1974 when history intervened. Watergate was taking down the president. The so-called Saturday Night Massacre, in which Elliot Richardson

21. *Id.* at 28.
22. *Id.* at 31.

and William Ruckelshaus both resigned rather than obey Richard Nixon's order to fire special prosecutor Archibald Cox (Robert Bork eventually did the deed), brought Laurence Silberman to the number two position in the Justice Department, and he pushed to have Scalia hired as the new assistant attorney general for the Office of Legal Counsel, a position that most considered to be the conscience of the Justice Department. Following Nixon's resignation in August 1974, Silberman continued to campaign for Scalia, who got the job roughly two weeks later.

There was not much time to get cozy. Nixon was still trying to get his tape recordings and other potentially inculpatory documents back to his home in San Clemente, California, claiming that they were his private property. President Gerald Ford decided he needed a formal legal opinion on who owned the materials, and Scalia went to work. On September 8, the Justice Department released Scalia's fourteen-page opinion, which concluded that the papers indeed belonged to Nixon. "To conclude that such materials are not the property of former President Nixon would be to reverse what has apparently been the almost unvaried understanding of all three branches of the Government since the beginning of the Republic, and to call into question the practices of our Presidents since the earliest times," Scalia wrote.[23]

Scalia's handiwork was overshadowed by another news story coming out of the executive branch that day—the full and unconditional pardon of Richard Nixon. Amid high public resentment over the pardon, Congress was not about to let Nixon walk away with the evidence. Virtually ignoring Scalia's opinion, Congress enacted the Presidential Recording and Materials Preservation Act, ensuring that the materials would remain in the public domain. "The episode would be one of several that caused Scalia to guard jealously executive power and, in an atmosphere of distrust and suspicion, to consider Congress an adversary," wrote Biskupic.[24]

With openness in government the order of the day, Congress now passed a series of important amendments to the Freedom of Information Act (FOIA). There was a split within the Ford administration on whether to sign the legislation. White House counsel Philip Buchen urged Ford to sign the bill immediately, before Silberman and Scalia could talk him out of it. Scalia simply was not persuaded by the major premise of the FOIA. The Act could not be salvaged so long as "we are dominated by the obsession . . . that the first line of defense against an arbitrary executive is do-it-yourself oversight by the public and its surrogate, the press," he wrote. Some people requested information under the Act out of "idle curiosity," and federal judges were not well equipped to handle classification disputes.[25] How could the executive branch be expected to do its job if

23. *Id.* at 43.
24. *Id.* at 44–45.
25. *Id.* at 45.

it had to do everything in the public eye? With a strong assist from Deputy White House Chief of Staff Dick Cheney, Ford was persuaded to veto the amendments. Congress promptly overrode the veto.

During the remainder of his time in the Justice Department, Scalia was one of the Ford administration's principal spokesmen for assertions of executive privilege against congressional demands for information. He famously traded verbal jabs with Senator Edmund Muskie of Maine when in 1975 Muskie sponsored legislation that would have required the administration to keep congressional committees regularly informed about executive branch matters, including national security. At about the same time, Scalia was appearing before a special committee that was investigating possible abuses by the intelligence community. Chaired by New York Democrat Otis Pike, the committee had recommended that Secretary of State Henry Kissinger be held in contempt for failing to produce classified documents about covert operations overseas. Scalia fell back on his debating skills to defend the administration's claims of executive privilege in this matter as well. Then, when the panel led by liberal Idaho Senator Frank Church turned up evidence of domestic warrantless wiretaps, Scalia opposed the removal of exclusive power to order such wiretaps away from the executive branch, calling such power a practical necessity. The Fourth Amendment does not require a warrant, argued Scalia; it requires reasonableness in searches and seizures. And, in the intelligence field, "reasonableness does not demand the service of a warrant."[26]

When Jimmy Carter defeated Gerald Ford for the presidency in 1976, Scalia and many of the conservatives in the Justice Department went into academic and think-tank exile. Scalia went to the University of Chicago Law School, where he became active in the free market–oriented American Enterprise Institute and the fledgling Federalist Society, a safe haven for conservatives in the decidedly left-leaning American legal academy. When Ronald Reagan was elected in 1980, Scalia's attention returned to government work. The Reagan administration was politically and intellectually up Scalia's alley, with its strong commitments to deregulation, free markets, federalism, and executive branch prerogatives. He was bitterly disappointed when he lost out to Rex Lee for the solicitor general position in 1981, and then declined an offer of a seat on the Seventh Circuit Court of Appeals in spring 1982. He was holding out for a seat on the District of Columbia Circuit, which better fit his administrative law expertise; too, Washington was a much better fit for the Scalia clan than the Midwest. By late 1982, he had his appointment to the D.C. Circuit.

Sitting on the nation's most prominent and powerful federal circuit court, Scalia's star continued to rise quickly. Patrick Buchanan, the pugnacious former Nixon speechwriter who had been appointed Reagan's communications director

26. *Id.* at 57.

in 1985, was a strong advocate of making Scalia the administration's next Supreme Court appointee. The next year, when President Reagan nominated William Rehnquist to replace retiring Chief Justice Warren Burger, Reagan tapped Scalia to take Rehnquist's seat as an associate justice. Given how ideological and outspoken Scalia was, it could have been a bruising confirmation battle, but for the fact that the Senate took up Rehnquist's nomination first. The Democrats on the Judiciary Committee spent all their bullets on Rehnquist and Scalia received a relatively free pass.

* * *

In 1985, two years after Circuit Judge Scalia published his article on standing and separation of powers, the National Wildlife Federation (NWF) sued the Secretary of Interior and the Bureau of Land Management (BLM), claiming that over the previous decade they had violated federal law in carrying out a plan to return certain protected federal lands to the public domain, where they might then be subject to mining claims or oil and gas leasing. There were multiple and confusing layers of legal protections on these lands. In 1976 Congress had passed the Federal Land Policy and Management Act, which had mandated review of the lands' status. But it wasn't until 1981, when James Watt, President Reagan's first Secretary of the Interior, accelerated the lifting of some of the lands' protections that the process became highly controversial. The NWF worried that mining claims in particular would lead to environmental harm, which in turn would diminish recreational opportunities for NWF members. The complaint alleged that approximately 170 million acres had been illegally returned to the public domain, and it requested a preliminary injunction stopping the process.

The case came before federal district judge John H. Pratt, a Johnson appointee known for ruling in favor of plaintiffs in several prominent civil rights cases. The government moved to dismiss the case on multiple grounds, including lack of standing. On December 4, 1985, Pratt denied the motion and issued a preliminary injunction effectively invalidating the lifting of protections on lands going all the way back to 1981.

The government appealed to the D.C. Circuit and the case was assigned to a three-judge panel consisting of Abner Mikva, the celebrated liberal ex-congressman from Chicago; Stanley Weigel, a liberal but erratic Kennedy appointee; and Stephen F. Williams, a scholarly conservative Reagan appointee with considerable expertise in public lands. Almost exactly two years after Pratt's ruling, the panel affirmed in full. Speaking through Mikva, the panel found that the NWF had adequately alleged harm to its 4.5 million members nationwide, who wished to use parts of the affected 170 million acres for aesthetic or recreational purposes. The government insisted that this blanket assertion of harm was insufficiently specific; it did not establish that any particular NWF members intended to use any particular lands at any particular times. In that sense, the government argued, the complaint was defective under *Sierra Club v. Morton*, the Mineral King case. But the panel rejected the comparison to *Sierra Club*, instead finding that *SCRAP* was the precedent most on point. "Given the holding of SCRAP," wrote Mikva, it was hard to figure exactly why the government thought it could win on standing. Judge Williams filed a lengthy dissent sharply criticizing the scope of the injunction. "The majority today upholds a district judge's self-appointment as *de facto* Secretary of the Interior over 180 million acres," he wrote. "[T]here is no basis for the sweeping injunction here issued."[27]

As the case went back to Pratt for trial, things got strange. Mikva and Weigel seemed to have a sudden case of buyer's remorse. Only four months later, in denying rehearing, the panel issued a memorandum to the effect that its patience was wearing thin:

> "It has been over two years since the preliminary injunction was issued," the panel stated. "We noted then, and continue to believe, that some of the criticisms of the breadth and scope of the preliminary injunction offered in [Williams's] vigorous dissent are not without force. . . . For these reasons, we believe that the disposition of millions of acres should not continue to rest any longer than necessary on the foundation of a preliminary injunction which was entered on consideration of the brief affidavits and cursory materials presented to the court below.[28]

Oddly, Pratt exhibited no sign of resentment toward the panel's new attitude. He himself seemed to have had a change of heart. Assessing the case on remand, Pratt noted that the previous finding of the NWF's standing was made in the context of a motion to dismiss. In that posture, the courts were required to construe the complaint's allegations most favorably to the plaintiff, which in this case meant tolerating a high degree of vagueness about the details of which BLM decisions harmed which of NWF's members, and in what way. But the case was no longer at that preliminary stage. The government was now moving for summary judgment. According to Pratt, this meant that, in order to maintain standing, the NWF had to produce some actual evidence to prove that BLM decisions harmed NWF members. He pointed to the Supreme Court's important 1986 decision in *Celotex Corp. v. Catrett* as requiring this strict standard on summary judgment motions.[29]

The NWF submitted two affidavits of members, Peggy Peterson and Richard Erman, to prove the harms necessary for standing. As is generally true in modern civil litigation, they were written up by lawyers in boilerplate language. In this case, they were written with an eye toward satisfying *Sierra Club*. The Peterson affidavit claimed that she used lands in the vicinity of the South Pass–Green Mountain area of Wyoming for recreational and aesthetic enjoyment, which had been adversely affected by BLM's decision to open the lands to prospective

27. 835 F.2d at 327, 338.

28. 844 F.2d 889, 889 (D.C. Cir., Apr. 29, 1988) (memorandum opinion).

29. 477 U.S. 317 (1986).

mining and oil and gas exploration. The Erman affidavit made similar claims with respect to federal lands in the vicinity of the Grand Canyon National Park, the Arizona Strip (Kanab Plateau), and the Kaibab National Forest. The Arizona Strip is an area of approximately 5.5 million acres, about one-eighth the area of Arizona.

Judge Pratt found both affidavits "vague, conclusory, and [lacking] factual specificity." He stressed that both affidavits had repeatedly used the term "in the vicinity." Even if that had been sufficient for standing to challenge BLM decisions in those particular areas, what about all the other areas? "[P]laintiff's claims of injury reach hundreds of decisions affecting 180 million acres spread over seventeen states," Pratt wrote.

One had to think that the original panel dissenter, Williams, had a good chance of getting Mikva and Weigel to go along with an affirmance this time. But on this go-round the case drew a different panel: Harry T. Edwards, the liberal former law professor whom Jimmy Carter appointed to replace David Bazelon on the D.C. Circuit; Ruth Bader Ginsburg, another former law professor who had written extensively on sex discrimination; and Frank Kaufman, an ornery old Johnson appointee to the district court in Maryland.[30] They saw the affidavits in a different light. It was true that neither Peterson nor Erman had stated the precise coordinates of the lands they used and enjoyed, and, in that sense, the court could not independently verify that the BLM decisions in question actually affected the lands being used by the two affiants. Where Judge Pratt had seen this as a question of specificity, however, the panel saw it as a question of veracity. Peterson and Erman had sworn under penalty of perjury that the BLM decisions had affected the lands they actually used, whichever precise acres those were. "If Peterson was not referring to lands in [the affected areas], her allegation of impairment to her use and enjoyment would be meaningless, or perjurious," Edwards wrote.[31] And yet Pratt had not challenged the honesty of the affidavits, only their specificity. In any event, Edwards continued, Mikva's opinion for the first panel had settled all this. That opinion had considered the very same affidavits and found that they had "specifically identif[ied] locations where its members' interests [were] threatened by the Department's actions."[32] It was true, Edwards conceded, that the first panel was dealing with Judge Pratt's denial of a motion to dismiss, as compared to summary judgment this time around. But, Edwards argued, in that first go-round Pratt also had a motion for a preliminary injunction before him, which meant that the standards for construing the affidavits were just as stringent as if it had been a motion for summary judgment.

With one future Justice, John Roberts, arguing for the government, and another, Ruth Bader Ginsburg, on the panel whose decision was under review,

30. National Wildlife Federation v. Burford, 878 F.2d 422 (D.C. Cir. 1989).
31. 878 F.2d at 431.
32. 835 F.2d at 325.

the Supreme Court voted 5–4 to reverse. The Court divided along stereotypical ideological lines, with Rehnquist (now the Chief Justice), Byron White, Sandra Day O'Connor, Anthony Kennedy, and Scalia voting to reverse and Harry Blackmun, Brennan, Thurgood Marshall, and John Paul Stevens voting to affirm. Rehnquist assigned the opinion to Scalia who, now into his fourth year on the Court, would have his first opportunity as a Supreme Court justice to apply the standing doctrine in a major environmental case.

The narrowest route for Scalia would have been to adopt the approach of the district court. Pratt had had the unenviable task of explaining why he thought the NWF had standing the first time around but not the second. His explanation was plausible—the standards on a motion to dismiss were different than on a motion for summary judgment. Indeed, Scalia's opinion for the Court began with that point. Citing the combination of *Sierra Club* and *Celotex*, Scalia made it clear that, in order to prevail on summary judgment, the government need not affirmatively disprove the NWF's case for standing. The burden was on the NWF to set forth specific facts supporting the elements of that case. Turning to the Peterson and Erman affidavits, Scalia quoted at length from the district court's opinion finding them insufficient, then quoted from the portion of Judge Edwards' panel opinion stating that the district court was obliged to resolve any ambiguity in the affidavits in favor of the NWF, the party resisting summary judgment.

"That is not the law," Scalia stated. A district court may not assume that general averments in an affidavit include the specific facts necessary to survive a summary judgment motion, he said. There is some room for argument about how specific is sufficiently specific in any given case, Scalia acknowledged, but the summary judgment standard was certainly not satisfied "by averments which state only that one of respondent's members uses unspecified portions of an immense tract of territory."[33] Then, with one swift stroke, Scalia marginalized *SCRAP*, the decision he had so excoriated in his article. "The *SCRAP* opinion, whose expansive expression of what would suffice for Section 702 review under its particular facts has never since been emulated by this Court, is of no relevance here, since it involved not a [summary judgment motion] but a . . . motion to dismiss on the pleadings," he stated.[34] Scalia had authoritatively portrayed *SCRAP* as nothing more than an outlier among precedents, limiting it to its facts and effectively excusing lower federal courts—and future Supreme Court majorities—from having to engage the case in any serious way.

The next portion of Scalia's majority opinion struck at the heart of the NWF's litigation strategy. The NWF's complaint sought to paint the government's lifting of protections on these federal lands as a bureaucratic monolith, a unitary

33. Lujan v. National Wildlife Federation, 497 U.S. 871, 889 (1990).
34. 497 U.S. at 889.

edict carried out systematically in various geographical locations. The NWF did not want to be forced to litigate each BLM decision piecemeal; the costs would be prohibitive. It was, for all intents, a nationwide class action. But class actions are generally only appropriate where the alleged harms radiate from a common source, so that the issue of liability can be dealt with in a centralized way, as where a certain make and model of automobile suffers from a distinctive kind of brake failure or sudden acceleration, injuring a large number of people. The NWF verbally characterized the series of BLM decisions lifting protections as "the land withdrawal review program," thus implying that the BLM's individual decisions to lift protections on particular lands were so substantially similar that their legality or illegality could be determined in gross. The court of appeals panel accepted that characterization without discussion.

Scalia, the former administrative law professor, found a textual portal through which to attack the characterization. The APA permits judicial review of "final agency action." Did this series of BLM decisions fit that phrase? Scalia said it did not:

> The term "land withdrawal review program" (which as far as we know is not derived from any authoritative text) does not refer to a single BLM order or regulation, or even to a completed universe of particular BLM orders and regulations. It is simply the name by which petitioners have occasionally referred to the continuing (and thus constantly changing) operations of the BLM in reviewing withdrawal revocation applications and the classifications of public lands . . . . As the District Court explained, the "land withdrawal review program" extends to, currently at least, "1250 or so individual classification terminations and withdrawal revocations."[35]

Writing for the dissenters, Justice Blackmun questioned Justice Scalia's assertion that the NWF was not challenging truly final agency action. The choice to view the BLM decisions as disconnected from one another was contestable. Sometimes "agency action" consists of a rule of broad applicability, Blackmun noted, in which case a victory for the plaintiff will, as a matter of precedent, invalidate the rule as to everybody, not only the plaintiff. "Under these circumstances a single plaintiff, so long as he is injured by the rule, may obtain 'programmatic' relief that affects the rights of parties not before the court," he wrote.[36] Blackmun and Scalia could have had precisely the same argument about "facial" versus "as applied" challenges of statutes or executive orders. Scalia and the majority believed that courts functioned to settle claims of right between individuals (some of whom might work for government); Blackmun and the dissenters believed that, in the modern state, governmental coercion often and

35. 497 U.S. at 890.
36. 497 U.S. at 913 (Blackmun, J., dissenting).

most powerfully operated through vast bureaucracies, directly and indirectly against large groups of individuals.

Roughly a decade earlier, some academics had offered a theoretical account in support of the Blackmun/Brennan view of adjudication. In 1978, Joseph Vining of the Michigan law faculty published a book called *Legal Identity: The Coming of Age of Public Law.*[37] It was alternately a technical exposition on the standing doctrine and a philosophical meditation on the protean quality of personhood in an increasingly interconnected society. He celebrated *Data Processing*'s loosening of strictures on judicial review of agency action because it implicitly recognized that the legal order is founded in a community of shared ends and public values. The legal right test, inherited from common law, was premised on a hopelessly anachronistic view of society as essentially atomistic. Time and again Vining referred to what he called "the Donne effect," in honor of Justice Blackmun's citation in *Sierra Club* to the "no man is an island" epigram. "The consequences of an accident, or, to choose an example much in the mind of modern lawyers, a misleading corporate press release, ripple through the existing system of mutual dependencies," wrote Vining. "What we are witnessing is nothing less than the breakdown of individualism as a basis for legal reasoning," he declared.[38] Courts were not mere umpires of private disputes, but rather "one agency in a system of multiple decision-making agencies pursuing emerging public values."[39] Vining's dreamy prose made the book more of a "connoisseur's piece"[40] than a manifesto, but it captured a sense among activists, students, and many academics that American society had outgrown its traditional model of courts and adjudication.

The next year, Owen Fiss published a foreword to the *Harvard Law Review* that continued down Vining's path. Fiss, a Yale law professor who had clerked for Brennan, very nearly inverted the conventional story about adjudication. Where orthodox wisdom saw dispute resolution among individuals as the paradigm and sweeping "structural reform" injunctions as outliers that threatened the legitimacy of the federal judiciary, Fiss deemed the structural reform cases as central and conventional disputation as secondary. His descriptive claim was breathtaking:

> The function of adjudication, whether in the nineteenth century or twentieth century, torts or criminal law, contract or antitrust, *McCulloch v. Maryland* or *Brown v. Board of Education,* has not been to resolve disputes between individuals, but rather to give meaning to our public values.[41]

---

37. Yale University Press.

38. JOSEPH VINING, LEGAL IDENTITY 2 (Yale Univ. Press 1978).

39. *Id.* at 22–23.

40. Richard B. Stewart, *Standing for Solidarity*, 88 YALE L. J. 1559, 1576 (1978) (reviewing Vining).

41. Owen M. Fiss, *Foreword: The Forms of Justice*, 93 HARV. L. REV. 1, 36 (1979).

This process of assigning meaning was especially present in the cases seeking reform of mass state-run institutions: "At the core of structural reform is the judge, and his effort to give meaning to our public values."[42] The real threat to freedom and equality, Fiss thought, was not individual bad actors but massive, dehumanizing bureaucracies. The role of the judge was not to stand apart as a passive neutral, but to distill specific propositions from abstract shared ideals and then to remake bureaucracies in accord with those propositions.

Precisely what were these "public values" of which Vining and Fiss spoke so lyrically? For his part, at least, Fiss believed that they were norms that underlay the grand phrases in the Constitution—liberty, equality, due process, freedom of speech, no establishment of religion, property, no impairments of the obligation of contract, security of the person, no cruel and unusual punishments. "They are capable of a great number of different meanings," Fiss stated. "There is a need—a constitutional need—to give them specific meaning, to give them operational content, and, where there is a conflict, to set priorities."[43] He did not explain how his conception of "giving meaning to constitutional values" differed, if at all, from the conventional notion of constitutional interpretation according to text, history, and structure, yet he seemed to suggest an enterprise more oracular than technical.

But if judges were oracles of sorts, they were hemmed in by procedural requirements. Unlike legislators, judges had little control over their agendas. They were stuck with the litigation that came before them. They could not reach out to decide matters not before them, nor could they ignore issues that were before them. They were not free to speak to just anyone involved with the litigation; their dialogue was limited to the proper representatives of the named parties. And it had to be a true dialogue. Judges were required to listen, and they were required to respond. At least with respect to impactful decisions, they could not simply say, "I prefer this result," or "I say so." They had to give reasons.

Fiss insisted that this process was not at all the same thing as judges simply giving voice to their personal political beliefs. "The task of the judge is to give meaning to constitutional values, and he does that by working with the constitutional text, history, and social ideals," he wrote. "He searches for what is true, right, or just. He does not become a participant in interest group politics."[44] Fiss was relying on a kind of moral realism. The grand phrases of the Constitution rest on moral precepts that possess an objective reality. They are not posited by authorities, nor are they dependent upon what majorities of people think. They are, as the philosophers say, mind-independent. This was the problem with the law and economics obsession that began to grip the academy in the

42. *Id.* at 17.
43. *Id.* at 1.
44. *Id.* at 9.

1970s, and the love affair with markets that Reagan would touch off in the early 1980s. "We have lost our confidence in the existence of the values that underlie the litigation of the 1960s, or, for that matter, in the existence of any public values," Fiss complained. "All is preference."[45]

Although neither Vining nor Fiss spoke of environmental protection as a "public value" that needed to be given meaning through adjudication, doubtless many other liberals believed something like that. Despoilment of the environment was a "tragedy of the commons": individuals received full economic benefit from certain types of polluting conduct, but suffered only a tiny fraction of the resulting environmental degradation. In that sense, protection of the environment is a classic collective action problem, and the solution is regulation. But to the degree that regulatory agencies operate on the basis of interest group pluralism, they will be unable to overcome this collective action problem, as individual demographic or other interest groups do not feel the need for environmental measures with the sufficient intensity to bring them about. Some of the D.C. Circuit environmental opinions from the 1970s appear to have been premised on something like this "public values" view of adjudication.

Scalia ridiculed this view. Courts were not there to give "meaning" to any kind of values. They were there to settle disputes. The politically accountable branches were there to make value choices. This was elementary separation of powers—high school civics, really. Beyond that, Scalia held the environmental movement in low regard. He thought it elitist, a bunch of rich, privileged Ivy-leaguers sanctimoniously telling people from economically developing communities that they shouldn't pollute and shouldn't develop land. Whether intentionally or unintentionally, upper-middle-class environmentalists were pulling the ladder of social mobility up behind them.

In 1992, Scalia drew the assignment of writing the majority opinion in *Lujan v. Defenders of Wildlife* (sometimes referred to as *Lujan II* despite being entirely separate litigation). It would be his most important standing opinion and his most important environmental decision. It provided him with a perfect opportunity to put into action the ideas set forth in his earlier standing-and-separation-of-powers law review article.

Under the Endangered Species Act of 1973 (ESA), the Secretary of the Interior was required to draw up a list of endangered species and their habitats. The Act further requires every federal agency, "in consultation with . . . the Secretary," to ensure that none of its actions jeopardizes any of the listed species or habitats. During the Carter administration, two federal agencies promulgated a joint regulation stating that this statutory consultation requirement extended to agency actions overseas as well as domestically. A few years later, however, the Reagan administration issued a superseding joint regulation reinterpreting

45. *Id.* at 17.

the ESA not to require such consultation for agency action overseas. Defenders of Wildlife and other wildlife conservation organizations sued the secretary in federal court seeking an injunction that would require him to draw up a new regulation restoring the original statutory interpretation. The district court dismissed for lack of standing, but the Eighth Circuit reversed, and on remand the district court issued the requested injunction.[46]

Justice Scalia began with the proposition that the purpose of standing doctrine was to preserve separation of powers. He then recited what had become the orthodoxy since the early 1970s about the Article III underpinnings of standing:

> Over the years, our cases have established that the irreducible minimum of standing contains three elements. First, the plaintiff must have suffered an "injury-in-fact"—an invasion of a legally protected interest which is (a) concrete and particularized . . . and (b) "actual or imminent," not "conjectural" or "hypothetical." Second there must be a causal connection between the injury and the conduct complained of—the injury has to be "fairly . . . traceable to the challenged action of the defendant, and not . . . the result of the independent action of some third party not before the court." Third, it must be "likely," as opposed to merely "speculative," that the injury will be "redressed by a favorable decision."[47]

Scalia also drew a distinction between plaintiffs who are "objects" of agency regulation (regulated parties) and those who are not (intended beneficiaries of the enabling statute). In the latter cases, standing is not precluded, he wrote, but "it is ordinarily 'substantially more difficult' to establish."[48]

Beyond these general statements about standing doctrine, Scalia came to two holdings: the plaintiffs had failed to demonstrate sufficiently imminent injury-in-fact; and they had failed to demonstrate that the requested injunction was sufficiently likely to remedy their claimed injury-in-fact.

With respect to injury, the Court of Appeals had found standing requirements satisfied by focusing on two main affidavits, those of Joyce Kelly and Amy Skilbred. Kelly stated that she had gone to Egypt in 1986 to observe the habitat of the Nile crocodile and would like to do it again, with the hope of actually seeing the crocodiles; however, American support for the rehabilitation of the Aswan Dam endangered the habitat. Skilbred stated that she had been to Sri Lanka in 1981 in an unsuccessful attempt to view the endangered

46. The panel opinion reversing the original dismissal is *Defenders of Wildlife v. Hodel*, 851 F.2d 1035 (8th Cir. 1988). The opinion affirming the district courts actions on remand is at 911 F.2d 117 (1990).

47. Lujan v. Defenders of Wildlife, 504 U.S. 555, 560–61 (1992) (citations and bracketing omitted).

48. *Id.* at 562.

elephant and leopard. She too said she would like to return to these habitats, but they were endangered by a development project that was funded by the Agency for International Development. When asked when she intended to return, she demurred. "There is a civil war going on right now," she said. "Not next year, I will say. In the future."[49] The Court of Appeals found that these affidavits established sufficiently imminent injury-in-fact.

Scalia and the majority disagreed. The affidavits contained no facts showing how damage to the species would produce "imminent" injury to the two women. The fact they had visited the animals' habitats in the past contributed nothing to the likelihood of future injury, Scalia wrote, citing the chokehold decision. And their professions of intent to return to the habitats were too vague. "Such 'some day' intentions—without any description of concrete plans, or indeed even any specification of *when* the some day will be—do not support a finding of the 'actual or imminent' injury that our cases require."[50]

In the next section, Scalia concluded that the plaintiffs had failed to demonstrate redressability. He made it clear that the plaintiffs had deliberately chosen a litigation strategy that was judicially disfavored. "Instead of attacking the separate decisions to fund particular projects allegedly causing them harm," he wrote, "respondents chose to challenge a more generalized level of Government action (rules regarding consultation), the invalidation of which would affect all overseas projects."[51] It was the same sort of tactical decision the National Wildlife Federation had made in the first *Lujan* case: litigate a series of similar practices in gross. From the perspective of public interest organizations, there was no other way to check bureaucratic abuses. Litigation of individual, yet virtually identical, bureaucratic actions was like trying to clean up a spilled bag of flour with pinched fingers. It was like forcing 10 million purchasers of a defective 29-cent ballpoint pen to each bring their own lawsuit. Unless they could challenge an entire pattern of illegal bureaucratic actions, plaintiffs had no effective way to stop them. Scalia conceded the efficacy of this tactic, but not its legitimacy. "[S]uits challenging, not specifically identifiable Government violations of law, but the particular programs agencies establish to carry out their legal obligations . . . are, even when premised on allegations of several instances of violations of law, . . . rarely if ever appropriate for federal-court adjudication," he asserted.[52] If public interest organizations wanted federal agencies to change their policies, they could help elect a different president.

The technical problem with redressability in this case, Scalia explained, had to do with whom the plaintiffs had sued. The defendant was the Secretary of the Interior. But the source of danger to the animals' habitats was not the actions of

49. *Id.* at 564.
50. *Id.*
51. *Id.* at 568.
52. *Id.*

the secretary, it was the actions of the agencies funding the Aswan Dam rehabilitation and the development project in Sri Lanka, respectively. The district court could order the secretary to revise his regulation to make it clear that the consultation requirement extended to agency action overseas. Unless the funding agencies were bound by any such revision, however, the danger to the animal habitats would remain unabated. The dissenters argued that the agencies would have been bound, but Scalia insisted that such binding effect was unclear, at best.

The Court of Appeals had upheld standing on one other theory, namely, that plaintiffs had suffered a "procedural injury." The ESA contained a "citizen-suit provision," which was Congress's way of extending the "any aggrieved person" authorization of judicial review to its farthest reaches. The provision stated, "Any person may commence a civil suit on his own behalf . . . to enjoin any person, including the United States and any other governmental instrumentality or agency . . . who is alleged to be in violation of any provision of this chapter."[53] This provision appeared to create a vested legal right in every person to see government adhere to the consultation requirement of the ESA. If it did create such rights in everyone, however, Justice Scalia cautioned that not just anyone could have a judicial remedy. Congress lacks the power to confer upon "*all* persons . . . an abstract, self-contained, noninstrumental 'right' to have the Executive observe the procedures required by law." Only those who can demonstrate their own concrete injury-in-fact can sue. Allowing people to sue without such injury would violate the so-called "prohibition against generalized grievances" exemplified by *Fairchild v. Hughes*, *Frothingham v. Mellon*, and, more recently, *United States v. Richardson*, Scalia wrote.

In a footnote, he added a rather scholarly observation about procedural rights and redressability, one whose significance would not become obvious until years later:

> There is this much truth to the assertion that "procedural rights" are special: The person who has been accorded a procedural right to protect his concrete interests can assert that right without meeting all the normal standards for redressability and immediacy. Thus, under our case law, one living adjacent to the site for proposed construction of a federal licensed dam has standing to challenge the licensing agency's failure to prepare an environmental impact statement, even though he cannot establish with any certainty that the statement will cause the license to be withheld or altered, and even though the dam will not be completed for many years. . . . What respondent's "procedural rights" argument seeks, however, is quite different from this: standing for persons who have no concrete interests

53. 16 U.S.C. Sec. 1540(g).

> affected—persons who live (and propose to live) at the other end of the country from the dam.[54]

It is worth noting what Justice Scalia acknowledged as settled in the law of standing. As an expert on administrative law, he could not ignore the many cases in which a person has obtained judicial review of an agency's failure to adhere to procedures, even though it was clear that, in the real world, it would do nothing but delay the agency's ultimate action. Thus he conceded that, where a procedural right is concerned, the normal standards of redressability and imminence are relaxed. What he did not ask was how this could be squared with his statement earlier in the opinion that the irreducible minima of Article III include imminent injury and redressability. Did Article III have two standards, one for "substantive" rights and one for "procedural" rights? Did Congress have the power to relax redressability and imminence standards that originate in Article III, and, if so, from whence did that power come?

Justice Kennedy joined Justice Scalia's opinion, with one exception. He carefully withheld his vote from Scalia's conclusion that Defenders of Wildlife had failed to demonstrate redressability, instead basing his concurrence on the holding that the alleged injury had not been sufficiently certain. He was obviously more comfortable with the public interest litigation model than Scalia was:

> As Government programs and policies become more complex and far reaching, we must be sensitive to the articulation of new rights of action that do not have clear analogs in our common-law tradition. Modern litigation has progressed far from the paradigm of Marbury suing Madison to get his commission . . . . In my view, Congress has the power to define injuries and articulate chains of causation that will give rise to a case or controversy where none existed before, and I do not read the Court's opinion to suggest a contrary view. In exercising this power, however, Congress must at the very least identify the injury it seeks to vindicate and relate the injury to the class of persons entitled to bring suit.[55]

Kennedy was ceding to Congress a broad power to authorize judicial review of agency action, so long as there was some nexus between the plaintiff and some specified injury.[56] For him, the only constitutionally mandated rule of standing prohibited Congress from enacting something like the following: "any person may sue to challenge any agency action that violates the law." The problem with the citizen-suit provision in *Lujan II* was that it came too close to this locution.

---

54. 504 U.S. at 573.

55. 504 U.S. at 580 (Kennedy, J., concurring in part).

56. Kennedy's belief that Congress should have broad latitude to authorize standing to seek judicial review of agency action closely paralleled that of Cass Sunstein. *See* Sunstein, *Standing and the Privatization of Public Law*, 88 Colum. L. Rev. 1432, 1477–79 (1988). I am indebted to Ash Bhagwat for pointing this out to me.

Kennedy had no problem with courts engaging in robust scrutiny of agency action, but he believed that the congressional authorization for such scrutiny had to be relatively specific. In his view, specificity in the congressional warrant meant the courts were more accountable to the democratic process.

Lujan II was widely taken as a major defeat for environmental public interest litigation and a major victory for the rigid separation-of-powers view of standing. Scalia's opinion appeared to set the bar high for imminence and redressability of injuries. But careful examination of Kennedy's critical concurrence, and even of Scalia's own discursive footnote on "procedural rights," should have alerted observers that the Court was leaving a great deal of discretion in Congress for future judicial review of agency action, including in the environmental area.

* * *

On October 20, 1999, a group of nineteen private organizations petitioned the Environmental Protection Agency (EPA) to regulate greenhouse gas emissions from new motor vehicles under the Clean Air Act. Four years later, the EPA denied the petition on two distinct grounds: first, that the agency lacked authority to regulate greenhouse gases; and second, that even if it had such authority, the agency chose not to exercise it. The organizations, now joined by a large number of states including Massachusetts, sued unsuccessfully in the D.C. Circuit to obtain judicial review of the EPA's denial.

Writing for a 5–4 majority, Justice Stevens reversed, finding that the state of Massachusetts had standing to seek judicial review of the EPA denial.[57] The state's injury-in-fact was the potential loss of its coastal lands to rising sea levels. The most arresting feature of Stevens' opinion was his reach back to a 1907 Oliver Wendell Holmes, Jr., opinion to support the proposition that states, when suing in their capacity as quasi-sovereigns, were not to be treated as mere private litigants, but were instead "entitled to special solicitude in [the] standing analysis." The ancient case was *Georgia v. Tennessee Copper Co.*, in which Georgia was held to have standing to sue for the purpose of protecting its citizens from air pollution originating from outside its borders.[58] Stevens explained that states had special standing to sue on behalf of their citizens as part of a *quid pro quo* at the time of their admission to statehood. "When a State enters the Union, it surrenders certain sovereignty prerogatives," wrote Stevens. "Massachusetts cannot invade Rhode Island to force reductions in greenhouse gas emissions, it cannot negotiate an emissions treaty with China or India" and some of its usual powers to reduce emissions within Massachusetts might be federally preempted. If Massachusetts has ceded to the federal government certain of its powers to protect its citizens, then it should have a role in judicially reviewing the federal government's use (or non-use) of those powers. In dissent, Chief Justice Roberts

57. Massachusetts v. Environmental Protection Agency, 549 U.S. 497 (2007).
58. 206 U.S. 230 (1907).

correctly noted that *Georgia v. Tennessee Copper* "had nothing to do with Article III standing," but he failed to mention why: the doctrine of Article III standing, as we have seen, did not exist until the 1920s.

Even conceding the "special solicitude" point for the sake of analysis, Roberts and the dissenters did not think Massachusetts had satisfied Article III standing requirements. First, as the Court (especially Scalia's majority opinions) had sometimes said, injury-in-fact had to be "particularized" to the plaintiff at bar. This was another way of saying that the alleged injury could not be a "generalized grievance." In the case of Massachusetts, "[t]he very concept of global warming seems inconsistent with this particularization requirement," Roberts wrote. "Global warming is a phenomenon 'harmful to humanity at large,' and the redress petitioners seek is focused no more on them than on the public generally—it is literally to change the atmosphere around the world."[59]

Second, Roberts argued, Massachusetts had not demonstrated that the regulation of new motor vehicle emissions in the United States would redress Massachusetts' claimed injury, the loss of coastal lands. Eighty percent of greenhouse gas emissions already originate outside the United States, and that will only increase as China and India develop further economically. Thus, the redressability of Massachusetts' claimed injury will depend on the behavior of third parties not before the court. If China and India do not drastically curtail greenhouse gas emissions, the alleged changes in climate would still occur, the sea level would still rise, and Massachusetts would still lose land.

But not as much as it otherwise would, Stevens responded for the majority. Here was Stevens' key conceptual move: rather than view redressability as all-or-nothing, he viewed it as a matter of degree. Rather than ask whether the regulation of new vehicle emissions in the United States was likely to completely reverse the process of global warming, Stevens asked whether such regulation was likely to lead to some diminution in global warming. For purposes of standing, it did not matter that China and India were much larger emitters of greenhouse gases, or that they were unlikely to make drastic reductions in such emissions. "A reduction in domestic emissions would slow the pace of global emissions increases, no matter what happens elsewhere," Stevens wrote. Even if domestic emission reductions only made a small dent in climate change, that presumably meant a small decrease in the loss of coastal lands, or a small decrease in the risk that coastal lands would be lost. And that, in turn, would constitute redress—however partial.

Stevens' move from a binary concept of redressability to one of degrees allowed the majority to conclude that Article III standing requirements had been met. Stevens now called upon the ideas latent in Kennedy's *Lujan II* concurrence and in Scalia's discursive *Lujan II* footnote—namely, that Congress

59. 549 U.S. at 541 (Roberts, C. J., dissenting).

had substantial control over the standards for redressability and imminence. Stevens wrote:

> [A] litigant to whom Congress has "accorded a procedural right to protect his concrete interests"—here, the right to challenge agency action unlawfully withheld—"can assert that right without meeting all the normal standards for redressability and immediacy." When a litigant is vested with a procedural right, that litigant has standing if there is *some possibility* that the requested relief will prompt the injury-causing party to reconsider the decision that allegedly harmed the litigant.[60]

Congress had granted Massachusetts (and all other aggrieved persons) a "procedural right" to challenge agency action wrongfully withheld. Against the argument that Massachusetts' loss of coastal lands was too temporally remote, one could say, based on Scalia's *Lujan II* footnote, that Massachusetts did not have to meet the normal standard for "immediacy" of its injury. Against the argument that regulation of new vehicle emissions was not likely to reverse global warming, one could say that Massachusetts did not have to meet the normal standard for redressability. It merely needed to show that there was "some possibility" that such regulation would somewhat diminish the risk that coastal lands would be lost, Stevens said. At first glance, *Massachusetts v. EPA* seemed a long way from *Lujan II*, but upon closer examination, the distance between the two was not that far.

By 2007, then, it looked as if the Court might be headed toward a significant revision in the standing doctrine, measured against the orthodoxy of the 1970s through the early 2000s. Kennedy's *Lujan II* concurrence now appeared to have won the positive assent of all other members of the Court. The only aspect of standing doctrine actually compelled by Article III was a prohibition against "citizen suits to vindicate the public's nonconcrete interest in the proper administration of the laws." In other words, *every plaintiff must possess a concrete and personal injury-in-fact*, and Congress may not waive this requirement. Congress may, of course, bestow upon individuals property or other concrete interests, the deprivation of which would create standing, but not otherwise. Congress may relax the redressability and (presumably) causation requirements, for they are products of the Court's prudence rather than of constitutional exegesis. This conceptualization of standing was in stark contrast to the Court's oft-repeated insistence since the early 1970s that the minima of Article III standing were injury-in-fact, causation, and redressability.

The acceptance of Kennedy's *Lujan* position had implications throughout standing doctrine. Since the early 1970s, the Court had begun to treat the "prohibition against generalized grievances" as if it were supplemental to and

60. 549 U.S. at 517–18 (citations omitted) (emphasis added).

separate from the injury, causation, and redressability requirements. Moreover, the Court could not decide whether the generalized grievances rule was prudential or constitutionally mandated. But the adoption of Kennedy's *Lujan* concurrence appeared to settle the matter: the requirement of concrete and personal injury-in-fact *was* the prohibition against generalized grievances. They were not separate rules at all. The requirement of concrete and personal injury, without more, achieved the constitutional objective of seeing that the courts permit the executive branch to act as the primary enforcer of congressional enactments.

Looking forward, this rule assumes that courts can ascertain what injuries are sufficiently "concrete" and "personal" to surmount the Article III threshold. The Court has never really defined "concrete" in so many words. It seems that concreteness primarily concerns the likelihood that the alleged injury will be suffered, as in *Lujan, Summers,* and *Lyons.* The Court found it too speculative whether those plaintiffs would be denied the opportunity to see the Nile crocodile, be denied the right to comment on proposed public land dispositions, or be subjected to future chokeholds, respectively. These alleged injuries were found too abstract for Article III standing. The question of whether the alleged injury is too speculative (*will* it happen?) ought to be distinguished from the question of whether the injury is sufficiently "imminent" (assuming it happens, when?). The question of imminence should be seen as a question of ripeness rather than of standing. Concreteness versus abstractness also has to do with the type of injury being claimed, with traditional common law property and liberty interests on the concrete end of the continuum, and the general citizen interest in government obeying the law at the abstract end. After *Sierra Club v. Morton,* the Court has consistently accepted aesthetic and recreational injuries as sufficiently concrete, so long as the plaintiffs are among the injured.

The triumph of Kennedy's approach would seem to call Brennan's misbegotten "personal stake in the outcome of the controversy" principle into question. Although the Court continues to insist upon concrete injury, it now openly acknowledges that Congress may authorize standing to challenge agency action even where it is highly unclear that the agency action will bring about the claimed injury, and even where it is relatively unlikely that judicial review would redress the plaintiff's claimed injury. Recall Justice Scalia's own observation that plaintiffs have routinely been accorded standing to challenge a failure to file an environmental impact statement even where the underlying development project would be unlikely to produce injury to the plaintiff, and even where the challenge would be unlikely to lead to any changes in the project. But if the plaintiff is unlikely to be harmed by the project, and if judicial review is unlikely to lead to any reduction in that likelihood of harm, then where is the plaintiff's "personal stake in the outcome of the controversy"? The real-world story is almost certainly that the plaintiff has an ideological opposition to the development project and is suing to stall it; the failure to file an environmental impact statement simply creates an opportunity for the plaintiff to get his foot in the door.

To put it differently, the fact that Congress can relax redressability and likelihood-of-harm standards effectively means that Congress can relax the "personal stake" requirement. Generally speaking, if people can sue to challenge actions that are relatively unlikely to harm them, or if they can sue for relief that is relatively unlikely to redress harms they would otherwise suffer, then they have standing to sue without more than a token personal stake. They are basically ideological plaintiffs. It seems the Court must now acknowledge that the notion of "personal stake in the outcome of the controversy" is a policy norm—valuable for whatever historical wisdom it holds—and not a rule of constitutional law.

The pendulum continues to swing. The Court goes through periods of aggressive judicial review and periods of aggressive judicial restraint. It seems reasonable that people should have judicial remedies for violations of their vested legal rights, but it seems unreasonable that the courts should decide so many cases with profound political consequences. That is the enduring conundrum of judicial review in a constitutional democracy. As Justice Kennedy says, we have come a long way from the days when Marbury sued Madison for the delivery of his commission. "Legal rights" occupy a vastly larger field today than in 1803. We would do well to remember this when considering the creation of new legal rights. In the end, however, what can be said on behalf of a society that creates legal rights enforceable only through the political process? It is not, I would think, a society in which most would want to live.

POSTSCRIPT: THE PEOPLE, THE COURT, AND THE ACADEMICS

This book has traced the origins of judicial restraint doctrine in the Supreme Court. Because my goal has been historical rather than normative, I have not surveyed the considerable 1970s and 1980s academic literature critiquing the judicial restraint doctrines, primarily the Burger Court's treatment of standing. But there is another body of academic literature that I do want to recount here, not only because of its importance, but because it provides an interesting narrative of its own. The literature to which I refer concerns the reconciliation of judicial review and popular sovereignty.

As seen throughout this book's narrative, the history of judicial activism and judicial restraint in America has a pendular quality. Aggressive regulation in the late nineteenth and early twentieth centuries was portrayed as an attack on the institution of private property, which would be parried by the doctrine of liberty of contract through substantive due process, among other devices. Frustrated proponents of regulation then cried "judicial activism," advocating the repeal of the diversity jurisdiction and the Due Process Clause. When those desired reforms were not forthcoming, Progressives and New Dealers insisted upon a two-stage protection for legislation and regulation: first, courts should avoid constitutional questions whenever possible (the Brandeisian credo); and, failing that, they should review legislation and regulation in as deferential a manner as possible (the Thayer rule of clear error). But this regime of avoidance and deference proved unduly hospitable to the oppression of Blacks, particularly in the South, and to police abuse of criminal defendants everywhere. Judicial restraint, on these occasions, might have been more aptly described as judicial abdication in the face of wholesale deprivations of rights. In stepped the Warren Court with *Brown v. Bd. of Education* and (much later) its implementation of *Brown*; with *Baker v. Carr* and *Reynolds v. Sims* (the voting decisions); with *Mapp v. Ohio* (extending the exclusionary rule to state court defendants); and eventually with *Gideon v. Wainwright* (right to counsel). If these decisions did not go too far for White, middle-class Americans, the Court gave them *Griswold v. Connecticut* (right to contraceptives) and *Roe v. Wade* to boot. The cries of judicial activism led to the second ascendancy of standing and other avoidance devices; interestingly, they may have had more adverse impact on environmental and welfare rights plaintiffs than on reproductive rights or racial egalitarianism claimants.

Predictably, this ebb and flow has also characterized the literature of the law professoriat. Professor Felix Frankfurter, egged on by Justice Louis Brandeis, led the academic charge against substantive due process and the diversity jurisdiction (and the antilabor injunction as well). Brandeis, Frankfurter, and Learned

Hand became the intellectual progenitors of the Legal Process scholars, including Henry Hart and Paul Bator at Harvard, Herbert Wechsler at Columbia, and Alexander Bickel at Yale. While the scourge of fascism properly repulsed them from moral relativism as a metaphysical matter, they remained highly skeptical about whether judges had any corner on the truth. What followed, for them, was an emphasis on refining the process of judicial decisionmaking. In his 1959 Holmes Lecture at Harvard, and later in his famous article *Toward Neutral Principles of Constitutional Law,*[1] Wechsler criticized *Brown* for its lack of principle. Wechsler defined a neutral principle as one resting on "reasons quite transcending the immediate result that is achieved." By that definition, he thought *Brown* unprincipled because it was motivated not by the general principle of racial equality, but by a desire to integrate public education. Bator argued against the Warren Court's far-reaching decisions liberalizing federal habeas corpus.[2] No court can ever really know the truth of whether a criminal defendant is guilty or innocent, he wrote. The rational course for society was to see that he receive a full and fair adjudication and then to enforce that decision as final, without remorse and without the endless reopening of the judgment.

In 1969, with Earl Warren about to leave the Court that now bore his name, Alexander Bickel was called to deliver the Holmes Lecture at Harvard. It was precisely a decade after Wechsler had given the Holmes Lecture, and Bickel would strike a similar chord of judicial restraint. Until the late 1960s, Bickel was a political liberal, but jurisprudentially a Frankfurterian. Bickel's thesis, later published as a book titled *The Supreme Court and the Idea of Progress,* was that the Warren Court had taken a gamble on history. The Court had bet everything that history would vindicate its decisions in the desegregation and reapportionment cases. The Court's opinion writing in those cases was often shoddy, Bickel wrote. Some of the Court's assertions proved too much and could not be sustained over a broader range of fact situations. At the other end, the Court sometimes applied principles incompletely, failing to explain why they did not govern other areas. The Court's analysis had not been sufficiently rigorous—had refused to "submit to the discipline of the analytically tenable distinction," said Bickel. In lieu of judicial craftsmanship and technical virtuosity, the Court was instead counting on history to prove the righteousness of its actions.

Writing at the close of the Warren Court, it appeared to Bickel that the Court was on its way to losing its bet. Bickel had by then become something of a student of school desegregation and its discontents. "If my probe into a near-term future is not wildly off the mark . . . the upshot is that the Warren Court's" two main enterprises—school desegregation and reapportionment—"are heading

1. 73 HARV. L. REV. 1 (1959).

2. Paul M. Bator, *Finality in the Criminal Law and Federal Habeas Corpus for State Prisoners,* 76 HARV. L. REV. 441 (1963).

toward obsolescence, and in large measure abandonment."[3] Bickel did not put much stock in the argument, popular among liberal academics, that courts owed less deference to the political branches when acting to protect "discrete and insular minorities" from prejudice that tended to exclude them from the political process. In such cases, runs the argument, there is no conflict with democratic theory because the Court enhances rather than derogates from the democratic process. (Chief Justice Harlan Stone had first made this suggestion in footnote four of *United States v. Carolene Products*, which is surely the most famous footnote in the history of American law.)

Bickel found the argument "question begging." Take apportionment, he said. "The question whether one or another method of constructing a legislative institution is more democratic is the very question for decision." For Bickel, the "discrete and insular minority" theory, like so much of the Warren Court's reasoning, was grossly oversimple at best, and disingenuous at worst. After the Great Migration of Blacks from the South to northern industrial states in 1910–30, were Blacks really a "discrete and insular" minority? Did segregated schools directly exclude Blacks from the political process? The "footnote four" theory did not address these questions, nor did it have much to say about the precise contours of the remedies. Are legislatures to be districted? Is minority representation necessary, and how is it to be assured? "A resolution of the problem that will enhance the democratic process is far from obvious if the slightest degree of complexity is allowed to infect populist assumptions," Bickel wrote. Surely there were situations where judicial intervention was warranted by breakdown in the political process, he conceded. "A coup d'etat abolishing elections and representative institutions or excluding an immutably and arbitrarily defined group from the political process would be something else again," he wrote, "[a]nd so would a measure flatly forbidding political speech and association." Bickel did not explain why he thought a history of slavery and Jim Crow segregation fell short of this standard. Bickel subscribed to his Yale colleague Robert Dahl's brand of interest group pluralism and was loathe to permit judicial interference in the settlement process.[4]

Of particular interest today are Bickel's views about the people's role in constitutional interpretation. The Court had the final word on the meaning of the Constitution in only the narrowest sense—its word was the law of the case at bar. The long-term precedential effect of the decision, as a practical matter, depended on its widespread acceptance. "To realize the promise that all others similarly

3. ALEXANDER BICKEL, THE SUPREME COURT AND THE IDEA OF PROGRESS 173 (Harper & Row 1970).

4. Although some of Dahl's early work comes to quite a contrary conclusion: that the Court (up until 1957, at least) had a pronounced tendency to reaffirm majority values. *See* Robert Dahl, *Decision-Making in a Democracy: The Supreme Court as a National Policy-Maker*, 6 J. PUB. L. 279 (1957). I am indebted to my colleague Dorit Reiss for this point.

situated will be similarly bound, the Court's judgments need the assent and the cooperation first of the political institutions, and ultimately of the people."[5] A landmark constitutional decision was the *beginning* of a conversation between the Court and the people. In some cases, the decision is followed by a series of complex events, two steps forward and one back, ultimately rooting the norm in society. In others, the Court's pronouncement ends up being nothing more than a speech. "The Court is often incapable of generating the necessary consent by itself, and it does not command the resources of administration."[6] For Bickel, the Court's power in the real world rarely extended much beyond the persuasiveness of its arguments.

If he was indeed right that history would look askance on the desegregation and reapportionment cases, what lesson should be learned? In Bickel's view, the Court should have stuck to what it does best, namely, filling in the cracks and crevices left by private ordering on the one hand and by the politically accountable branches on the other. (Although he did not use their terms, Bickel was heavily influenced by the notions of efficiency and markets then coming out of the Chicago School. He despaired of federal district courts, through use of the structural injunction, engaging in the "central planning" of society.) The restraint called for by such a path of judicial modesty would come in large part from adherence to analytical coherence. "The insistence on . . . principled judgment no matter how narrow its compass, is traditional," he wrote, citing Wechsler with approval.[7] Oliver Wendell Holmes, Jr., Brandeis, and Frankfurter had tried to adhere to this reign of reason, Bickel said, even if they had not always succeeded, and even if the value choices sometimes required for constitutional adjudication could not always be extracted from reason itself. "They were in this sense also men of the Enlightenment, holding to reason as a civilizing force, and holding that clarity and candor, what Felix Frankfurter called the 'conscious recognition of the nature' of the process, tend to be warrantors of validity, or at least of quality."

Bickel had unmistakably carried forward the Thayerian concern with the "countermajoritarian difficulty," and in doing so, set the stage for a popular constitutionalism of sorts. Put simply, the Court had no corner on constitutional truth. "The true secret of the Court's survival is not, certainly, that in the universe of change it has been possessed of more permanent truth than other institutions," Bickel concluded. The Court's authority "is in practice limited and ambivalent, and with respect to any given enterprise or field of policy, temporary. . . . For, by right, the idea of progress is common property."[8] Bickel's problem was not with

---

5. BICKEL at 90.
6. *Id.* at 91–92.
7. *Id.* at 81.
8. *Id.* at 181.

judicial review per se, it was with judicial supremacy, the idea that the Court's interpretation of the Constitution is and must be the final word.

The Legal Process scholars, then, were concerned with "who decides, and in what way."[9] Courts needed to distance themselves from interest group politics, which meant deciding only on the basis of generally applicable principle and not on the basis of litigant identity. In those cases where no such principle was available to resolve the matter, judicial decision had to be avoided. Legislative, agency, or local action should be allowed to stand under such circumstances because those bodies were politically accountable. Political accountability, in turn, excused some degree of arbitrariness or caprice. If a legislature thought that teenage girls should have to notify their parents before obtaining abortions, then who were courts to say otherwise? There was no objective right answer to this question, thought the Legal Process scholars, just as there was no such answer to many or most political or social controversies. Perhaps the legislature would bring its most solemn moral reasoning to bear on the problem; perhaps the legislature would simply resolve it by oiling the squeakiest wheel; perhaps it would resolve it by log-rolling and featherbedding. But it didn't matter. Political accountability meant automatic decisional legitimacy. If courts were to take on the question, they would either have to decide it on the basis of generally applicable principle, in which case it would be legitimate, or they would actually have to get the answer right. Because the Legal Process scholars were deeply skeptical that one could objectively know the right answers to these kinds of questions, and because they could think of no general principle by which to decide them, final resolution had to be left with the majoritarian branches. It is sometimes said that the Legal Process school was animated in part by discontent with the perceived moral relativism of Legal Realism, for no one in the postfascist environment following World War II could have been insensitive to relativism. But deep epistemological skepticism was a constitutive element in Legal Process.

Defenders of the Warren Court immediately returned fire in the pages of the *Harvard Law Review*. J. Skelly Wright, an early leader in the implementation of *Brown* as a federal district judge, had since joined Chief Judge David Bazelon to become the twin titans of the Left on the District of Columbia circuit. Wright took dead aim at the "scholastic mandarins" of the Brandeis/Frankfurter legacy in an article called "Professor Bickel, the Scholarly Tradition, and the Supreme Court."[10] He fairly bridled at Anthony Lewis's declaration in the *New York Times* that Bickel's Holmes Lecture had been "an event in the law." Wright's message was decidedly pragmatic: all that talk about principle and analytic rigor is fine in theory, but it won't work in practice. A Louisiana native who had gotten both his

9. Akhil Reed Amar, *Law Story*, 102 Harv. L. Rev. 688 (1989) (reviewing Hart & Wechsler, The Federal Courts and the Federal System) (3d ed., Paul M. Bator, Daniel J. Meltzer, Paul J. Mishkin, & David L. Shapiro, eds.).

10. 84 Harv. L. Rev. 769 (1971).

bachelor's and law degrees at Loyola University of New Orleans, Wright deftly played the "elitism" card against Bickel, the Harvard-trained Yale professor.

He offered a point-by-point rejoinder to Bickel's critique of the Warren Court's work product. Where Bickel claimed the Court's aggressive assertion of judicial review was in tension with the social contractarian premise of "consent of the governed," Wright offered his own philosophical response. The people may not legitimately consent to government action that violates the Constitution. Constitutionality was a hard side constraint on the operation of consent to governance. Wright, of course, assumed that *courts* were the proper institution to enforce this side constraint. This move recalled Wright's celebrated decision in the 1965 case of *Williams v. Walker-Thomas Furniture Co.*, in which he invalidated an onerous retail sales contract as "unconscionable" because of gross inequality in bargaining power.[11] Wright and other liberals were highly skeptical about the meaningfulness of consent given in a real world shot through with inequality. Liberals would call it realism; conservatives labeled it paternalism.

As for Bickel's embrace of interest group pluralism, Wright accused him of being behind the times. By the late 1960s this "complacent" theory was no longer the unchallenged conventional wisdom among political scientists. The notion that minorities could protect themselves through the political process by compromising and banding together with other minorities was "nonsense," Wright sneered. "The big winners in the pluralistic system are the highly organized, wealthy, and motivated groups skilled in the art of insider politics."[12] This rejection of interest group pluralism at least partly explains Wright's willingness to liberalize judicial review of agency action, at least in certain areas.[13] Wright also rejected Bickel's charge that the Court had made America overly litigious. Rich people had always been able to mobilize the legal system in service of their interests. It only became "litigiousness" when poor people and minorities started to do it too. Wright impugned the sincerity of Bickel's attack on the Warren Court in another way as well. If the desegregation and reapportionment cases were illegitimate because of methodological deficits, as Bickel implied, then the criminal procedure decisions were equally illegitimate—yet Bickel approved of them. Bickel's real objection wasn't about method or process, it was about the merits. All the sermonizing about process was an attempt by conservatives to monopolize the high ground.

But neither elitism nor hypocrisy was Wright's most heartfelt criticism of the Legal Process school. The heirs to the Brandeis and Frankfurter legacy were simply old and out of touch. A new generation of lawyers and law professors had

---

11. 350 F.2d 445 (D.C. Cir. 1965). The case has become a staple of first-year contracts classes in law school.

12. J. Skelly Wright, *Professor Bickel, the Scholarly Tradition, and the Supreme Court*, 84 Harv. L. Rev. 769, 789 (1971).

13. *See* Schiller, *supra* note 40, Ch. 4.

no patience for square corners and double-stitching, or for the endless husbanding of political capital. For this new generation, "there is little charm in an interminable discussion of the complexity and subtlety of life and of how resistant it is to rational solution."[14] These young lawyers were energized by the justice of human equality. Justice delayed was justice denied. Picking on Bickel's acknowledgment that even he would permit judicial intervention in the face of a coup, Wright retorted, "An institution that sits back, always emphasizing its weakness and its reasons for inaction, is unlikely to be in a fighting stance when the tanks roll down Pennsylvania Avenue."[15] Of course this new generation would eventually grow old, but their cause would endure. "[N]o amount of experience will substantially dull the inspiration of the 1960s," Wright proclaimed.

But there was already a popular indignation toward the Warren Court's criminal procedure decisions, and then came *Roe v. Wade.* Though *Roe* took no more interpretive liberties than did *Griswold v. Connecticut* eight years earlier, the stakes with abortion were considerably higher than with contraceptives. Debate over judicial activism versus judicial restraint broke out anew in the constitutional law professoriat, this time under the aegis of "interpretivism" versus "noninterpretivism," with *Roe* and *Griswold* supposedly representing the latter. Most interpretivists were political moderates or conservatives, but by the end of the 1970s they had been joined by some leftists, who began tilting away from judicial review as the Court began to tilt toward conservatism. In 1980, John Hart Ely published a book called *Democracy and Distrust*, defending the Warren Court against this new wave of criticism. Ely, one of Warren's favorite former clerks, did not hide his admiration for the Chief. "For Earl Warren," penned Ely. "You don't need many heroes if you choose carefully."

Ely claimed to be charting a course between interpretivism and noninterpretivism. "Clause-bound interpretivism," as he called it, was untenable. One could not interpret each clause of the Constitution as if it were a disembodied technical code. Some of the clauses, such as "equal protection," "privileges and immunities," and the Ninth Amendment were so designedly capacious that a narrow interpretation could only be disingenuous. On the other hand, "noninterpretivism," which Ely portrayed as the imposition of the judge's own values without any serious attempt to engage the parchment, was unacceptably undemocratic. There had to be some way to give broad meaning to the grand phrases of the Constitution without resorting to the judge's subjective values. Ely found it in footnote four of *United States v. Carolene Products Co.*, and he now offered a full elaboration of Chief Justice Stone's famous musing.

---

14. Wright at 805. Wright did not abjure principle altogether. Judges should make reasoned arguments to one another and decide on the basis of principle when possible, but the dictates of the real world required courts to make adjustments to those principles going forward on a case-by-case basis.

15. Wright at 804.

In *Carolene Products,* the Court upheld Congress's power to prohibit the shipment of adulterated milk in interstate commerce. In testing the defendant's claim that it had been deprived of its property without due process, the Court asked whether Congress had a rational basis for enacting the legislation, a question Chief Justice Stone answered in the affirmative. In the process of so holding, however, Stone ruminated aloud about the occasions on which the Court might employ a more searching level of scrutiny:

> There may be a narrower scope for operation of the presumption of constitutionality when legislation appears on its face to be within a specific prohibition of the Constitution, such as those of the first ten amendments, which are deemed equally specific when held to be embraced within the Fourteenth.
>
> It is unnecessary to consider now whether legislation which restricts those political processes which can ordinarily be expected to bring about repeal of undesirable legislation, is to be subjected to more exacting judicial scrutiny under the general prohibitions of the Fourteenth Amendment than are most other types of legislation. . . .
>
> Nor need we enquire whether similar considerations enter into the review of statutes directed at particular religious, or national, or racial minorities, whether prejudice against discrete and insular minorities may be a special condition, which tends seriously to curtail the operation of those political processes ordinarily to be relied upon to protect minorities, and which may call for a correspondingly more searching judicial inquiry.[16]

Here Ely found the key to reconciling judicial review with democracy. In a pluralist system, groups had to jostle, cajole, and horse-trade for desired outcomes. This was the process of values settlement in a heterogeneous society. But if a particular group had been obstructed from its place at the bargaining table, the process had broken down. If those in power were using the apparatus of the state to block access to outsiders, one could no longer have confidence in the democratic quality of the outcomes. The integrity of the process could then only be restored by intervention from outside the political system. That intervention could never legitimately be aimed at achieving particular outcomes; it could only be aimed at restoring the excluded group to its rightful position in the bargaining process. So long as the intervention was limited in that way, it was both the maximum and the minimum that the judiciary could do.

Ely argued that the Constitution was not a repository of moral and social values, but instead a blueprint establishing a complex set of processes for governance. "[T]he original Constitution was principally, indeed I would say overwhelmingly, dedicated to concerns of process and structure and not to the

16. United States v. Carolene Products Co., 304 U.S. 144, 152 n.4 (1938) (citations omitted).

identification and preservation of specific substantive values," Ely asserted.[17] Certainly the first three articles, establishing the tripartite framework of the federal government, fit that description. But so did much of the Bill of Rights. The First Amendment was largely a way of ensuring that a citizenry charged with the task of self-government could remain informed and check government when it gets out of bounds. The Fourth Amendment's prohibition against "unreasonable searches" surely protected a substantive value, privacy, but the amendment also covers seizures and arrests, and it covers them whether they are in private or out in the open. The Fourth Amendment is thus in significant part about limiting official discretion and avoiding indefensible inequities in treatment, which are more procedural concerns, Ely claimed. The Fifth Amendment's prohibition against the taking of property without just compensation reflects the substantive value of private property, but because it permits such takings where recompensed, it also demonstrates a commitment to spreading the cost of public goods throughout society—a structural concern. Similarly, wrote Ely, the Eighth Amendment's prohibition against "cruel and unusual punishments," while aimed at outlawing certain forms of torture, was more generally aimed at the "tremendous potential for the arbitrary or invidious infliction of 'unusually' severe punishments on persons of various classes other than 'our own.'"[18]

Ely saved his hardest and most critical argumentative push for the Reconstruction Amendments. With the obvious exception of the Thirteenth Amendment, banishing slavery, these amendments "do not designate substantive values for protection from the political process."[19] The Due Process Clause "is concerned with process writ small, the processes by which regulations are enforced against individuals." The Equal Protection Clause recognizes that "technical access to the process may not always be sufficient to guarantee good-faith representation of all those putatively represented." The Fifteenth Amendment, banning race discrimination in voting, was an obvious attempt to unblock access to the political process for historically oppressed races. Looking beyond Reconstruction, the Seventeenth Amendment made for direct election of senators; the Nineteenth Amendment extended the vote to women and the Twenty-Third extended it to residents of the District of Columbia; the Twenty-Fourth abolished poll taxes; and the Twenty-Sixth lowered the voting age to eighteen. All these provisions of course broadened voting rights with an eye toward opening the political process and enforcing "the representative's duty of equal concern and respect to minorities and majorities alike."[20] Ely paused to note that one of

---

17. JOHN HART ELY, DEMOCRACY AND DISTRUST: A THEORY OF JUDICIAL REVIEW 92 (Harv. Univ. Press 1980).

18. *Id.* at 97.

19. *Id.* at 98.

20. *Id.* at 99.

the very few constitutional provisions that placed a substantive value beyond the reach of the political process—the Eighteenth, mandating Prohibition—did not last long "because such attempts to freeze substantive values do not belong in a constitution."[21]

Democracy and Distrust made two normative arguments in favor of Ely's "representation reinforcement" theory as a simultaneous justification for and limitation on judicial review pursuant to the open-ended provisions of the Constitution. First, unlike Skelly Wright's thinly veiled belief that judges had a duty to do what they knew to be just and right, representation-reinforcing judicial review was "entirely supportive" of democracy. Courts were required to intervene where "market" mechanisms had been corrupted, but ultimately, choices among fundamental values remained where they belonged—in the hands of the people's elected representatives. Second, the representation-reinforcing approach would give judges a role they were functionally competent to perform, Ely claimed. The process was corrupted whenever those in power had effectively choked off the channels of political change to ensconce themselves in office, or representatives of a majority were systematically disadvantaging a minority out of simple hostility or prejudice, "refusing to recognize commonalities of interest," and thus keeping the minority from dealing at the table of pluralism. Incumbents could not be trusted to blow the whistle on either of these situations, just as one could not be trusted to judge one's own cause. As relative outsiders who generally need not worry about their job security, however, appointed judges are in a position to make fair calls about whether the normal channels of change really have been blocked off. Ely conceded that judges would be faced with all kinds of tough judgment calls, but even the toughest of those calls could be made fairly. "The whole point of the approach is to identify those groups in society to those needs and wishes elected officials have no apparent interest in attending," he wrote. "If the approach makes sense, it would not make sense to assign its enforcement to anyone but the courts."[22]

How much sense, then, does the approach really make? In the real world, how does a judge know whether the normal channels of change have really been blocked off? What are the telltale signs of blockage, assuming the offending majority has not been so obnoxious as to take away the outgroup's formal right to vote? Let us take the example of gays and lesbians. *Circa* 2010, have the normal

21. One problem here is that Ely assumes all efforts to extend the franchise are meant to be exclusively "representation-reinforcing" and not enshrinements of the substantive value of moral equality for previously oppressed groups. That is surely true with respect to the Seventeenth and Twenty-Sixth Amendments, but probably untrue with respect to extending the vote to Blacks and women, and may even be untrue with respect to giving the vote to residents of the District of Columbia, given the disproportionately large population of Blacks there.

22. Ely, *supra* note 17 of this chapter, at 151.

channels of change been blocked off to "the gay community"?[23] Without question there is an abundance of prejudice and misinformation about gays and lesbians, distorting the cognition of many politicians and preventing them from realizing how enormous the shared interests between straights and gays. On the other hand, the political battle against discrimination on the basis of sexual orientation is fought by multiple organizations of considerable size and sophistication on the national and state levels. And, while it is certainly a myth that "most gays are well-educated and well-to-do," there is no reason to believe that most gays are poorly educated and impoverished, either. Based purely on these data about process, should the courts in 2010 exercise some type of heightened scrutiny against government classifications working against gays?

Some will immediately answer this negatively and others will immediately answer it affirmatively, but many of us would throw up our hands, desperate for more information. Before long, someone will say, "Didn't the voters in California and Maine just reject same-sex marriage? Doesn't that prove that gays and lesbians have been systematically blocked off from the political process, given that there is no nonmakeweight reason to deny same-sex marriage other than bias against gays?" But of course this is not an assertion about process at all. It is an assertion about the fundamental equality of people notwithstanding sexual orientation (the political rejection of which is taken, *ipso facto*, to indicate that the process is broken). In this reasoning, "process" is a fifth wheel, with substantive values driving the other four. Or, to put it more succinctly, I doubt that in the real world judges can make any important calls about blockage in the political process without interpreting data through the lens of substantive values.

There are other well-known critiques of Ely's thesis. One is that he wrongly equates simple majoritarianism with the more contestable concept of democracy.[24] It is certainly true that federal judges are not elected by popular majorities, but our constitutional system quite conspicuously eschews simple majoritarianism at critical junctures, including, but not limited to, the Electoral College (remember 2000?), the filibuster, the veto override, and the three-quarters requirement for ratification of constitutional amendments under Article V. Although not all would agree, one might plausibly assert that two of the preconditions for democracy are themselves substantive values: that government treat all classes of citizens as moral equals and that all acts of government coercion be subject to articulable justification. If this assertion is true, then appointed judges

---

23. Scare quotes because it is highly problematical to posit the existence of a monolithic "gay community," "Black community," "Asian community," or other metaphorical collection of individuals. Nonetheless, many in society base their biases and prejudices on the assumption that such monolithic groups exist, and so the law's response to those biases and prejudices will ignore the assumption at its own peril.

24. W. B. Gallie's phrase was "essentially contested." See his *Essentially Contested Concepts*, 56 PROCEEDINGS OF THE ARISTOTELIAN SOCIETY 167, 184–85 (1956).

(along with the clergy, journalists, and academics) would seem to be among the leading candidates to insist upon adherence to such values, and, arguably, they have.

Another common critique is that Ely wrongly equates the work product of legislatures with the work product of the people.[25] Much legislation is the product of professional lobbyists, log-rolling, and rent-seeking. The work product of administrative agencies has even less claim to being the voice of the people. Ely's response was that, however imperfectly democratic legislatures may be, they are certainly more democratic than appointed judges, but it is not clear to me that a man who drinks half a quart of whiskey when he gets up every morning has any less of a drinking problem than a man who drinks a whole quart.

One thing is for sure: Ely didn't think much of the Frankfurterian/Bickelian belief in husbanding political capital. "Throughout its history," wrote Ely, "the Court has been told it had better stick to its knitting or risk destruction, yet somehow the possibility of judicial emasculation by way of popular reaction against constitutional review by the courts has not in fact materialized in more than a century and a half of American experience."[26] Ely also pointed out that some other observers who had wrung their hands over the Court's credibility had been surprised. "In 1967 [Harvard law professor] Louis Jaffe, characteristically candid in his refusal to 'revise and extend' his earlier remarks, confessed: 'At least some of us who shook our heads over Baker v. Carr are prepared to admit . . . that it has not impaired, indeed that it has enhanced the prestige of the Court.'"[27]

By the 1980s, constitutional scholars had started to shift their attention from the institution of judicial *review* to the institution of judicial *supremacy*. The conventional assumption had been that, save the formal amendment process in Article V, the Court always had the last word on constitutional law by way of judicial review. But now constitutional scholars began to argue that the principle of popular sovereignty required the People, not the Court, to retain the last word. Although populism is not the sort of idea normally associated with the high theorists who do their conjuring among the Gothic details of Cambridge and New Haven, this strain of scholarship became known as "popular constitutionalism." In 1983, Bruce Ackerman delivered his Storrs Lectures at Yale, declaring that "We the People" engage in a transcendent, "higher lawmaking" at special moments in constitutional history, and that those decisions cannot be undone by

25. A related critique is one based on accountability. *See* Jane Schacter, *Ely and the Idea of Democracy*, 57 STAN. L. REV. 737, 755 ("there are grounds for substantial skepticism about any robust dynamic of retrospective political accountability" of legislatures) (symposium issue in honor of John Hart Ely).

26. ELY, *supra* note 17 of this chapter, at 47–48.

27. *Id.* at 121.

ordinary politics, however democratic it may be.[28] Four years later, his Yale colleague Akhil Amar, viewing the Constitution and its history as a whole, argued that a majority of citizens nationwide could legally ratify a constitutional amendment even though Article V's requirement of ratification by three-quarters of the states was not satisfied.[29] And, in 2000, the well-known leftist law professor Mark Tushnet sent shudders through the legal academy by publicly imagining an America without judicial review at all—and by suggesting that, after a while, the People might do a better job of constitutional interpretation than the Court.[30]

The most recent academic endorsement of popular constitutionalism has been by Larry Kramer. In 2001, Kramer's outpouring of frustration in response to *Bush v. Gore* concluded with these lines: "The Supreme Court has made its grab for power. The question is: will we let them get away with it?"[31] In his 2004 book, *The People Themselves: Popular Constitutionalism and Judicial Review,* a calmer Kramer admitted that his earlier article had been "tendentious" in its history, but he continued to insist that the contemporary notion of judicial supremacy was anything but preordained. It was the aristocratic High Federalists, including John Marshall, who had expected the Court to have the last word on constitutional matters. They were the ones who distrusted the lower urges of the common man—who wanted to interpose the Court between property rights and any intemperate redistributionist measures that might issue from democratic legislatures. In order for the Court to discharge this duty, it had to be supreme on constitutional matters. Its word had to be final. The popular branches had to be bound by its pronouncements.

Thomas Jefferson, James Madison, and the Republicans, on the other hand, believed in an arrangement whereby each department would be the ultimate arbiter of its own constitutional interpretation. Under this theory of "departmentalism," the Republicans accepted the institution of judicial review. The Court, no less than any other department, was bound by the Constitution. If the Court were called upon in litigation to enforce an unconstitutional law, it would of course have to refuse. The Court, itself a product of the Constitution, could never exercise any power that contradicts the Constitution. But who else would be bound by the Court's constitutional interpretation was another matter entirely. Under departmentalism, "the Judiciary have no more right to prescribe, direct or control the acts of the other departments of the Government, than the other

28. Bruce Ackerman, *The Storrs Lectures: Discovering the Constitution,* 93 YALE L.J. 1013 (1984). Ackerman followed it up with numerous writings, the most important of which is WE THE PEOPLE: FOUNDATIONS (Harv. Univ. Press 1991).

29. Akhil Reed Amar, Philadelphia *Revisited: Amending the Constitution Outside Article V,* 55 U. CHI. L. REV. 1043 (1988).

30. MARK V. TUSHNET, TAKING THE CONSTITUTION AWAY FROM THE COURTS (Harv. Univ. Press 2000).

31. Larry D. Kramer, *Foreword: We the Court,* 115 HARV. L. REV. 4, 169 (2001).

departments of the Government have to prescribe or direct those of the Judiciary."[32] Kramer traces the move from a conservative, customary constitution to a progressive, popular constitution in the election of 1800. The Federalists had seen judicial review as the means by which Constitution and Court would protect minorities from majorities. But now the Republicans had swept to victory on a theory of judicial review whereby the Constitution and the Court would protect the People from its own government. On this view, judicial review was a less radical, less destabilizing substitute for outright popular rebellion.[33] "Judicial review was yet one more device with which to force popular reconsideration of possibly unconstitutional methods," Kramer wrote.[34] The Court was acting as a surrogate for the People. All three branches were agents of the People, working with and against each other to maximize the People's welfare and liberty. Playing the agency metaphor to its logical conclusion, it made no sense for one agent (the Court) to "bind" the other two agents (Congress and the executive) to its constitutional interpretations. Each agent had to be free to serve the principal's interests directly and fully, even if that meant adopting a different view of constitutional meaning than the Court had adopted.

The Jacksonian era, however, made judicial supremacy more attractive. First, party politics began to dominate. The Federalist Party all but disappeared after the War of 1812, leaving a single party that had been renamed the "Democratic-Republican" party. A Jacksonian coalition including Martin Van Buren gradually created a new Democratic party, restoring old party rivalries, and first took the White House in 1828. "[P]opular politics was in effect swallowed up by party politics: and because party politics was all about winning office, popular politics started to lose its salience as a check operating from outside to control political institutions," according to Kramer.[35] The "voice of the people" was now spoken by elected representatives who responded to party signals. The people had lost their capacity to speak "as a corporate entity; they became incapable of 'independent action.'"

Second, a series of major political controversies with constitutional underpinnings threatened to pull the nation apart. In 1828, South Carolina attempted to "nullify" tariff legislation that, in the South, at least, was perceived to benefit northern industrial interests. Over the next five years, Jackson denied the power of individual states to "nullify" federal legislation; he also denied the power of a state to secede from the Union. Finally, in 1833, after agreeing to lower the tariffs, Jackson procured from Congress a bill authorizing military force to enforce them.

---

32. Larry D. Kramer, The People Themselves: Popular Constitutionalism and Judicial Review (Oxford U. Press 2004) 144 (quoting speech by John Bacon, 11 *Annals of Congress* 983 (Jan. 1802)).

33. *Id.* at 132.

34. *Id.* at 80.

35. *Id.* at 168.

The same year, Jackson withdrew federal funds from the Second Bank of the United States, having vetoed the rechartering of the bank the year before. The withdrawal of funds led to a period of great financial instability, eventually culminating in the Panic of 1837 and a deep depression. And, throughout his administration, Jackson favored a policy of "Indian removal," forcing them west of the Mississippi River. This sharpened sectional cleavages, as the policy was largely favored in the South but often sharply criticized in the North. It was the 1832 decision in *Worcester v. Georgia*, upholding tribal sovereignty against state law, that supposedly prompted Jackson to say, "John Marshall has made his decision; now let him enforce it."

This "series of constitutional altercations . . . had made the problem of settling constitutional differences into a major public headache," Kramer lamented. At this point many, including Madison, "came round to thinking that the judiciary might, after all, be the right place to turn for finality."[36] Kramer's fuller description of the phenomenon is worth considering:

> What ultimately moved a greater number of Americans to embrace the idea that judges should have the preeminent word on constitutional meaning, in other words, was experience, which seemed to teach that popular constitutionalism in its traditional form might not work in a society as diverse and dynamic as the United States. Someone more definite and distinct than "the people" was needed to resolve constitutional disputes, which if left unsettled threatened to break apart the Union.[37]

In American history, at least, Exhibit A against judicial supremacy has to be *Dred Scott v. Sandford*.[38] In 1853, after unsuccessfully suing for his freedom in the courts of Missouri, Dred Scott brought an action against his owner in federal circuit court. Jurisdiction was alleged on the basis of the parties' diverse citizenship. The defendant, whose sister was the widow of Scott's original owner, was alleged to be a citizen of New York, and Scott alleged himself to be a citizen of Missouri. When the jury brought back a verdict for the defense, Scott sued out a writ of appeal to the U.S. Supreme Court.

Chief Justice Roger Taney (and president-elect James Buchanan) desperately hoped that a decision in *Dred Scott* would quell the massive national unrest over slavery by putting the matter beyond political debate. In fact, it did nothing of the sort. Taney's opinion began with the question of jurisdiction—was there diversity of citizenship? Taney wrote:

> The question is simply this: Can a negro, whose ancestors were imported into this country, and sold as slaves, become a member of the political community

36. *Id.* at 172.
37. *Id.*
38. 60 U.S. (19 How.) 393 (1857).

> formed and brought into existence by the Constitution of the United States, and as such become entitled to all the rights, and privileges, and immunities, guarantied by that instrument to the citizen?[39]
>
> We think they . . . are not included, and were not intended to be included, under the word "citizens" in the Constitution, and can therefore claim none of the rights and privileges which that instrument provides for and secures to citizens of the United States.
>
> It is very clear, therefore, that no State can, by any act or law of its own, passed since the adoption of the Constitution, introduce a new member into the political community created by the Constitution of the United States.[40]

It did not matter that Missouri might consider Scott a citizen; he was by definition ineligible to be a citizen of the nation. He therefore could not have the rights appertaining to citizenship, such as suing in the federal courts.

At this point one would think Chief Justice Taney's opinion would end, having found that the circuit court had no jurisdiction. And yet Taney could not let it end there; he had said only that slaves were not and could not be citizens. This was not, to put it mildly, one of the principal points being contested in 1857. With Kansas bleeding profusely, and with the Missouri Compromise effectively having been laid asunder by the Kansas-Nebraska Act of 1854, Taney had to go much further to bring about peace. He needed to settle the question of whether slavery could be banned in the Territories.

Proceeding to this question was a bit tricky; Taney had to somehow justify reaching the merits of the case despite having found that the lower court utterly lacked jurisdiction. He conceded that, if the court below had been a state supreme court, the U.S. Supreme Court would have no choice but to dismiss the appeal. But a writ of error to the circuit court was different, he said. Longstanding practice established that the appellate court was entitled to reach all questions decided by the lower court. The circuit court had found that he was not entitled to his freedom, and now the Supreme Court would seize this opportunity to validate this holding and make it into a rule of general application.

On the merits, Taney and the majority had little difficulty. Scott claimed his freedom on the basis of his then master, U.S. Army Major John Emerson, having taken him to Fort Snelling in the Wisconsin Territory (present-day Minnesota). In the Missouri Compromise of 1820, Congress had prohibited slavery in the Wisconsin Territory. But did Congress have that power? If slaveowners had vested property rights, Taney reasoned, then separating masters from slaves upon entry into a territory was no different than separating a man from his chattels upon entry. To say that a slaveowner relinquished his property rights by entering one of America's territories was to say that the Bill of Rights had no

39. *Id.* at 403.
40. *Id.* at 404.

application in the territories. "[N]o one, we presume, will contend that Congress can make a law in a Territory respecting that establishment of religion, or the free exercise thereof, or abridging the freedom of speech or of the press, or the right of the people of the Territory peaceably to assemble, and to petition the Government for the redress of grievances," Taney wrote.[41]

The only logical way out was to distinguish ownership of human beings from ownership of things. Taney so much as conceded that the modern mind, circa 1857, might well see it that way. But he chastised those who would project modern racial sensibilities onto the Framers, who clearly had believed that the "African race" was inherently inferior and thus suitable for enslavement. There were two explicit provisions in the Constitution countenancing slavery, without speaking its name: the clause stating that "Migration or Importation of such Persons as any of the States now existing shall think proper to admit, shall not be prohibited by Congress prior to the year One Thousand Eight Hundred and Eight,"[42] and the clause stating that "No Person held to Service or Labour in one State, under the laws thereof, escaping into another, shall, in Consequence of any Law or Regulation therein, be discharged from such Service or Labour, But shall be delivered up on Claim of the Party to whom such Service or Labour may be due."[43] The Framers had salved their sectional wounds with a compromise accepting the right of men to own other men. The slate was unclean. Now peace could only be had if this right was placed beyond the reach of politics, Taney believed. Thus he found the Act of Congress purporting to ban slavery in the Wisconsin Territory unconstitutional and unenforceable.

There was one loose end. Scott also claimed that he had become free when Emerson had taken him to Fort Armstrong, Illinois. Illinois was a free state. Upon his return to Missouri, Scott argued, his status as a free man was uninterrupted. But Taney and the majority would not stand for it. The laws of Missouri, not Illinois, governed his status upon return. And, even if Missouri law at the time of Scott's return was ambiguous on the matter, it had subsequently been settled. Scott had again become a slave when he returned to Missouri. Now Chief Justice Taney and President Buchanan could only hope that *Dred Scott* had settled federal law on slavery to the point where men would put down their swords.

It was, of course, a vain hope. Abraham Lincoln's response was departmentalist: he agreed that the decision ought to be enforced between the parties, but, under the circumstances, rethought by the population at large:

> [T]he candid citizen must confess that if the policy of the government upon vital questions, affecting the whole people, is to be irrevocably fixed by

---

41. *Id.* at 450.
42. Art. 1, Sec. 9, Cl. 1.
43. Art. 4, Sec. 2, Cl. 3.

> decisions of the Supreme Court, the instant they are made, in ordinary litigation between parties, in personal actions, the people will have ceased to be their own rulers, having to that extent practically resigned their government into the hands of that eminent tribunal.[44]

As Kramer noted, this version of departmentalism was muted down from the full-throated Jeffersonian version. Lincoln's qualifications on the purer version made sense. Neither plaintiff nor defendant in *Dred Scott* was a government official or even a public interest organization with full-scale litigating capacity, yet they both virtually represented the positions of millions of interested persons. Why should the Court's far-ranging opinion preempt the independent judgment of the other branches? At least, as Lincoln hinted, the Court's opinion should have to stand some test of time before it was accorded wide deference.

Dred Scott is the star witness in the case against judicial supremacy. But there remains the cross-examination of the star defense witness—*Cooper v. Aaron*, the high drama 1958 decision in which the Court finally put an end to delays in the desegregation of Central High School in Little Rock, Arkansas.[45] No case, with the possible exception of *Marbury* itself, is cited more often for the proposition that it is the duty of the *courts* to say what the law is, and therefore that the courts have the last word in constitutional interpretation. Does *Cooper* really support that proposition, and, if so, is *Cooper* itself sound?

Here is what the Court said:

> [*Marbury*] declared the basic principle that the federal judiciary is supreme in the exposition of the law of the Constitution, and that principle has ever since been respected by this Court and the Country as a permanent and indispensable feature of our constitutional system. It follows that the interpretation of the Fourteenth Amendment enunciated by this Court in the *Brown* case is the supreme law of the land, and Art. VI of the Constitution makes it of binding effect on the States "any Thing in the Constitution or Laws of any State to the Contrary notwithstanding." Every state legislator and executive and judicial officer is solemnly committed by oath taken pursuant to Art. VI, [Para.] 3 "to support this Constitution."[46]

On its face, *Cooper* was the Court's declaration of supremacy in constitutional interpretation.

My colleague Ash Bhagwat has pointed out that *Cooper* has nothing to say about departmentalism because the case involved state, not federal, officials.[47]

---

44. Abraham Lincoln, First Inaugural Address (Mar. 4, 1861), quoted in KRAMER, *supra* note 32 of this chapter, at 212.

45. 358 U.S. 1 (1958).

46. *Id.* at 18.

47. Ashutosh Bhagwat, *Cooper v. Aaron and the Faces of Federalism*, 52 ST. LOUIS UNIV. L. J. 1087 (2008).

But *Cooper* does raise the equally important questions of whether and to what extent state and local officials are bound to the U.S. Supreme Court's pronouncements about the federal constitution, even when they are not parties to the litigation in which the pronouncements are made. Bhagwat frames the questions thusly: First, were state and local officials in Little Rock under a legal obligation not to enact legislation, or take other official actions, designed to obstruct the implementation of *Brown* or to encourage others to obstruct it; and second, did these officials have a positive legal duty to assist federal officials in implementing *Brown*? Bhagwat answers both questions in the negative, arguing that in our federalist system, state and local officials have a valuable role to play in shaping constitutional meaning, and that this role often includes disagreement with and even defiance of federal court decisions.[48] He does concede that state officials are limited by "principles of contempt, supremacy, and the rule of law."

As for Bhagwat's first question, I think state or local officials who take official action with the *conscious object* of obstructing the enforcement of court orders, directly or through intermediaries, are in contempt.[49] Any contrary rule would license state and local officials (or anybody else, for that matter) to nullify any federal (or state) court order, whether because they sincerely disagree with the ruling or simply to make hay with the public. Perhaps they can be named as parties to the injunction, but the officials will of course structure their obstructive acts in waves to take advantage of this rule. I simply do not see how courts can function under such a rule. If the officials are unaware that their actions have the effect of obstructing courts orders, then they cannot be held in contempt, nor do they have any legal obligation to forswear from such conduct. The hard theoretical case is the one in the middle—if officials are *aware* that their actions will have the effect of impeding a judicial decree, but such effect is not their purpose, then what? Conceding for present purposes that such conduct would not qualify as contempt, the important point is the first one: that official action consciously directed at undermining a judicial decree violates the law.

With respect to Bhagwat's second question—whether state officials must positively assist federal courts in carrying out their edicts—I agree they have no such legal duty, unless of course they are properly named in the injunction. But even here, I would reiterate my position on the first question. Just as an official may not take action with the conscious purpose of undermining a court order, he or she may not forebear from discretionary action with that same purpose. To be sure, it will often be hard to prove that officials omitted to take action for a particular reason, and that will be tough darts for the party seeking

48. *Id.* at 1113.

49. *See* United States v. Hall, 472 F.2d 261 (5th Cir. 1972) (contempt lies against a nonparty who willfully interferes with a court order, even where the nonparty did not act in concert with a party); Lynch v. Rank, 639 F.Supp. 69 (N.D. Cal. 1985) (explaining the holding in *Hall*).

to enforce the injunction. If, however, a certain official's refusal to act is sandwiched between routine actions in seemingly indistinguishable circumstances—if a desire to undermine court orders is the only plausible explanation—then that too must be contempt.

Kramer's advocacy of departmentalism is a bit more vague than Bhagwat's proposal in favor of popular constitutionalism for state and local officials, and it is not entirely clear which version of departmentalism he favors. It seems clear that he does not advocate what might be called the Jeffersonian model, under which all court orders to the executive branch are considered legally ineffective, for one branch may never dictate the meaning of law to another. Jefferson subscribed to this view; if the Court had ordered his administration to deliver Marbury his commission, Jefferson and Madison would have promptly ignored it. The best that can be said for this model is that it is logically coherent. Presumably it would have led to different results in *Youngstown Steel* (the steel mill seizure case) and in *Nixon v. United States* (the Watergate tapes case). Presumably it also means that a termed-out war president could *legally* disregard a Supreme Court order to relinquish office to a newly elected antiwar president by simply asserting that his interpretation of the Twentieth Amendment provides for an implicit exception on the basis of exigent circumstances or national security.

The version of departmentalism that Kramer appears to favor might be called Lincolnian departmentalism. Court orders to the executive branch are legally binding within that litigation (they become "the law of the case"), but there is no legal obligation for the executive to abide by the orders outside that litigation. This appears to have been Lincoln's original response to *Dred Scott.*

This model has a surface appeal. It takes care of *Youngstown Steel, Nixon,* the hypothetical warmonger who would not leave the White House, and all other litigation against the president confined to a single case, or a small handful of cases. But it does not reach litigation that is spread out over hundreds of thousands of cases where individuals are up against a federal administrative agency. Suppose the Supreme Court hands down a decision, *Jones v. Smith, Secretary of Health and Human Services,* finding that a particular practice of the Social Security Administration (SSA) in making eligibility determinations for disability benefits violates constitutional rights. Further suppose that this practice leads to the wrongful denial of benefits for approximately 100,000 people every year. Secretary Smith is the named defendant in this action, and she is now under a court order to cease the offending practice, so Jones's benefits will be restored. But what about the other 99,999 people whose benefits were wrongfully denied because the SSA used the very same practice?

Under the Lincolnian departmentalist model, the SSA is legally entitled to instruct its administrative law judges to continue denying them benefits. If these denied applicants have the wherewithal, both financially and longevity-wise, to complete the multilayered SSA appeal process, they will eventually be entitled to sue in federal district court, which will of course be obligated to restore the benefits. We know from actual experience that many of these applicants will never make it to court. The federal government could cut its entitlements budget significantly by simply forcing all these applicants to exhaust their administrative appeals. Perhaps the hypothetical is too fanciful to persuade; maybe someone would file a nationwide class action in federal court for an injunction to stop the SSA from continuing the offending practice. But certifying a nationwide class takes months, if not years, and it is no cinch that relief would be provided during the pendency of that litigation. And the underlying facts of the hypothetical are not exactly science fiction; in the early years of the Reagan administration, the SSA used quotas and biased physicians to terminate disability benefits for some 200,000 recipients. Although most of them were eventually able to get their benefits restored, many of them suffered unspeakable hardship during the pendency of their administrative appeals and litigation, and some of them died.[50] Nor is it too much of a stretch to imagine a federal agency refusing to accept the *stare decisis* effects of federal appellate decisions. In fact, from the 1960s to the mid-1980s, the SSA often instructed its administrative law judges to ignore applicable federal circuit precedents if they conflicted with the agency's own interpretation of the statute. Then attorney general Edwin Meese invoked Lincoln as authority for this practice of "nonacquiescence,"[51] and was roundly criticized for it.

Lincoln had indeed claimed that the executive branch was not legally obligated by Supreme Court precedent, but his claim predated the modern administrative state. In the years prior to the Civil War, the federal government simply did not have that many opportunities to exercise coercive force against the liberty or property of most individuals. The war changed that, of course, as did the martial law of Reconstruction throughout the former Confederacy. At the time of Lincoln, however, there was nothing like a Social Security Administration, an Internal Revenue Service, or even a federal civil service. With the advent of the federal bureaucracy, the executive branch became a much greater threat to the rights of individuals; departmentalism becomes a much higher-stakes game under today's conditions.

Never mind the administrative cases, departmentalists may say, what about *Dred Scott*? We can fashion some kind of exception to departmentalism for bad faith, large-scale manipulation of individual administrative matters. But how can judicial supremacists answer to a case in which the Court has frozen a manifestly evil and incorrect interpretation into the Constitution? If, in defiance of *Dred Scott*, the president had sent troops to the Wisconsin Territory to liberate slaves, isn't a supremacist forced to say that he had broken the law? A departmentalist, of course, could say with clear conscience that the president had no

50. The tragic story is chronicled in *Schweiker v. Chilicky*, 487 U.S. 412 (1988).

51. Edwin Meese III, *Perspective on the Authoritativeness of Supreme Court Decision: The Law of the Constitution*, 61 TULANE L. REV. 979 (1987).

legal obligation to abide by this wretched decision. A supremacist would seem to have no choice but to condemn the president's action as illegal.

As I view it, the problem with the preceding sentence is that it confuses morality and law. It is true that a supremacist must label the hypothetical liberation action as illegal, but no "condemnation" is necessarily involved. Not all illegal acts are immoral. We need go back no further than civil disobedience of the 1960s and the Declaration of Independence to see that. At some point it becomes morally permissible—and, in very rare occasions, morally imperative—to disobey unjust laws. But wishing that unjust laws are not laws does not make it so, and that is why the immorality of *Dred Scott* ought not be taken to add any weight to the argument for departmentalism.[52] The morality of liberating slaves provides the president with a weighty reason to order the troops in, but it does not alter the legal status of such an action.

Why is it normatively attractive to label the hypothetical slave liberation illegal, given that *Dred Scott* itself was both morally and legally wrong? The answer is institutional settlement. This is not the place to explicate the full argument for institutional settlement; Larry Alexander and Fred Schauer have done that elsewhere.[53] In brief, however, society is better off making it illegal for individuals to make independent judgments about the desirability of laws. Actors have to be able to rely on some considerable number of basic legal questions to have been settled. Without some critical mass of settlement, actors can have little confidence in their choices, never knowing whether the coercive force of the legal system will be available to back them up. Without that core of settled issues, it becomes difficult or impossible for individuals to engage in complex sorts of mutually beneficial arrangements because one can never have confidence that all parties who benefit will be held to their corresponding obligations. This isn't just true in private markets; it applies wherever complicated kinds of human cooperation are required. Admittedly, the means of settlement need not always be a court or courts, and the mode of settlement need not always be formal. But the virtue of formality is certainty, and few institutions are better suited than courts to operate on formal terms.[54]

---

52. Here I suppose I have sided with Hart in the so-called Hart-Fuller debate. *See* H. L. A. Hart, *Positivism and the Separation of Law and Morals*, 71 HARV. L. REV. 593 (1958) (no necessary logical relationship between law and morality); Lon L. Fuller, *Positivism and Fidelity to Law: A Reply to Professor Hart*, 71 HARV. L. REV. 630 (1958) (law has its own inner morality).

53. The most fully developed justification of judicial supremacy has been formulated by Professors Larry Alexander and Frederick Schauer, and is based primarily on the critical settlement function of law. *See* Larry Alexander & Frederick Schauer, *On Extrajudicial Constitutional Interpretation*, 110 HARV. L. REV. 1359 (1997); Larry Alexander & Frederick Schauer, *Defending Judicial Supremacy: A Reply*, 17 CONST. COMM. 455 (2000).

54. While accepting the general proposition that settlement is an important function of law, Tushnet insists that Congress, rather than the Court—or perhaps Congress *and* the Court, working in conjunction—could provide that service. *See* TUSHNET, 28–29.

Can civil disobedience be squared with the principle of settlement? I believe the answer is yes. Making it illegal to engage in independent judgments about the desirability of laws is not the same thing as saying one should never do it. It is simply to say that one will be sanctioned (or technically eligible for sanction) if one does it. This arrangement discourages gaming—that is, engaging in profitable illegality, then claiming that it was dictated by conscience. Some genuine civil disobedience will be deterred by the possibility of legal sanctions, but it is worth the price. A society in which there is insufficient legal settlement is not only inefficient and open to being gamed, but one in which people suffer from paralysis and emotional insecurity.

On the other hand, too much settlement invites ossification. If the elected branches always have an obligation to abide by constitutional precedents, how can the courts ever have any opportunity to reconsider them? Take *United States v. Morrison*, in which the Court held that Congress lacked authority under either the Commerce Clause or Section Five of the Fourteenth Amendment to enact the Violence Against Women Act.[55] Suppose twenty or thirty years go by, during which time the Court's views of the commerce power or the Section Five power have somewhat expanded. Is Congress still *legally* forbidden from enacting a new Violence Against Women Act in order to test the viability of *Morrison*? I believe not, so long as a reasonable observer would think that circumstances had changed sufficiently that the Court's answer might be different. I am not wedded to this formulation; suffice to say that I am in favor of some kind of exception aimed at officials who sincerely wish to test the current state of the law. To take one more example, suppose Congress enacts a criminal prohibition for flag burning, contrary to *Texas v. Johnson*.[56] A U.S. attorney (who happens to be running for a senate seat) immediately brings a prosecution, which is promptly dismissed. He vows to renew the prosecution following each dismissal. I do not think we want to limit our condemnation of this prosecutor to the moral and ethical variety. I think we want to say that his conduct is illegal and ought to be met with the full panoply of legal remedies.

Would the Nation truly perish if the executive branch were under no legal compulsion to follow Supreme Court precedent? I tend to think not, but I also think it is the wrong question. Would the Nation be better off, all things considered, if the executive branch were under no legal compulsion to follow Supreme Court precedent? The burden of proof is on those who would answer this question affirmatively, since judicial supremacy is the status quo. Tushnet correctly argued that the Court's ability to provide stable constitutional norms is compromised by many factors, including weak constitutional *stare decisis*, changes in court membership, and politicization in the nomination and confirmation of the justices. Despite all that, however, there is no good reason to think that the

55. 529 U.S. 528 (2000).
56. 491 U.S. 397 (1989).

elected branches could provide greater settlement value than the Court. Weak *stare decisis* can be expected to bring about more stability than none at all. And changes in the Court's membership are numerically dwarfed by changes in congressional and presidential leadership. For dynamism and political accountability, the elected branches have the Court beat; for clarity and stability in the expression of norms, the Court has all the advantages. If the Constitution is law, and if a principal purpose of law is to achieve settlement, then the judiciary should be the branch that plays the primary role in constitutional interpretation.

What, then, of popular constitutionalism? How can the People play their role in constitutional interpretation when the Court occupies the field, surrounded by the moat of supremacy? Part of the answer, at least, lies in the inevitably political situation of the Court. As Barry Friedman has recently written, in the long run, the Court always follows the people.[57] The real stakes are not who will control the interpretation of the Constitution in the long run. The real stakes are limited to provisional control. If judicial review were abolished, or even if Lincolnian departmentalism were adopted, the elected branches and the interest groups would have no reason to take the Court's view of the Constitution seriously. They would have no incentive to engage the Court in any kind of conversation about constitutional values because in either case the Court would have no coercive force over them. Under judicial supremacy, on the other hand, the elected officials and interest groups have no choice but to focus their attention on the Court's binding edicts. If their opposition to the Court's interpretations are sufficiently intense and enduring, the Court will eventually relent, in full or in substantial part. If their reaction to an interpretation is qualified acceptance, the Court may eventually adjust the interpretation to respond to the qualification. The dialectic may lead to a superior final product. And why should the Court ever heed the reactions of the elected branches, the interest groups, and the People? As Alexander Hamilton said—modernly, through Alexander Bickel—the Court is the "least dangerous branch," on account of the fact that it has neither purse nor sword. Without supremacy at least in the short run, it would fast become the most useless branch.

The proffered justification for doctrines of judicial restraint is that judicial review cuts against the grain of democracy. The standing doctrines, the deferential "rational basis" standard of review for much legislation, the various abstention doctrines, and other Brandeisian constitutional avoidance devices are thought to smooth off judicial review's sharp edge. These doctrines reduce the number of occasions on which judicial review can be exercised or make it less likely that legislation will be overturned. They help restrict judicial review to the matters in which it is indispensable to private rights, as opposed to matters that

57. Barry Friedman, The Will of the People (Farrar Straus 2010).

have a more public and political character. Those matters should be resolved not by courts, but by politically accountable officials, and by the people themselves. Some, like Kramer and Tushnet, feel these devices of judicial restraint are insufficient to preserve the people's role in constitutional interpretation, so they propose going farther, either the adoption of departmentalism or the abolition of judicial review altogether.

It is perhaps embarrassing that my thinking on this can be captured in an old bumper sticker from the 1960s: "Question Authority." Rather than work so hard to keep judges from saying what they think the Constitution means, we should be constantly and actively questioning their interpretations. We should never entirely cede the power of moral reasoning to anyone else, elected or unelected. Humility requires that we listen to others' views with as open a mind as we can manage, but in the end, the decision of whether to obey and what to believe always rests with us.

It is my hope that this book has demonstrated that the actual development of the judicial restraint doctrines was the product of forces more varied and more complicated than a simple desire to protect democracy, or simple obedience to the principles of constitutional government. That is not to say they have no tendency to protect democracy, or that they cannot be seen as part of a sensible system of constitutional government. It is merely to say that the judicial restraint doctrines ought not be given a free pass in the marketplace of normative policy analysis. Let us examine the evidence about whether judicial restraint doctrines tend to promote democracy rather than shield them from such scrutiny with trumping declarations about history and tradition. And, even more so, we must look very hard indeed at the actual benefits likely to accrue from even more drastic regimes such as departmentalism or the abolition of judicial review altogether. We must insist on real benefits in light of what we already know is the cost of the judicial restraint doctrines, departmentalism, or the abolition of judicial review: *ubi jus, non ibi remedium.* For a person who is told his rights are without remedies, the promise of law is an empty one indeed.

INDEX